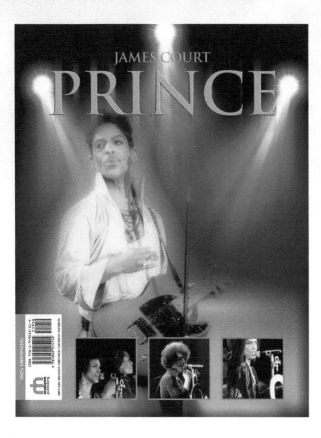

PRINCE
THE LIFE
THE GENIUS
THE LEGEND

❖

Prince Rogers Nelson

**Guitarist, Drummer, Bass Player, Pianist, Keyboardist,
Song Writer, Producer, Programmer, Arranger, Vocalist, Business entrepreneur, Actor, Director, Dancer, Choreographer.**

James Court has been an avid collector, writer and follower of Prince and his work for more than thirty years. Upon Prince's death in April 2016, James set about the colossal task of revealing every part of this fascinating ever-changing musician, leaving no stone unturned.

The Biography tackles the issues that plagued the Superstar, his fight for Musical freedom and his constant need to write, record and perform without restriction or filter.

Often described as the greatest Musician of his generation, Prince remained at the very top of the game, a multi-instrumentalist with the ability to write cutting edge songs at will, his talent, ability and influence were simply unmatched.

The results make this the most comprehensive, detailed and exhaustingly accurate depiction of one of the most popular, misunderstood and elusive musicians in modern day music....

New Haven Publishing Ltd
Email: newhavenpublishing@gmail.com
Website:
newhavenpublishingltd.com

Published 2021
All Rights Reserved

....

....

Cover and interior design © Pete Cunliffe
pcunliffe@blueyonder.co.uk

Photographs (unless credited otherwise)
© Jason E Abrams

Copyright © 2020 James Court

ISBN 978-1-949515-11-4

CHAPTER ONE

A SMALL BOY AND A PIANO

LIFE:
THE PERIOD BETWEEN BIRTH AND DEATH, OR THE EXPERIENCE OR STATE OF BEING ALIVE;

GENIUS:
EXCEPTIONAL INTELLECTUAL OR CREATIVE POWER OR OTHER NATURAL ABILITY.
EXCEPTIONALLY INTELLIGENT PERSON OR ONE WITH EXCEPTIONAL SKILL IN A PARTICULAR AREA OF ACTIVITY.
VERY CLEVER OR INGENIOUS;

LEGEND:
SOMEONE VERY FAMOUS AND ADMIRED, USUALLY BECAUSE OF THEIR ABILITY IN A PARTICULAR AREA.

Musical Geniuses **are born just like everyone else. In fact, any type of genius, in any field, starts life in the same way as you and me; where the path diverts from mere mortal to talented individual to complete genius is worth investigating.**

Prince was a masterful polymath who flirted with his audience both on record and onstage. He possessed an unmatched gift of all the ingredients needed to be the 'ultimate pop star'. He was a brilliant songwriter and a stunning singer in a variety of voices and harmonies. He was an electric and riveting performer, amazing dancer, gifted drummer, innovative programmer, jaw-dropping guitarist, funky bass player, prolific producer, and exceptional keyboardist - Prince was simply without equal.

He was a fascinating and utterly intriguing musical blend who transcended his influences. He was a rare artist who also excelled in business, and fought for the right to excel along the way. He was a complete workaholic who operated on virtually no sleep and could outperform anyone in front of him. He tested cultural and gender direction with a unique changing image. He was profoundly solo with a limitless fountain of grooves, ideas and significance. So, how did it all start?

The early years of Prince do not give much of an indication as to how he would become one of the most influential and talented musicians, songwriters and performers of modern times. There are certain attributes shown in his early life that are worth noting. He suffered a broken home, with his father walking out on the family - he did however leave his piano behind for the young Prince to console himself with. And of course, he was black, or perceived to

be, with a huge afro; he was certainly 'non-white' and for Minneapolis in the 1950s and 60s black people were very much the minority. Minneapolis was even nicknamed 'the vanilla state' for its whiteness. This was not somewhere you would expect a musically obsessive workaholic rock/pop/funk genius to hail from, or more importantly remain and set up an entire musical empire.

So, before the music - and there's a lot to get through - let's examine the foundations prior to this extraordinary individual stepping foot into a recording studio or onto a stage. It's not a simple journey; in fact there is so much music it's extremely difficult to digest. This was ultimately, though, his genius.

Prince Rogers Nelson was born on 7th June 1958 at Mount Sinai Hospital in Minneapolis. If you were to turn on the radio on the 7th June 1958 to hear what was number one on the Billboard pop chart you would not be surprised to hear that it was *'The Purple People Eater'* by Sheb Wooley - a fitting coincidence to what was to come. In the UK, it was The Everly Brothers with *'All I Have To Do Is Dream'*. Lovely.

Prince's Father, John L Nelson, was a musician and composer who played locally at parties and events around town. His style was described as jazz but it was more a free-flowing jazz fusion than pure jazz. Certainly, no covers of Sheb Wooley or The Everly Brothers would be played in any of the venues where he would perform. His day job was not so glamorous: he was a plastic moulder at a local company going by the name of Honeywell Electronics. Music however was what John Nelson was about and the evening job was very much his first vocation in life with the day job just there to pay the bills. John never got further than the clubs and bars to perform in and needed the day job to make ends

PRINCE'S EARLY LIFE WAS TROUBLED, WITH BOTH PARENTS FREQUENTLY ARGUING, MAKING IT AN UNHAPPY ATMOSPHERE FOR THE YOUNGSTER.

meet. He would be an inspiration to Prince, who watched his father perform at an early age. Although they were often estranged there were many occasions when Prince would reach out and involve his father in his life and success throughout the years, even giving him writing credits on some songs, although this is disputable and more likely a financial donation rather than a true collaboration.

Prince's mother, Mattie Shaw, played in John's jazz band as a backing singer before they were eventually married. She later left the band to acquire a steadier income. She gained a masters degree in social work and went onto to work within the local school system in Minneapolis. Both parents originated from Louisiana and chose to move to Minneapolis as it was then perceived to be a more liberal state, and it certainly was in comparison to Louisiana in the 1960s. Prince's early life was troubled, with both parents frequently arguing, making it an unhappy atmosphere for the youngster. Some scenes in the loosely autographically movie Purple Rain reflect this relationship and the effect it had on Prince. The family consisted of Prince and Tyka (Prince's sister born two years later) with Lorna, Sharon and John Junior who were from John's first marriage. The family lived at 915 Logan Avenue in the northern district of Minneapolis, a mainly black area of the city at this time.

There are many clues and hints within Prince songs about his childhood and his early days. Often, he was more comfortable talking to an audience or through his lyrics than at any interview he gave, although this was due to his natural shyness and not some record company's fictionalized marketing scheme.

In 1968 Prince's parents separated and they filed for divorce after a thirteen-year marriage, his father leaving the family home. Significantly, he left his piano behind. Prince missed his father being around and for a while the piano started to gain attention with Prince replicating tunes from TV shows, a sort of coping mechanism when no one was around. This changed however when Prince's mother remarried, to a man named Haywood Baker. Mr Baker was, in comparison to Prince's father, a strict disciplinarian and inevitably the relationship became hostile, making for a very unhappy time in Prince's early life. He was passed frequently from pillar to post during this period and did briefly live with his real father again, but this ended badly when he caught Prince with a girl and subsequently threw him out. Prince pleaded with his father to be able to move back but his father refused. So again, he was shuffled around relatives. Musically the young boy was now starting to develop rapidly on a variety of instruments, showing a freakish ability to play whatever he had in front of him. He seemed to able to pick up any instrument at school and play it instantly.

Eventually, and significantly, Prince was taken in by his best friend Andre Anderson's family. Andre's mother, Bernadette Anderson, soon became the main authority figure in Prince's life. He moved into the basement with Andre and the pair split the basement in two. However, this was soon to be transformed into a makeshift music studio and rehearsal space.

Musical history is littered with certain duos meeting for the first time and becoming significant in the development of any band with longevity: McCartney meeting Lennon, Jagger meeting Richards and so on. Prince met Andre Anderson (later Andre Cymone) in third grade at John Hay Elementary School in 1965

where they became friends, along with Prince's second cousin Charles Smith. Andre did not stay with Prince for long as a musical partner, with Prince inevitably branching away, but the significance lies in how Prince became a part of Andre's family, and how the two became young early musical collaborators as well as best friends, living in the basement of Andre's house. Andre would be in Prince's first band on bass touring with him in the early days before later leaving to pursue a solo career of his own - but these early basement collaborations and jams would shape a foundation for the musical sound Prince was later to achieve, famously known as the *'Minneapolis sound'*.

The *'Minneapolis sound'* was a form of funk developed by Prince. Not all future songs featured this style but it became more prominent as Prince progressed and had the ability and technology to record. It had some distinguishing characteristics that Prince made unique to him. Synthesizers replaced horns, and were used more as accent than as fill or background, while the rhythm guitar was often faster and less narrow than traditional funk. It owed much to the new wave pop music that emerged in the early 1980s. Guitars were usually played cleaner for rhythm sections and were frequently louder and more aggressively processed during solos than in most traditional funk. The bass was less heavy and drums and keyboards filled more of the bottom sound. The drumming was more highly processed and of course with the advent of the drum machine, in Prince's case the *Linn LM-1* drum computer, this made for a unique and distinctive sound that Prince owned and would later become famous for.

Manufactured by Linn Electronics Inc. the *LM-1* was the first drum machine to use digital samples of acoustic drums. It was conceived and designed by Roger Linn. It was also one of the first ever programmable drum machines and Prince loved it; not only did it have a unique soft sound, it also enabled Prince to speed up his process, and he became obsessed with it, taking it to a new level of programming over his recordings. It was introduced in early 1980 and was upgraded when additional features were incorporated. It became discontinued after the release of its successor, the *Linn Drum*. Prince though loved the sound of the original and stuck with it for most of his early work. Both amateur and professional musicians used it for its rarity as well as its characteristic sounds. It can be heard on the recordings of other artists such as Herbie Hancock, Michael Jackson, the Human League, Peter Gabriel, Kraftwerk and many others during the 1980s. Prince was a fantastic drummer but this machine gave him speed and continuity in the studio, and also freed him up to play more instruments, in particular keyboards. The drum sound of the adopted *LM-1*, alongside the other techniques Prince had naturally developed, led to the sound being dubbed the *Minneapolis Sound*, and many replicated it, or tried to, during the early 1980s. The present-day replica of the sound would be Bruno Mars with *'Uptown Funk'* and *'Gorilla'* which are current examples of using this style.

At this time though, in the basement/studio of Andre's house, the two friends were still thrashing through songs moving towards this future sound. Prince's musical ability was now becoming evident at music lessons in school and he was fast gaining a reputation for his talent. The shift in his personal life moved this underlying talent to the foreground and from this point it can be argued that his preoccupation with music began. His legendary appetite for creating and recording was unstoppable by any conventional means, whether that be technology, other musicians and engineers, or even his own sleep.

Making space in the basement, the boys could now practice as and when they wanted, with Prince now fully competent on drums, guitars, keyboards, piano and bass. Whether this early freedom is linked to later events is up for debate but it's worth looking at the context and effect it must have had on the young Prince. He went from arguments, being passed around various relatives, kicked onto the street by his father, and a strict unhappy regime, to almost complete musical freedom where he could thrash out his talents at will in the basement with his best friend Andre. It was an early Emancipation.

In 1973, a year or so after Prince and Andre had started jamming in the basement, the two young boys decided it was time to start a band. Prince invited his second cousin Charles Smith to join them on drums with Andre placed on bass. They settled on the name Phoenix for the band, which came from the album by *Grand Funk Railroad, Flight of the Phoenix* from 1972. This was one of their favorite acts at this time, a blend of loose seventies-style rock funk fusion not dissimilar to the kind of music Prince would go on to jam on in later studio sessions. This name was short lived however and after various discussions the boys finally settled on the name *Grand Central*.

Grand Central would jam for hours at a time, with Prince now becoming more musically prominent within the band. They would often set up in Charles' backyard causing neighbors to come over and watch the boys show off their musical skills. They mainly covered hits at the time by Jimi Hendrix, Earth Wind and Fire, James Brown and Sly and the Family Stone, becoming a competent cover band around the neighborhood. Prince often taught the rest of the band chords and arrangements having learned certain songs by ear, such was his early virtuoso. One of the early original pieces they did perform was a song called *'Do You Feel Like Dancing'*, an early effort in songwriting for the young band.

A year later in 1974 a significant shift happened within this first Prince band. Drummer Charles Smith was repeatedly missing rehearsals due to football commitments. For Prince, this was not acceptable. Even at this early age he was showing signs of getting increasingly frustrated with the musical limitations of others around him; the early signs of the band leader and frontman he would later become. The band cast a vote and Charles was voted out. He was replaced by a young drummer and recent friend by the name of Morris Day.

<hr/>

Impressed with the level of musical ability Prince and Andre possessed, Morris introduced his cousin William Doughty to Prince and after a brief rehearsal he took the role of percussion within *Grand Central*. The new percussionist's mother, Lavonne Doughty, seemed to have some loose connections within the music industry. She set the boys up with a small finance deal where they

paid themselves a small dividend, and this led them to change their name to the more financial sounding *Grand Central Corporation*.

At this time the Minneapolis music scene was light years behind the mainstream. There were virtually no venues for touring bands to play; the Met Centre for example, which Prince would play at in later years, did not open until October 1967 (it was later demolished in December 1994). Radio was far behind anything up to date to draw inspiration from or find a modern view of where things were heading. A young aspiring musician would not be as exposed to new sounds and new bands as they would if they hailed from LA or New York. Radio stations, and charts, were split between white and black, the white radio stations playing mainly country, and the black playing a mixture of old hits that wouldn't provide much inspiration. Prince, even at this early age, was already unhappy with any kind of categorizing of music, especially when you were instantly categorized because of your appearance as opposed to what you were playing. Prince struggled with this categorization for many years - he never understood it, especially when he was playing many different styles of music: his natural ability crossed over into all different areas, so he was hard to place within a certain category.

The one area where there was some kind of atmosphere was situated in the centre of Minneapolis. Here lay the hub of the emerging club scene which Prince named and continued to reference as *'Uptown'*. This was the location of First Avenue, the club later made famous in *Purple Rain* and the venue that Prince would go on take ownership of for trying out new songs and indeed new band members. Local bands would play at various locations in Uptown trying to drum up a following. *Grand Central Corporation* were now renting themselves out regularly, playing at various events and parties and continuing to tour the local circuit of bars and venues.

It was in 1974 that *Grand Central Corporation played* at a ski party, an event attended by a musician named Pepe Willie who stood and watched the young band perform. Pepe had married Prince's cousin Shantel Manderville and had recently moved to Minneapolis. Pepe was very impressed with the young band and arranged for a friend who co-owned a recording studio to take a look. They were invited in to the studio and spent time jamming and recording some of their own early compositions; it was the first time the band had been in this environment. To Pepe, Prince's talent was starting to look bewildering, as he was excelling at anything put in front of him. He stood out not only within his own band but amongst other seasoned musicians who were regulars to the studio. He also had a strong work ethic and a desire to finish anything he started. Pepe moved to capitalize on this young prodigy and in 1975 approached Prince and asked if he could employ him as a studio musician alongside his own band for some songs he had written and wanted to record demos for. It made commercial sense: why employ four or five experienced studio musicians when this young kid could play everything just as well? They recorded five tracks at this time, one being *'If You See Me'*, which Prince took back and rerecorded in 1982, proving he was impressed with this early track. Another track *'Games'* went on to be released in 1986 on an album Pepe released called *Minneapolis Genius The Historic 1977 Recordings*; this album was attributed to *94 East*, a name Pepe came up with as he couldn't find a name for the band. Other songs from these sessions ended up on the album *Symbolic Beginnings* in 1995, much to the disappointment of Prince who would, unsurprisingly, not have been happy with these early demos becoming released by Pepe and having Prince attributed to them.

Prince was now playing regularly at local events, his band fast becoming lodged in so-called *'Battle of the Bands'* competitions around town. One significant band on the scene in Minneapolis around this time was called *Flyte Time* and consisted of the soon-to-be-famous Jimmy Jam and Terry Lee Lewis. There was also Prince's future bass player Sonny Thompson's group called *The Family*, although this was not the group of the same name Prince would later create. These bands, which later on would all fall under Prince's employ, were rival platforms in the emerging Minneapolis club scene.

In early 1976 *Grand Central Corporation* recorded several of their own compositions at a small studio on the north side of Minneapolis. It was the first time that Prince and the band felt they had enough quality material of their own to record, with six songs eventually recorded. Prince took lead vocals, guitars and keyboards, with Andre on bass and Morris on drums. Prince also took on producing this early demo session, as well as playing a little saxophone, an instrument he had recently picked up. Engineering the sessions was David Rivkin who would later become a significant collaborator for Prince in the coming years. Rivkin would go on to assist in engineering *Purple Rain* and *Parade* as well as the multi-selling album *FYC* by *The Fine Young Cannibals*. He went on to achieve a long list of other credits throughout his career as an engineer and producer.

After these sessions, Prince did his first ever interview, which was published in the *Central High Pioneer Minneapolis*. The article titled *"Nelson finds it hard to become known"* sees Prince claiming that if he was born in LA or New York he would have made it already, a bold claim for someone of such a young age. He praises his school music teachers as they let him 'work' on his own. The article notes his musical ability on several instruments and he goes on to say that 'he now sings' - apparently a recent development. He gives advice in the article and discusses the importance of learning musical scales. He also states that he learns music by ear and has no formal training as such. He speaks of an ambition to record an album of his own material and then return to school later on when he is older to continue his studies. The photo for this article sees Prince sitting at a piano looking straight at camera, befitting the headline questioning how hard it is to become known in Minneapolis. This was a frustrating time for Prince, as he had an ambition to break out and become famous; he was acutely aware of his talent and ability but getting a record deal or some other avenue to success was nearly impossible. Of course, he could continue playing in bars and at functions, touring the event circuit, but his father had already proved that this was not a route to success.

Larry Graham would become a central part of Prince's life in the late 1990s, but for now, in early 1976, he had just left as bass player for *Sly and the Family Stone* to form his own band *Graham Central Station*. This name sounded too close to *Grand Central Corporation* so Prince and the band decided they would change their name again. They clearly felt they would become big enough to cause confusion out there, and so, in spring 1976, *Grand Central*

Corporation became *Champagne*.

After the earlier recording session *Champagne* continued to look for recording studios to keep the band moving towards the ambition of making an album. There had recently been a few arguments around this time, with musical disagreements coming to the surface as you would expect with such a young band, all still only aspirational teenagers. It was also frustrating for other members in the band as Prince was now fast becoming the band leader, becoming ever more competent at arrangements and basic musicality. He would frequently put his own instrument down and show others how to play a particular part on their instrument before going back to continue.

———◆◆◆———

Moonsound was a recording studio based by Lake Nokomis, not far from the downtown or 'Uptown' district of Minneapolis. It was owned by Chris Moon, a promoter for local concerts around town. Moon was an aspiring musician and had recorded several commercials, trying his hand at a few demo tapes. He had been writing poetry and lyrics for many years but lacked the musicianship to turn his poems and lyrics into songs. In spring 1976 Moon watched as a bunch of teenagers called *Champagne* set up in his studio to record some tracks. After watching the band, he quickly spotted Prince and eventually offered a proposal. The deal was a simple one: Prince would let himself in after school and work on music to add to Moon's lyrics, which he would leave on the piano. In return, Moon would show Prince around the studio, teaching him basic producing methods and engineering. They agreed to share any profits that might be acquired equally. Moon recalls a quiet reaction from Prince as he listened to Moon's offer, giving just a single nod to agree the terms. So, on top of this extraordinary musical talent, Prince now, still a teenager, was being taught studio producing techniques and engineering in a professional environment. In addition, Prince enrolled in Music Business classes, an early exposure to business acumen within music. All of the above made for a perfect storm, creating a musical force about to rise to the surface in the years ahead.

On his 18th birthday Prince graduated from Central High School and immediately began working at Chris Moon's studio. He also began spending weekends there working on compositions to Moon's lyrics. Over the next eight months Prince worked tirelessly on songs, laying down all the instruments on each and every track. He also recorded music for commercials and various jingles. Moon showed him certain studio techniques to help him create more effectively, one such being multi track recording, a technique Prince would go on to use frequently in the years ahead. Future engineers working with Prince often comment on how they have never worked with anyone like him. A common and reoccurring method was Prince having all the instruments ready to go in a studio around him. He would punch himself in and record drums, in one take, from scratch, with no breaks. The song was in his head and he would stop, pause, and fill for the entire track. Then he'd pick up the bass and repeat the process - if he couldn't punch himself in then an engineer would be required to lean in and assist - it was then guitars, keyboards, piano and so on. Once the instruments were laid down the engineer was sent out and Prince would record vocals and layered harmonies alone while sitting at the control booth, microphone hanging down in front of him with a lyric sheet taped up. The song was then sent to be mixed. Everything was done in one session, every day, every night. This consistent churning out at speed was made possible by the techniques the teenager was learning, and now fast developing, at the studio with Chris Moon through these summer months in 1976. It was a one-man-band recording technique that would go on to be the favored way in which Prince would create his vast amount of recorded work.

With material now stacking up the pair decided to vamp up the lyrics, a technique they called *'implied naughty sexuality'*: fill the lyrics with suggested innuendoes, enough to get noticed but not enough to cause offense. This early technique was not really around in this context back in the 1970s: the charts were full of love songs and devotion, or party anthems and disco. What there wasn't was anything like *'Soft & Wet'*, a recently recorded track. It was innuendo that you could, if it was subtle enough, just about get away with; *'Soft & Wet'* was the first example of Prince using this tactic. With material now ready, it was time for Prince to look for some kind of record deal.

In around September of 1976 Prince decided to try his luck and opted for record companies in New York. He wanted Moon to be his manager but Moon had no interest. Prince decided to travel alone and so, with his demo tapes safely packed, he traveled to New York. He stayed with his half-sister there, with Moon making some arrangements from Minneapolis to record companies, trying to get some interest. *Atlanta Records* agreed to meet with Prince but they could not identify a hit from the selection of songs he played them, many of them being long extended jams. He was offered one deal through a friend, but it meant Prince would have to sign over publishing rights. Prince refused. He was still only a teenager, and he had no one with him at the time, but he was bright enough to understand that this meant losing artistic control. It was an early sign of the savvy business mind that would later emerge as he battled for, and succeeded in winning, the rights to own his own masters.

Back in Minneapolis, Chris Moon contacted Owen Husney. Husney owned an advertising agency in Minneapolis and had a background as a promoter and publicist for bands. Moon met with Husney at his office and played him a selection of songs. Impressed with the quality and musicianship Husney asked who the band was, and whether they were from Minneapolis. Moon explained it was one person, writing everything, singing everything, playing all the instruments, producing everything; and he was just a kid. Husney called Prince in New York and offered to be his manager. Intrigued by this offer Prince flew back from New York to meet with Husney face to face.

In December 1976 Prince signed with Owen Husney's newly formed company *American Artists Inc*, and he became Prince's manager. An office was rented with rehearsal space for Prince who regularly invited musical friends including Andre Anderson and Bobby Z Rivkin to jam. Husney, seeing the potential that he now had, left his advertising company to be run by others so he could concentrate 100% on Prince, the objective being to get a recording contract with a major label. Husney was an astute businessman,

with a background in advertising and promoting, and he felt he knew just how to do this; he was not looking for a small contract, he knew what he had, he could see the major talent he now represented, and he also saw the marketing possibilities within Prince's personal persona. He was incredibly shy, barely audible to those who first met him, but with instruments and a stage he was a completely different person, absolutely gold marketing material if used right with a commercial mind. It wasn't an act either, it was the way Prince was, and Husney knew this and felt he knew how best to pitch it.

This was an important time and another shift in the attitude that Prince would acquire. He now, still at a young age, had a fully-fledged manager devoting his time to him, allowing him to create every day. The management team gave him an allowance and he had musical instruments purchased for him through the management company. Crucially he moved out of the basement in the Anderson family home and into a one-bedroom apartment in downtown Minneapolis. Chris Moon at this time also withdrew from working with Prince, leaving Husney and his team to manage the youngster's affairs. This must have been an interesting time for Prince. He had the family basement with a selection of musical friends to jam with for fun, and he had a recording studio with a gentlemen's agreement to mess around in. Moon and Prince never had any contract of any kind, which could be the reason why later on in his career Prince was so against getting tied down in legalities and giving up control of what he was producing.

Now Prince had his own place and a management company pushing forward - he was ready to launch on the big players in the music business.

Husney and Prince had many conversations about how the songs should be structured. Prince now had a substantial backlog of material and Husney wanted him to concentrate on structuring the songs with hooks and bridges to make them catchier to the untrained ear. Prince was used to free-flowing extended jams and Husney wanted this approach condensed to make it more appealing to the pop market. He also wanted to shave a year or so off Prince's age to make him even more of a prodigy, and crucially tell as little about him as possible, thus building up the mystery behind the music, building essentially on his natural shyness in face to face scenarios.

Prince now transferred to one of the major studios in Minneapolis, Sound 80, where he continued to work on a demo worthy of putting in front of a major record company. He spent most of the winter months in 1976-1977 locked away here, again with David Rivkin as engineer. He wrote new songs as well as polishing up the old demos previously recorded at Moonsound. Crucially at this time Prince was first introduced to the synthesizer, a newly developed piece of futuristic kit, which would later go on to envelop his unique sound. Prince also during these months guested on some Pepe Willie tracks as well as joining some sessions with Sonny Thompson's band. He was well established already as the *'go to guy'* if you wanted a particular arrangement adding to a song.

At the start of 1977 Owen Husney started putting together some press packs to promote Prince and get him in front of record companies. He had 15 deluxe kits made, each with a silver colored wheel, for the demo material.

Prince performing in 1986

Inside were pictures of Prince in various poses giving the impression of mystery and mystique; the idea was to blow them away and make them feel they were missing out on a major talent. This approach gathered momentum and it wasn't long before record companies were in competition with each other to meet with him. Husney managed, using this method, to meet directly with Warner Bros, CBS, A&M, RSO and ABC/Dunhill.

Prince flew out to Los Angeles with his management team to meet with the record companies. The team, polished and in expensive suits, pitched to the recording companies while Prince waited outside. Prince came in after for effect, but Prince being Prince he said very little and would often avoid any eye contact, sticking to simple yes or no answers to questions. Prince wanted a 3-year record contract and full control over producing his own records. At this time in early 1977 this was practically unheard of, especially with someone so young. CBS, interested in the claims Husney had made, set Prince up for a recording session in front of senior executives and producers. He recorded, from scratch, *Just As Long As We're Together'*, which went on to appear on his first album. He played every instrument and produced the whole song in breathtaking speed. Despite this they still wanted a producer for the first album because of Prince's age, and they offered Verdine White who was the brother of the frontman of Earth Wind and Fire.

To market Prince, Husney arranged for an interview with *The Minnesota Daily* based around Prince's search for a record contract. Ironically, in this article Prince talked about having a future pseudonym to produce music in other avenues. Even at this very early age he was already planning ahead.

In May of this year RSO and ABC/Dunhill turned Prince down but Warner Bros, A&M and CBS entered into a bidding war. The management team flew out several times during this period to hold meetings, again with Owen Husney's strategy for playing one against another in order to generate the best deal. ABC's offer would only stretch to two albums which Prince rejected. CBS and Warner Bros offered Prince a 3-album deal, exactly what he wanted, but neither would allow him to produce himself. Some kind of compromise would have to be made.

Owen Husney had a good working relationship with executives at Warner Bros and felt that they best understood Prince and what he was about. The deal offered was for Prince to receive an $80,000 advance. He would be given the title co-producer, and would not be guaranteed to have full producing rights just yet; he would need first to prove himself in this area. He would need to produce 3 albums in 27 months and the first within 6 months of signing. The budget for spending on the 3 albums was set at $60,000 each. If after the period Warners offered him a new deal he would get a further $225,000 on top of the original deal. There would be another option for an extension offering him $250,000 which was dependent on albums and release dates. Although these may look like modest numbers in 1977 this was one of largest contracts ever offered to a solo artist - and in particular to a teenager.

<hr />

And so, in June 1977, Prince Rogers Nelson, aged just 19, signed with Warner Brothers records. It was a relationship that would in the years ahead catapult him to the top of the music world making him one of the most famous, exciting, controversial, unique and influential pop stars on the planet. Prince's rise to stardom had begun.

CHAPTER TWO

SIGNED

As the recording contract stated Prince was to have an executive producer present on the making of his debut album, Tommy Vicari was flown in to meet Prince and subsequently co-produce *For You.*

Vicari was an experienced producer and engineer, having previously engineered a host of records for names including Quincy Jones and Santana amongst others. He was ten years older than Prince and would, in the months ahead, prove to be a sort of mentor to him. As with previous people who encountered Prince, Vicari found that he had an ability to learn the knowledge he had been shown, absorb it, then reproduce it and move on to the next level. Vicari would later go on to engineer and co-produce Warner's 1993 compilation The Hits The B Sides during Prince's much publicized dispute with the label, and he would also be drafted in to produce *4Ever* in 2016.

Prince now moved in with Owen Husney and his wife in a three-level apartment in California. Vicari also moved into the house at this time. Prince and Vicari worked in the studio six days a week from around 5pm to 3 or 4am, a practice Prince would be familiar and comfortable with in the years ahead. He practically became nocturnal, such was his work ethic. Andre Anderson was a frequent visitor, still keen to jam and play music with his old school friend and roommate. Vicari quickly realized that there was little room required for his input or creative improvising. Prince had a large body of work already and he had an exact idea as to how each track should sound. He was never going to ask an opinion on anything: he knew what he wanted and how to achieve it, and the co-producer quickly became a kind of redundant assistant.

The process would be the same as before with Prince working on one song at a time, firstly laying down drum tracks, then synthesizer, bass, and finally guitars, rhythm and leads. As before, he seemed to have the song entirely in his head before recording, playing often over 25 different instruments. It was at this time that Prince began to start to layer synth sounds and add fluidity to synth lines, which he chose to replace traditional horns. Prince wanted a different sound, which was difficult to achieve with standard horns, so he started experimenting in the studio by multi-tracking the synthesizer and guitar sounds. This technique would later emerge as the 'Minneapolis sound'. David Z Rivkin was flown in to

engineer the album's vocal sessions with Tommy Vicari remaining as the primary engineer. Warners, concerned that the budget was expanding, sent senior executives to check progress. The message was clear: speed it up.

Prince recorded many more songs during these sessions, with David Rivkin coming in for added vocals on some tracks. Andre Anderson continued to join in on bass for jam sessions. During this time, Prince also got to meet some previous heroes of his, namely Chaka Khan (who he loved), Carlos Santana and Sly Stone, all of whom would be heavy influences in the coming years and whom Prince would work with and write for.

At the start of 1978 Prince moved out of the three-level apartment and rented a house in the Hollywood hills with Owen Husney and his wife, David Rivkin and now Andre Anderson, who moved away from Minneapolis to join Prince on his newfound road to stardom. Prince now began working on overdubs and mixing now that the basic tracks were completed. In late February, the debut album was finally completed. It took 5 months of studio work to complete, lightning speed for 99% of bands out there but an eternity for Prince. *For You* smashed its budget; indeed it nearly went over the total amount allocated for the first 3 albums. It was, though, finally completed.

If the young Prince was to turn on his radio in 1978 to listen to a countdown of the year's bestselling singles in the US - and of course there were no other means of recording success of songs in the late 70s other than raw sales - it was a mix that he may not have derived a huge amount of motivation from. The Bee Gees sat in there with *'Saturday Night Fever'*, *'Staying Alive'* and *'How Deep Is Your Love'* - basically the Grease soundtrack. The Commodores, Eric Clapton, Billy Joel and Wings also sat happily alongside each other. The UK was even more uninspiring: the full-on double cheese of John Travolta and Olivia Newton John, the plodding *'Mull of Kintyre'* by Wings, and moms everywhere hit the dance floor to Boney M with *'The Rivers of Babylon'*, where we sat down. Others leaped at the chance to show they could make letters in the air with The Village People's *'Y.M.C.A'* and of course we cried at little bunny rabbits with eye infections as we contemplated *'Bright Eyes'* by Art Garfunkel. It's hard to see Prince finding anything in this mix he would have had any enthusiasm for.

On April 7th 1978 Prince's debut album *For You* was released. It would be the start of a list of albums unmatched in their quality, spontaneity, diversity and creativity. The lyrics are simple on the title track and significant when looking back at the vast amount of material he has produced. Prince's first song on his first album has the perfect lyrics: *"All of this and more is for you, with love sincerity and deepest care, my life with you I share"*. That's it. A sublime and absolute sentence that paves the way for the career ahead for this revolutionary artist; an a capella introducing himself simply, beautifully and perfectly to the music world. There isn't a huge amount on this debut album that would alert a listener to the phenomenon he would become, but as always with Prince, this deserves a closer look. With the exception of just a few, every Prince album from 1978 through to 2015 never sat perfectly with the time it was released. There needs a period of digestion, and patience - something that today's world of instant playlists and shuffles lacks. Albums were, in the late 1970s and indeed through the 1980s, a story of what the band or individual's identity was: it was a way of saying, this is me, this is us, this is what we can do, this is the direction we are going in at the moment, and ultimately, this is what we are about.

For You was Prince saying: look what I can do, I did this, all on my own. For the first time the album bore the classic line *'Produced, arranged, composed and performed by Prince'*, leaving the listener in no doubt who did this. And who did it all, completely. Prince was a single figure: no one else around, it was just him doing everything and giving it to you, or doing it *'For you'*.

'Soft and Wet' and *'Just As Long As We're Together'*, the two singles on the record, did relatively well for a debut. *'Soft and Wet'*, released June 7th 1978, became a minor hit on the US Billboard Top 100 but it did land in the top 10 on the R&B chart. This made Prince an instant teen pin up: posters and magazines all had his image. *'Just As Long As We're Together'* was released later in the year on November 21st and stalled around the edge of the R&B charts. The album itself reached number 21 on the R&B charts selling 150,000 copies in the US. It went on to sell a further 430,000 copies worldwide. Of course, as time went on and his popularity increased sales grew dramatically as fans searched out the back catalog.

Being placed within a category was something that annoyed Prince even at this early stage, and it was something he was keen to avoid. A crossover record was what he wanted and *For You*, for all its individual brilliance and diversity in sound, was looking like it would not manage to achieve this. Crossing over in 1978 meant quite literally a black artist, normally put in the soul chart category, crossing over to the main pop chart if he or she hit a certain threshold.

—◦◆◦—

In the summer of this year Prince did his first publicity tour, mainly focusing on the areas where the single *'Soft and Wet'* and the *For You* album had been most successful, focusing firstly on San Francisco, Chicago and Detroit. Warners promoted hard in these areas, giving away gifts and even waterbeds to local radio stations to gain publicity for Prince and the record. At one event in North Carolina over 3000 teenagers showed up and stormed the stage,

Prince's first exposure to fan hysteria. After this experience, Prince decided he did not want to do any more promotional touring and stayed at home, leaving promotional activity to his management team as he continued in the studio.

Prince now decided he wanted to live alone and moved away from Husney and into his first home, a relatively small yellow house at 5215 France Avenue in Edina. Edina is a small city situated immediately southwest of Minneapolis. Of course, he had as much equipment set up in the house as possible. The drum kit was in the basement along with all his guitars and keyboards, and he also had a 4-track reel to reel tape machine installed so he could record 24 hours a day if he wanted to. Prince also had a steady girlfriend at the time and she became a frequent visitor to the new home/studio. With this newfound musical freedom Prince now started shaping demos for his next album.

Rehearsals began next, with Prince renting rehearsal space to try out aspiring musicians. He did not want just any musician who could play; Prince was searching for individuals who could jam, who looked cool, with their own identity, and who could keep up with his creativity and stamina. He needed commitment. Again, being categorized was something Prince was keen to avoid so his band would be a mixture of white, black, male and female. He wanted a visual mishmash of styles and individuals, a group as diverse as possible both on the eye and in their musical styles and abilities.

Naturally Andre Anderson, now known as Andre Cymone, would play bass in the band. Prince held auditions for a drummer which included Morris Day amongst others but in the end he opted for Bobby Z Rivkin whom he had jammed with previously. Bobby was also white, adding to the multi-racial aspect of the band. With this core complete Prince, Bobby Z and Andre next flew to Los Angeles to continue rehearsals. Various aspiring young musicians came and went but Prince wasn't feeling right with any of them and the group returned to Minneapolis to continue the search. A young keyboard player named Gayle Chapman was next chosen.

Prince later said of Chapman's appointment to the band that she was white, she was blonde and she played funky keyboards, a perfect fit. Gayle had previously worked with Pepe Willie on a few tracks and was herself an aspiring songwriter. She was also a Christian and upheld strong Christian values. Prince wanted a second guitarist and keyboard player for his band but struggled again to find a fit with several unsuccessful auditions taking place. He instructed Owen Husney to advertise in the local paper and soon after several guitarists showed up for rehearsal. Dez Dickerson was chosen after only a short time jamming with the band. Dickerson was from St Paul and brought in a glam rock element. He had experience from playing with several bands and so jumped straight in to the loose jam session which set the tone for the rehearsal. He was also image conscious and added a visual concept that Prince liked. It's obvious to see this in the years that followed, as Dickerson played a key visual role in the videos for *'Little Red Corvette'* and *'1999'* which proved the starters for Prince's crossover success.

A second keyboard player was taking longer than expected, with Prince finding it hard to get a musician he could click with. Eventually a keyboard player named Matt Fink was chosen. Fink was a friend of Bobby Z and had expressed an interest after Bobby had played him a tape. He had many years' experience and had been playing competently since an early age. Matt Fink would become a pinnacle member of Prince's band and of all these early members would stay with him the longest. Even later on when *The Revolution* disbanded Matt Fink stayed with Prince; in fact he continued working with him right up until 1991 as an early member of the *New Power Generation*, although the band wasn't named as such until he left. Fink was also a member of the Prince jazz-fusion band *Madhouse*.

The band were put on the payroll with rehearsals five times a week. However, they soon realized what it meant to be in a Prince band, with rehearsals lasting as long as ten hours straight. Prince was a hard taskmaster and this wasn't work, it was simply what he did day in day out: the practice and application did not stop. Many of them had never experienced this level of commitment and drive and found it hard in the beginning to keep up with this work rate. However, during the close of 1978 Prince's first band was in place ready to take things forward to the next level.

The second single from the debut album was released on 21st November 1978. *Just As Long As We're Together* has a passage borrowed from a previous instrumental that was called *Jelly Jam* and Prince added this to the main track. It brushed the R&B charts but, crucially, failed to reach the pop charts. Prince and Husney had an argument relating to this with Prince feeling that things were not going to plan and more should have been done. The pair stopped communicating completely and it soon became clear that this was the end of Owen Husney. He walked away at the end of 1978, forcing Pepe Willie to step in briefly to assist Prince as new management was searched for. At the start of 1979 it was time for Prince to show off his new band to Warner Bros executives. The now famous concert would be Prince's first as a solo artist headlining his own show.

At the *Capri Theatre* in Minneapolis on 5th January 1979 Prince performed his first concert in front of about 300 people. There were a few technical difficulties in the first show but it was well received as he showcased songs from the *For You* album as well as a few new numbers. A second show on 7th January followed and although many were impressed with what they saw Warner execs were not fully convinced they could finance a full-scale national tour just yet, especially when he hadn't had a full-scale hit. They felt a bit more momentum was needed at this early stage. Prince's performance was extremely competent and it was clear that his musicianship and skill was impressive for such a young age, but Warners just wanted a little more time and maybe a second album to provide more material to tour with.

Pepe Willie now started searching for a manager and trailed through his contacts within the music industry, including Don Taylor who was the current manager of Bob Marley. Although a few candidates for the managerial role agreed to meet and worked with Prince briefly many found him difficult to work with. It was evident that this was a guy who would need their attention 24/7. Prince's ambition and drive simply outweighed his current position.

Prince now had no regular manager at the helm and his first debut album had failed to reach the dizzy heights he had envisioned. He also could not go on the road just yet to drum up a larger fan base.

In addition, *For You* was hugely over the entire budget which had been set for the first three albums. The message was clear: he needed a new record, he needed to record it fast, and it needed to be a hit. It was time to see if this young prodigy could turn it on when required. In early 1979 Warner Bros stepped in to assist in the search for a manager. It was clear that without this he could not concentrate fully on recording and so it was in their own interests to resolve this situation and get him back to the studio. They suggested Bob Cavallo and Joe Ruffalo, who already had connections with Warner Bros and Earth Wind and Fire. They agreed to take on Prince but initially didn't work with him directly, choosing instead to send an associate to Minneapolis to handle day to day matters. Prince then bought back his management contract with Owen Husney and the transition was complete. It was now back to the studio to concentrate on the second album.

In April 1979 Prince returned to the studio to record songs for his next album, scheduled to be called *Prince*. At the suggestion of his new management team Prince flew to Los Angeles to start work at a home studio owned by engineer Gary Brandt. Brandt was a good friend of Cavallo, who thought this home studio would be a good private place for Prince to work in. Prince rented a house not far from the studio to base himself. As before he had amassed a large body of work and started to pick through his already increasing back catalog of material for inclusion. He spent a full month at Brandt's home studio working at a frantic pace getting the album together. Brandt recalled Prince as a night person, routinely working twelve-hour sessions continuously through the night. He described him as secretive in personality but extremely driven and focused. Prince had all the songs in his head prior to recording so he simply had to be set up and he was away.

Brandt found Prince strange and different in his approach. He wanted things set up in unusual ways during recording, with certain blankets being laid down and cushions, Prince sometimes recording vocals lying down which meant that microphone pickups had to be arranged in certain places. Brandt found that Prince was open to new ideas and techniques but only as long as it didn't interfere with his own musical direction and the sound he wanted to achieve. Little bits of experimentation were starting to creep in to Prince's vocal set up even at this early stage. Prince was open to Brandt and his experience, especially with little tweaks here and there, and Brandt came to know when to offer his experience and when to leave Prince alone. *I Wanna Be Your Lover* is one example of engineer Brandt setting Prince up with the microphone in a certain way having had a long conversation about how to accomplish the sound Prince wanted. They experimented until they got exactly what Prince had in his head, and both Prince and Brandt thought the vocal on this record sounded great.

Interestingly, Brandt thought that Prince's best instrument were the drums and commented on how he always had a strong hook and a very rock orientated rhythm arrangement. Prince has said that from this point he knew exactly how to write hits; he now found it easy and the hits kept coming.

Initially he was booked in to Brandt's home studio for 30 days, and although these were marathon sessions, he ran over slightly and so was forced to finish off at Hollywood Sound, where he completed the album with overdubbing and mixing. Prince completed this with nine songs in nine days. He was fast gaining a reputation

AT ONE EVENT IN NORTH CAROLINA OVER 3000 TEENAGERS SHOWED UP AND STORMED THE STAGE, PRINCE'S FIRST EXPOSURE TO FAN HYSTERIA.

around engineers and music industry insiders as someone to watch.

People noticed that this kid was not your average rock or pop star. He was a pure musician, and unlike the majority of pop or rock stars he was not interested in large houses, cars, drugs or anything materialistic. It was only things that stimulated his creative urge that captivated him.

The *'Rebels'* is a recording session often collected by fans and searched for by Prince collectors far and wide. Shortly after the Prince album was completed, Prince and his band flew to Colorado to record sessions for this musical project. The whole project was a group effort with collaborations from band members Dez Dickerson and Andre Cymone as well as Prince. There were seven songs and a few instrumentals, with the sessions very much guitar based, nodding towards Dez Dickerson's influence. None of the songs recorded here would sit comfortably on the first two Prince albums, showing the diversity of sound Prince had in his band. Prince re-recorded some of the Rebels session songs later on for other artists, notably Paula Abdul and Mica Paris, as well as other side projects he worked on, as he would often do in the years ahead.

In August 1979 Prince and his band played a showcase gig for Warner Bros executives and media associates in Los Angeles. He showcased new material, in particular the two singles from the new album *'I Wanna Be Your Lover'* and *'Why You Wanna Treat Me So Bad'*. In contrast to the earlier show at the Capri Theatre, Warners were this time amazed at the transformation of Prince and his newfound confidence. Not only was he now showing increased musicianship onstage, he was also a fully-fledged front man, going to each band member during the performance to exchange moves and solos. They realized the major potential he had as a live act as well as a studio talent.

While in LA Prince also recorded the two videos for the singles, both showcasing Prince as a live act, with *'I Wanna Be Your Lover'* showing him as a multi-instrumentalist as well as singer. The video is a blatant attempt to show him as a complete one-man-band. There are two versions of *'I Wanna Be Your Lover'* available. The main version shows Prince in an unbuttoned leopardskin shirt and jeans singing alone in a black background with only a microphone, and significantly he has straight/wavy hair, clearly moving away from the large Afro he had the year before. Maybe this was another attempt to avoid categorization as a pure R&B or black artist. This is the version that was released, which the general public would see.

On the 24th August 1979 *'I Wanna Be Your Lover'* was released. It was Prince's first real success. It started slowly but eventually gained momentum, climbing the charts. It hit the number one spot on the soul chart and number eleven on the pop chart. It became certified gold in March the following year having sold more than one million copies. The B-side was *'My Love Is Forever'* from the previous *For You* album with Prince showing the listener there was another album out there, just in case you missed it. *'I Wanna Be Your Lover'* is a natural progression from *'Soft and Wet'* and it's better in every way. It shows Prince becoming more competent in tapping into hooks, melody and arrangement. Some even described

it as a masterpiece. It was the perfect record at the perfect time for him and the success led perfectly to the release of the Prince album. Warners were also pleased as he recorded it at breathtaking speed and it cost four times less than For You. They were delighted that he was proving that he understood the investment that he had been given and that he was enough of a businessman to give all involved a return.

The self-titled *Prince* album was released on 19th October 1979. It was a determined attempt to produce a hit record. It was Prince with something to prove. He succeeded. It went platinum, reassuring anyone at Warner Brothers that, if they had any previous doubts, this guy was bankable and a safe future asset to the music business. As before, Prince composed arranged, wrote and performed the entire album. In the credits, Prince mentioned Bobby Z and Andre Cymone, describing them as heaven-sent helpers. Throughout the album Prince uses his falsetto vocals, giving an innocence to the lyrics. The overall sound in contrast is less reliant on synths than *For You* with more piano on the tender tracks. Heavy guitar licks are showcased on the heavier numbers such as *'Bambi'* and *'Why You Wanna Treat Me So Bad'*. These two tracks also gave Prince ample opportunity to showcase his guitar work when performing live.

The album also sees Prince, as before, trying to stay away from any particular genre: it covers many styles from white pop, R&B, funk and full-on rock. Melodically it's more distinctive than *For You* and choruses and hooks are more prominent and instantly recognizable. Overall it's more satisfying, and easy to digest for the listener. The themes on the album continue as before with Prince falling victim to being mistreated by women, with longing and desire also at the fore. A theme of mistreatment would be something Prince would return to a lot in later years. While *For You* was a heavy nod to what was to come, Prince made the listener feel that he had finally arrived.

Many publications and critics were heralding him as a major future star with the 19-year-old catching attention for his unique blend of Smokey Robinson sounding vocals with urban R&B and funk sounding musicianship. He certainly avoided being pigeonholed into a particular category. The album itself reached number 3 on the R&B chart and stayed there for 23 weeks. Significantly it got to number 22 on the pop chart, so the crossover into mainstream pop was becoming clear.

Prince now wanted to hit the road, and with his band ready and rehearsed to breaking point he now launched his first major tour. It started at the *Roxy Theatre* in Los Angeles on 28th November 1979. There were many music industry insiders in the crowd and some famous faces connected with Warners, including amongst others Bob Marley and his manager Don Taylor, who months earlier was contemplating managing Prince.

The line-up was as before with Bobby Z on drums, Dez Dickerson on guitar, Andre Cymone on bass and two keyboardists, Matt Fink and Gayle Chapman. The shows were naturally based around material from *For You* and *Prince*. What was interesting to most who witnessed the show was how much heavier the sound was live compared to the recorded tracks. There were long drawn out guitar solos from Prince and Dez throughout and quite a rock spectacle, more in keeping with a raw rock band. The band looked uniquely different as well, far from your average R&B outfit ticking along at the time. Prince himself wore gold boots and a large blouse hanging over tight spandex. Dez had a black leather jacket and was shirtless underneath with leopardskin trousers. Andre had a black leotard with some sort of transparent trousers over the top. Fink on keyboards wore a type of bizarre jailbird outfit. All were visually very striking - not something you would see every day. The tour took in 13 major cities across the United States with a homecoming concert scheduled in Minneapolis for December 16th.

During this tour, Prince employed Steve Fargnoli. He ran the second half of the tour as promoter when Prince had problems getting to a concert in time and subsequently sacked the current team. He was soon promoted to a senior figure within Prince's organization working alongside Cavallo and Ruffalo as partner. Fargnoli remained a very close associate and manager to Prince and stayed with him for nearly ten years.

On the 21 February 1980 Prince started a nine-week tour alongside funk star *Rick James*. James was influenced by singers such as Marvin Gaye and Smokey Robinson and began his career performing with R&B groups as a teenager in his hometown of Buffalo, New York. He formed his first rock and R&B band *The Mynah Birds* in Toronto, whose line-up included Bruce Palmer and Neil Young. After serving a one-year prison term for refusing to be drafted into the army he resumed his career on release, moving to California.

While there he formed several rock bands under the name Ricky Matthews. In 1977 he signed with Motown's Gordy Records releasing his debut *Come Get It!* the following year. The album was an instant success selling in excess of two million copies. This launched his career as a funk and soul artist. His most popular album, 1981's *Street Songs*, launched him into superstardom thanks to the hit singles, *'Give It to Me Baby'* and *'Super Freak'*, the latter becoming his signature song.

Prince was touring with James on the crest of this new wave, with James very much the star on the scene having had an already established and colorful past. It would be no surprise to anyone then that Prince, as the young emerging star, and James, as the established act, would not sit quietly on the same stage night in night out. James, the self-proclaimed *"king of punk funk"* had lavish outfits and stage presence, later mocked by the likes of Eddie Murphy for this outlandish fusion of black male machismo. The promotional teams dubbed this tour *'the Battle of the Funk'* with Prince being the contender to the established star. Many critics and audiences favored Prince's showmanship over James's, leading to tensions backstage throughout the tour.

Prince also refused to socialize with James and his crew as there were continuously using drugs, alcohol and women. Prince instead would disappear to a nearby studio and record through the night. Prince also during this tour dressed more wildly than ever, wearing nothing more than leopard skin or zebra striped bikini briefs while strutting his stuff on stage. One night during this tour James wore a jailbird outfit, and Matt Fink was forced to change so there was

no conflict in dress. He scrambled together a surgical gown, stethoscope and mask. Matt Fink overnight became *'Dr Fink'*.

Unfortunately, things didn't work out well for James: he was later imprisoned again, this time for torturing and kidnapping two women while under the influence of crack. He was sentenced to three years. He tried several times to rebuild his career but finance issues blighted him and he never fully recovered. The only real saving grace was a successful claim of back royalties from MC Hammer for *'Can't Touch This'* when he was eventually credited for writing the song. Incidentally this finance claim led to the demise and financial problems of MC Hammer himself.

The tour concluded on 27th April 1980 with the two going their separate ways. It was also the end of female keyboardist Gayle Chapman who was increasingly finding it difficult to cope with Prince's sexually charged stage show and lyrics. She was replaced by a 19-year-old keyboard player and pianist named Lisa Coleman.

Lisa Coleman studied classical piano and had a musical father who was a percussionist. Although she had classical influences from an early age she had been inspired by jazz pianists. She was working as a shipping clerk when one of her friends mentioned that Ruffalo, Cavallo and Fargnoli were about to start to look for a keyboard player for Prince. She posted a tape and Prince asked her to come to Minneapolis for an audition. Prince was instantly impressed with her.

Up until this point he had received virtually no exposure to classical music or indeed jazz, and Lisa's light embellishments were an interesting and colorful touch to Prince's sound. She would later go on to be an established and very important part of his sound and indeed his legacy over the years.

Prince was now an emerging pop star with a growing reputation; he was becoming talked about by all that worked with him as a teenage prodigy and many felt it was only a matter of time before he exploded onto the mainstream. The *Prince* album gave him momentum and held him ready to cross over into the pop charts.

Warner Bros were now delighted: Prince had proved to them that he was someone who could write a hit easily, and they were looking forward to more of the same. They were excited about what would come next - more progress, more hits and more commercial songs that would reach radio and push Prince forward to be the inevitable star he was to become.

Unfortunately, they would have to wait, as Prince decided on something different. Rather than going for the commercial hits, which he now found easy, he decided to follow his artistic tendencies and go pure funk. The explicit nature of the songs he would write for his next album could not even be played on the radio at all. It left Warners scratching their heads. It would either be a commercial disaster or it would alienate him enough to give him a loyal fan base and a true loyal following. All you needed was a *Dirty Mind*.

CHAPTER THREE

I JUST CAN'T BELIEVE ALL THE THINGS PEOPLE SAY...

The next chapter in Prince's continuous rise to the top is a fascinating one. Prince recorded his next album, *Dirty Mind*, entirely in his home studio. This was small and extremely cramped and was limited to just 16 tracks, and he worked and completed it in just one month, in May 1980.

He was renting a new property in a more affluent area within the Minnetonka district. Prince wanted to release *Dirty Mind* just as he had recorded it but Warner Brothers wanted at least to have the opportunity to have Prince remix it at a fully-fledged studio. Prince reluctantly agreed and flew to Los Angeles to commence remixing. Only a fraction of what he had recorded during the month of May was to be on *Dirty Mind*, the rest of the songs shelved for future release or to pop up later on some ghost band or protégée he was working with. Again, it's important to highlight that this whole album and other recordings were all done in one month in marathon sessions at Prince's new house.

It was quite astonishing, and to Prince's eternal credit, that this record was so far away from what he had accumulated so far. It was an album of pure funk with lyrical content so graphic it could not be played on the radio. He was singing about incest, masturbation and oral sex with an overall sound that resembles a collection of demos rather than a polished constructed album built for the masses. *Dirty Mind* shows Prince's fearlessness and long term musical intuition for what he was doing.

Prince worked through the summer in Los Angeles on remixing songs for *Dirty Mind* amidst the obvious concerns from those at Warner Brothers. These concerns were again brought forward when the first single scheduled for release 'Uptown' failed to make the pop charts. It did however do well on the soul chart, reaching number 5. Prince was not, in any way, perturbed by these events; he knew in his own mind exactly what he was doing as the run up to the album's release got closer.

On October 8th 1980 *Dirty Mind*, Prince's third studio album, was released. Completely rebellious from the outset, nothing could

have prepared the legions of young Prince fans for what they were listening too. There is a cleanness in the melodies on the record which is in complete opposition to the lyrical darkness and positively filthy narratives. He wanted, and achieved, a single pop vision and by hiding himself away in his home studio he could be completely immersed in his own creation without any outside interference or influence. Radio play for *Dirty Mind* was, as expected, very minimal, with Warners even issuing stickers to radio stations beforehand warning them to listen first before playing. The overall theme, although obviously sexual, is liberation, freedom, and escaping the shackles of society. Society is a word that Prince uses a lot during this period as he rebels against these constraints urging all to be what they want to be without judgement. It's bordering punk in its attitude but the sound is a pure blend of funk rock. As before, critically the album caused confusion. Articles and reviews produced an ever-increasing list of individuals to compare Prince to as music journalists tried in vain to categorize him. This time though the list of comparisons was different from the last album, making the point that Prince was unique in his sound, look, and overall music. *Dirty Mind*, despite its controversy, reached number 45 on the pop and number 4 on the soul chart. It eventually sold in excess of 500,000 copies in the US, certifying it gold. Naturally it had a large uplift in sales after the success of *Purple Rain*.

On 4th December 1980 Prince took *Dirty Mind* on the road for a month-long tour. Prince's onstage persona and confidence grew rapidly while on this tour and his performances were captivating to those who attended. Not surprisingly the reviews of his performances were excellent and he was, despite the relatively poor sales of the *Dirty Mind* album at this time, becoming a must-see act when he toured. His reputation as a live draw was becoming talked about.

Significantly on the 9th December 1980 Prince reached New York for a concert at The Ritz. There was a large swell growing in the New York club scene about Prince and many celebrities attended this event to see this new wave wonder kid and his band perform.

He had amassed so much critical acclaim that he was fast becoming someone not to be missed wherever he was. In the audience that night was Andy Warhol, the members of rock band Kiss, Nona Hendryx and Nile Rogers amongst many others. The concert was a success and Prince brought the house down, so much so he gave another concert 3 months later with another star-studded crowd. Notably, watching with interest that night was Mick Jagger who contacted Prince's team after the show to ask if Prince would be interested in opening for them in October that year at the Coliseum in Los Angeles. Prince agreed and the concert was put into Prince's schedule. On the 26th December 1980 Prince concluded the *Dirty Mind* tour with a concert at Uptown Theatre, Chicago. The tour, despite poor sales in some cities, was a success in the fact that it gave Prince a loyal following and critical recognition as an incredible live act. He made fans that bought the album and attended his shows feel like they were part of a new movement, a private members' club just for those who got it. His reputation and fan base were growing with every stroke. To add to this momentum *Rolling Stone* magazine published its first article on Prince in February, reviewing the *Dirty Mind* album and adding more attention to Prince and his career to date. They cited Jimi Hendrix as a major comparison for future crossover success.

Prince performed on *Saturday Night Live* on US TV on 21st February 1981. He performed 'Party Up' and strutted around the stage with confidence; it was an incredible piece of showmanship and no one at Warner Bros after this performance had any doubts that he was going to go on to be a massive star. Warner Brothers were now for the first time starting to realize how problematic it could be to have an artist who could make hits at the drop of a hat, was so prolific and was constantly, without stopping for a break, creating music. He was by his very nature extremely bankable; but he would need to be somehow contained for commercial purposes. This was an issue that would manifest itself again and again throughout the years as Warners tried to contain Prince's output for their own financial gain. For now though, Prince had the answer.

The answer came in April 1981 when Prince created *The Time*. Prince signed a publishing deal with Warner Bros to allow him to record and work with other artists, and importantly it gave him an avenue to stay within a certain category without compromising any crossover that he himself was making. Now he had an act that he could write, record and produce music for under a pseudonym. His plan was brilliant.

During the *Dirty Mind* tour Prince had amassed a growing and loyal following of fans and critics alike. Because he was so prolific within the scene he had created he needed competition for himself, and what better way than to create your own competition? As far as the general public were concerned there was a new band on the

ROLLING STONE MAGAZINE PUBLISHED ITS FIRST ARTICLE ON PRINCE IN FEBRUARY, REVIEWING THE DIRTY MIND ALBUM AND ADDING MORE ATTENTION TO PRINCE AND HIS CAREER TO DATE.

scene. They were funky and they sounded a bit like Prince. Some even thought they were better. The point was it was all Prince from the beginning. Every note, every sound, every choreographed move on stage was controlled by Prince. He created his own competition, although the competition he created was his own creation and, ultimately, himself. Prince's vision for *The Time* was for them to be cool, and ultimately very funky. They would be streetwise and wear the best suits and shoes that money could buy. Morris Day would be the front man. He would be the ultimate ladies' man, controlling the band with ease, and using a self-assured strut throughout. Prince would write songs within this genre to allow Morris to make the most of his new identity giving ample room for posing and moving seamlessly with the band; it would be funky and entertaining, bordering comedy in its performances. One rumor as to why Morris was the front man in The Time was that Prince was paying him back for using the song *'Party Up'* on *Dirty Mind*. It was a track Day claimed to have written but Prince took it and re-worked it as his own.

Jimmy Jam and Terry Lee Lewis were members and founders of a Minneapolis funk band named *Flyte Time*. Prince decided that this group could be the backdrop to his new band and asked Andre Cymone to take over the project and approach them to see if they were interested. They had been on the scene for many years in different incarnations since around 1973. They agreed, and the new band was now in place and contracted to Prince; a fully-fledged ghost band as an outlet to release albums through. He quickly finished his demos and continued to Hollywood Sound to finish the mixes at the end of April 1981. He would then go on to teach his new creation the songs for future live performances.

Following on from the interest in Prince from the British press a few months previously, Prince now headed to Europe for the first time. Despite excellent reviews while performing in Holland, England and France, Prince would not return to Europe for many years when his stardom really took off and he crossed fully over to the mainstream of pop as a household name.

Dirty Mind had achieved everything Prince wanted it to, and he had established himself as a major force both live and in the studio. His new creation *The Time* were ready to go and he had a new home with a state-of-the-art studio built in. Things were looking good.

Prince's next album was already being worked on during the tour of *Dirty Mind*. Working seamlessly from one project to another, he had started to form the shape of the album over the course of the summer in 1981. The title track was recorded in his home studio in June and as before he followed up his studio recordings in Los Angeles.

Back at Hollywood Sound, Prince set the basic tracks down for *Controversy* with engineer Bob Mockler. Mockler recalled being blown away by Prince and described his experience later as like watching a modern-day Mozart. Trying to engage socially though was difficult. He did try to talk with him but Prince would be extremely quiet and never initiated a conversation; when asked about music Prince would simply say that he didn't listen to the radio or other bands. He would only really give polite instructions, just to say what he wanted and how he was going to do it: he was simply working and applying himself fully. There were no assistants

or other musicians around, just Prince and the engineer, and it became clear to Mockler that this guy wasn't your average musician; he knew instantly he was working with someone very special. Prince had no interest in anything outside that particular moment and he knew exactly what he wanted to achieve.

Mockler recalled feeling a sense of awe in watching him work, particularly in the way he recorded everything himself, drums first, in one take, with all the fills and gaps as before. Mockler recalled hearing just drums and nothing else coming through the consoles - the tape would be completely clean apart from drums. Next, without hesitation, he would put everything on the drums: bass, keyboards, guitars, and all backing and lead vocals. Mockler had simply not seen anything like it. There was no auto punch for recording back in 1981 so Prince got an engineer to get the sound he wanted and then excuse him/her while he punched himself in to record. All instruments were done in one or two takes. He would always proceed with one song at a time and continue until it was complete.

As well as *The Time* Prince also formed an all-girl group for the first time, to be named *The Hookers*. Prince recorded several songs for the group at his home studio. At this point, there were only two girls in the group, Prince's girlfriend at the time and his assistant. He got the girls to sing over his scratch vocals. He also got Morris Day to record this way during the summer for *The Time*'s songs he had recorded for their debut album. The method was a simple one. Prince would perform the entire song in the studio and then remove his own vocals to a minor whisper, enough for the singer in question to replicate it.

During a rare night off from recording, Prince attended a club and watched a band called Fantasy. Fantasy had an 18-year-old bass player who caught Prince's eye named Mark Brown. Brown was working as a cook at the time so immediately took up the offer when Prince approached him. Prince later renamed him 'Brown Mark' and the future *Revolution* member replaced Andre Cymone on bass.

On 21st July 1981, the debut album by new band The Time was released, titled *The Time*. Production on the album is credited to Morris Day and Jamie Starr, who was the mystery engineer on the *Dirty Mind* project. There are no songwriting credits anywhere on the record and the overall sound is very Prince-like in its production; heavy synth-laden sounds made it quite clear that he was behind the project. Of course, the band denied any involvement with Prince in interviews, although they were questioned, so the mystery was safe for now - most in the know though knew it was him all along.

Their first performance was for a small group of Warner Brothers executives in August 1981 at SIR Studio in Los Angeles. This was seen as a warm up to supporting Prince on his forthcoming tour to promote Controversy. With Prince at the control booth and the band fully rehearsed with Prince's musical tutorial and choreography, they provided a slick outfit and the show was given the green light. Jerome Benton also joined in on this performance as Day's onstage sidekick/valet, adding to Day's onstage persona; a double act that would remain part of any set that The Time did in the future. They performed comedy interludes that included certain dance steps and Benton holding up a mirror so Day could 'do his hair' during the songs. They went on to play a few local Minneapolis gigs to warm up and polish their performances for the forthcoming tour. Prince himself was scheduled to support The Rolling Stones in a few days at the request of Mick Jagger who had been impressed with the show at The Ritz in New York. For his warm up Prince played a 45-minute set at Sam's in Minneapolis. He showcased most of the *Controversy* album, playing all new songs. The gig advertised *Controversy* as the band, but word of mouth soon got around as to who Controversy really was and the venue was completely sold out. This was new member Brown Mark's first performance with Prince and the band.

Prince opened for The Rolling Stones at the Memorial Gardens in Los Angeles on October 9th 1981. He was one of the first on the bill of supporting acts scheduled for the day, onstage at around 2pm. At the start of the set Prince went down well as he belted out his own set of funk and rock fusion, but things soon went downhill. It was an environment that Prince had never been exposed to: objects started to fly onto the stage. First it was small items like plastic cups and bottles but soon the items got larger. Prince was forced to stop playing mid performance. The promoters and officials then regrouped and looked to Prince to come back on and continue his performance, but Prince was gone. He flew immediately back to Minneapolis and refused to perform the following night.

Fargnoli and guitarist Dez Dickerson talked to him and convinced him to play the second night, and Prince agreed; but this time the hostilities were worse with the crowd now in waiting and prepared even before he set foot onto the stage. Before he even started playing, a full chicken was thrown, followed by oranges and all kinds of vegetables. Prince carried on in vain but again after around 15 minutes was forced to stop. He cancelled all remaining scheduled dates even though Mick Jagger tried to convince him to do a couple more shows scheduled for Detroit which, ironically, was one of Prince's strongholds.

On 14th October 1981 *Controversy* was released. It was noted as "a musical outrage and a sincere statement of opposing views". It serves well as a natural follow on record from *Dirty Mind*. The sounds on *Controversy* however are more polished and more rounded, the arrangements are far more filled and expressive to the ear. Prince uses his recently found lower register in many of the tracks giving a different feel to the earlier full falsetto which his audience had become accustomed to. The themes are a mixture of topics from personal confusion and public curiosity towards himself in the title track, to politics, war and sexual liberation. The mix of religion and sex would be a blended theme throughout much of Prince's work to come. Religion and sex were, and still are, separated territories in both society and music which had never been put together in such a fashion; to some this was confusing, to others it was bordering offensive, but for Prince this was all the same ride. References to work were often seen as sexual, the implied suggestive lyrics having double meanings, as in 'Let's Work'.

Controversy outsold *Dirty Mind* and was met with positive reviews. It was a natural successor and, in many ways, it was Prince trying to answer certain questions that had been asked of him from the previous record. It went gold within two months, going platinum - 1 million copies - a few years later. It went to number 1 on the soul chart and hit number 21 on the pop chart in the US. It was voted the 8th best album of the year by an annual poll of critics.

Prince worked his new creation *The Time* through rehearsals and choreography through the summer of 1981, and he also spent time during a break from the tour to record their second album, *What time is it?* Prince recorded several tracks for them at his home studio again with Morris Day singing over Prince's pre-recorded vocals. He also recorded several songs during these home sessions that would surface on his own next album *1999* as well as others that would emerge as B-sides. After these sessions and with the bulk of The Time's second album completed Prince returned to the second leg of the *Controversy* tour, hitting Florida at the end of January 1982.

During this time in January 1982, while on the *Controversy* tour, Prince met another significant figure at the American Music Awards ceremony in Los Angeles. Denise Mathews was a young, confident and beautiful aspiring actress and singer. She started her young career by entering local beauty pageants before eventually moving to Toronto where she started modeling and entering various competitions. She won the Miss Niagara Hospitality title in 1977 and competed for Miss Canada in 1978. At just 17 she moved to New York City looking for her big break. She eventually signed to a professional modeling agency but because of her height she was restricted to photo shoots and commercials and not the full-on runway work which she craved. She moved into acting and had various small roles in some B movies going by the name of DD Winters. She eventually met with Prince while attending the American Music Awards, and she left with him and joined his entourage. He renamed her Vanity and she became the lead in his new girl group *Vanity 6*.

On 7th March at the Met centre in Minneapolis Prince's tour arrived for a performance which Prince decided he wanted to record for a live record and film. The Time, as before, opened the show before Prince took to the stage. The filming also featured backstage footage as well as interviews with members of the public who attended the show. Prince watched the footage back and planned a film, to be called *The Second Coming*, which would be a taste of the live show for those who hadn't had the pleasure of seeing it. The project however soon became problematic with the weight of ideas that started to spiral out of control, ultimately resulting in it being shelved. All was not entirely lost as *The Second Coming* put the thought clearly in Prince's head that a loose biography/concert movie could work, providing the right elements were present. Without *The Second Coming*, *Purple Rain* may never have come to pass; almost without skipping a beat the promotional tool was shelved and Prince started to visualize an autobiographical movie of some sort. Prince was now playing with the idea of a movie and his ideas were starting to develop as the tour continued.

The next hometown stop off was a day later at First Avenue. This was a venue Prince was fast becoming associated with and a place where he could try out new material and be a little more relaxed in his performances. The crowd at First Avenue would soon get accustomed to Prince playing songs for the first time and even showcasing new band members. Prince played to a capacity crowd in the packed venue. He played for around an hour, stating when he started the show that it wasn't a concert but a 'dance'. Morris Day and The Time joined Prince on stage as they closed the set with Morris playing the drums. The show ended with a rapturous version of 'Party up'.

On the 14th March Prince played the final concert of the Controversy tour at the Coliseum, Cincinnati. The atmosphere from the outset was mischievous with everyone in high spirits. The concert turned into a full-on food fight between The Time and Prince. While The Time were playing the opening act eggs started to be thrown from the side of the stage. Maybe Prince had drawn inspiration from his experience of supporting The Rolling Stones. The chaos then spilled backstage with members of each band armed with eggs and cakes chasing each other all over the venue. After Prince's performance members of The Time hunted him down and continued the fight. The mood clearly was one of success and accomplishment; the tour had been both commercially and personally lucrative and Prince's side project was proving a masterstroke, giving him an outlet to release songs that would ordinarily be shelved. His ferocious output and songwriting productivity were proving to be incredible, but he knew that it was simply not commercially viable to release this amount of material through his own name. The Time allowed for this and now, in addition, he had even more room for his creativity to flow with his new girl group. His star was definitely rising.

Prince was starting to focus more and more on the idea of an autobiographical film. He was now beginning to scribble notes and form ideas for this venture - a purple notebook started to appear. Also in March, while at his home studio, Prince started to write and perform songs for his new group Vanity 6, again with Prince recording everything, with the odd addition by Dez Dickerson. The set up was the same, with Prince singing all vocals and then Vanity singing over them for the finished track. Prince completed the Vanity 6 album at Sunset Sound as well as initial tracks for his next album, as yet unnamed, the first being 'Let's Pretend We're Married'.

In May 1982 Prince now, with the *Vanity 6* album completed and his own new album underway, set about recording songs for The Time's second album *What Time is it?* This was a period of prolific writing for Prince. Songs were simply pouring out of him and his creativity and obsession to write and record were unmatched. A lot of songs recorded during this time were later to go on to feature on future albums; notably he recorded 'Raspberry Beret', later to be released on *Around the World in a Day* in 1985. He also recorded 'New Position' which found its way onto *Parade* in 1986, 'Strange Relationship' which eventually settled on *Sign O' The Times* in 1987 and 'I Can't Stop This Feeling I Got' which made *Graffiti Bridge* in 1989. Productivity like this was always going to create a back catalog; it was an ongoing issue that needed consideration. Only on a few occasions did he go into a studio to record an album specifically for a certain project. He always had so much in the locker, or later 'vault', that he could at any time slot old songs into new projects, or re-record them, though often the re-recorded versions lost the edge of creativity as they were worked into a new arrangement. It was clear though that many songs he was completing would simply be shelved with the hope that maybe one day they would be resurrected for use either by himself or others. Either way, whether they would appear on an album or not, was irrelevant to Prince, whose only goal was to get the idea and song completed and move on to the next with studio engineers now revolving in shifts to keep up with him.

Prince continued during the summer of 1982 recording tracks with his band at Sunset Sound for his new album. One studio engineer working with Prince at this time was Peggy McCreary. Peggy had previously worked with Janet Jackson and Toto before Prince and The Time in 1982. Peggy commented on how different Prince was to others she had worked with, stating that he never worked in any conventional way - nothing was normal. He would come into the studio with a song in his head, record it, overdub it, sing it and mix it all in one go, from start to finish. Engineers would often wonder what he was up to. They all knew this guy was insanely talented and could turn out songs at will. He would go from recording drums, to bass, to guitars, to vocals and complete an entire song in hours, he had so much coming out of him. Sometimes it wasn't plain sailing for Prince though, as he would just keep going and if the songs turned out to be long they needed overdubbing, which meant more time and inevitably less sleep for all involved. Engineers like Peggy learned how to be fast around him, often setting him up quickly and leaving him to record before returning and setting up the next instrument.

To avoid breaks and distractions even more, Prince's home studio was also now fitted with state-of-the-art 24-track machines. This would be the same studio he would go on to record *Purple Rain* in, although the house at Lake Riley had not yet been painted purple. The studio set up was built in the basement - maybe nostalgia for Prince from his teenage years - and he had large monitors mounted on the walls. There was an isolation room built in and a full drum set in there. There was every state-of-the-art keyboard of the day as well as every guitar and amp set up money could buy. And of course, he had his Linn drum machine, which he could program at will for extra speed. Drummer Bobby Z recalls looking at this machine in wonder, like an assembly worker staring at a robot for the first time wondering if he had a future alongside it.

And so, when it was complete, in July 1982 Prince went back home and instantly recorded two tracks, 'Little Red Corvette' and '1999'. He knew both of these tunes were significant and paused on them while he headed back to Sunset Sound and completed the *What Time is it?* album for with The Time.

His band were also now becoming more of a central point in rehearsals. Prince as ever would jam all day and work things through. He now dubbed his band *The Revolution*, giving them a clear identity of their own. In August, still at Sunset Sound, he also completed the final work on his own new album, now to be entitled *1999*. The album now edited down from the vast amount of songs Prince had recorded during this period, Prince was happy that he had a clear signature track from the recent recordings.

It was also in August that the *Vanity 6* debut album was released. Vanity herself, ambitious and driven for success, was fired up for this and ready for fame. However, radio airplay was cautious, mainly due to the sexual nature of the songs. The image of Vanity 6 did not hide from this; whereas in some cases sexual references could be subtle and hidden in innuendo, the image and full-on nature of Vanity 6 left nothing to the imagination: it was obvious what the message was. This was ultimately, under the surface, about liberation and equality. However, this type of liberation and equality had a visual message that kind of got lost when Vanity 6 hit the stage or TV screen.

Prince's vision was for women to be ultimately sexy but to have control and independence. No one could tell them what to do, everything was their choice and they were out to have fun and break down stereotypes. Scantily clad in lace, dancing to Prince's choreography, they looked more like three strippers than a female band with an unshackling message of liberty. It was, to Prince's credit, ahead of its time.

The album itself peaked at number 45 on the pop charts, and fared better on the soul chart, which was now introduced as the black chart, landing at number 6. None of the singles charted on the pop chart, which Vanity herself was very disappointed with. It was,

crucially, not as popular as The Time's debut album, and they were now waiting in the wings to release their own follow up. The two ghost bands were in competition with each other, which is interesting considering it was all one person creating everything.

The Vanity 6 album did eventually get certified gold, selling in excess of 500,000 copies, but not until 1985 when Vanity herself was well gone, just before Prince had moved on to be the biggest star on the planet. For now though Prince was about to become even more popular, and the crossover he was searching for was just around the corner.

Prince performing during the Nude Tour in Tokyo, Japan in 1990

CHAPTER FOUR

DON'T WORRY
I WON'T HURT YOU...

On August 25th 1982, The Time's second album *What Time Is It?* was released. As before, Prince isn't mentioned anywhere on the credits but production is credited to The Starr Company. It was around this time that certain fractures started to appear with The Time.

Although *What Time Is It?* is a Time record it was essentially all recorded by Prince himself. The band wanted more input, particularly in recording songs, but as ever with Prince's ferocious appetite for recording by the time they had expressed a grievance for being shut out Prince had already recorded most of the songs already. Those in particular that were becoming frustrated were Jimmy Jam and Terry Lewis. During the *Controversy* tour Jam and Lewis had flown to Los Angeles to work on their own material, but they never introduced it for The Time as they thought it didn't match the image of the band. They both were under the impression that the whole concept of The Time was built solely around Morris Day and the rest of the band were just seen as backing musicians; and both had aspirations beyond this.

The new Time album was much improved from its predecessor both in melodic terms and in pure funk. The tracks are consistent and serve any audience who loved the first album well, maintaining the fan base as well as showcasing new funky tunes. It became an even bigger hit than its predecessor, reaching number 26 on the pop chart and number 2 on the black chart. They were now established as a funk band in their own right and their mix of tight choreography and live band imagery only added fuel to the growing fire surrounding them.

After the two released albums by Prince's bands *The Time* and *Vanity 6*, it was now time for Prince to release his own material starting with the single '1999' on 24th September 1982. Disappointingly it only reached number 4 on the black chart and number 44 on the pop charts. Despite being a brilliant piece of crossover music that Prince was convinced would fit the bill, it didn't land in the right area at the right time. It also had the superb B-side '*How Come U Don't Call Me Anymore*', the two songs together showcasing Prince's genius versatility. '*How Come U Don't Call Me*' was recorded by Prince alone in one take in the early hours of the morning. Simple harmonies on the chorus add a gospel tinge to the track and coupled with '*1999*' it is surprising that these two together didn't do better. Despite this initial setback '*1999*' would go on to become one of Prince's best-known songs and a defining

moment in his rise to superstar status. It has an apocalyptic yet upbeat message and it's a pure party anthem, and when Prince later re-released it on the back of the *1999* tour it became a smash hit. It peaked at number 12 in the US in July 1983, and at number 25 in the UK in January 1983, and eventually reached number 2 in the UK when re-released in January 1985, as part of a double A-side with '*Little Red Corvette*'. For now though it made decent progress and the core Prince fan base eagerly waited for the new album.

The *1999* album was officially released on 27th October 1982 and became his most commercially successful album to date. One of the keys to the success of *1999* was that it was simultaneously experimental as well as remaining commercial. It was Prince's fifth album and his back catalog was becoming widely looked at as he progressed forward. Again, Prince refused constant requests for interviews, preferring instead to let the music do the talking. This new album, his live reputation and the mystery surrounding him gave Prince even more popularity amongst the growing legion of fans and admirers in the music world.

As before it's the synth that dominates the sound and the LM-1 drum machine throughout gives a constant recognizable structure that weaves things together perfectly. It's a fusion of rock and funk that gives a new age feel to the music, with rhythmic and pulsing arrangements throughout. It showcases everything Prince was about at the time: pure pop, hard funk, soothing ballads and guitar led rock. The album also sees Prince acknowledging his band for the first time by adding *The Revolution* on the cover, although this is not instantly recognizable. He had to battle hard to get Warner Bros to let him release a double album, which on vinyl would consist of four sides of music. Each song continues longer than usually expected of a standard song at the time. When you consider that he also wrote the albums for *The Time* and *Vanity 6* at the same time, it is astonishing he had so much quality to record such an experimental and yet accessible body of work for himself. As expected with such progression in his musical stance the reviews of *1999* were excellent, and the album went platinum status and remained on the Billboard chart for an incredible 153 weeks.

Just a month after the release of *1999* Prince hit the road again for the *1999* tour of the US starting at The Memorial Auditorium in Tennessee. As before reviews of the shows were brilliant with Prince showcasing all his musical talent on stage. It was the full Prince show in every aspect, with Vanity 6 starting the show followed by The Time and then Prince, now with The Revolution.

Both Prince and The Time were well received by audiences and critics alike but Vanity 6 were less successful. The overall image of the girls, coupled with poor dancing and weak vocals, made some of the appearances awkward spectacles. In comparison, The Time as ever were humorous and slick during their own 40 minutes. Morris Day was perfect in his role as king of the pimps moving seamlessly throughout the tight choreographed songs. Dez Dickerson though was becoming more distant in the band and he started going AWOL on some rehearsals. Prince replaced Dez, at these rehearsals, with a friend of keyboardist Lisa Coleman's called Wendy Melvoin. Wendy played a bit of guitar and was traveling with Lisa on the tour bus. It was a sign of things to come. Vanity was also becoming unhappy, and her own band were becoming argumentative, with disagreements most nights after performances; one reason was that Prince was dating both Vanity and Susan Moonsie from the band, making things difficult for both girls. With such a large entourage now touring, it was inevitable that there would not be complete harmony. There were several tour buses, one for The Time and The Revolution, one for Vanity 6 and one for Prince, and whoever he wanted to have with him at the time.

As the tour continued Prince, on 21 November 1982, agreed to conduct an interview with *The Los Angeles Times*. He had agreed to participate in quite a few interviews, as his management thought it would be a good way of promoting the new album; but when things started to pick up, and the album was proving to be making great progress, Prince withdrew this commitment, just keeping this one interview which he had already agreed to. He was interviewed by the American pop music critic and author Robert Hilburn. He opened up, after a while, and talked about his name, his father, and emphasized the fact he was not gay, quashing rumors circulating around at the time. Prince's image was something that was ahead of its time: he didn't really see male and female boundaries and would often experiment with different looks. Like his music, his look was unique, and he always looked the star he was becoming.

Without exception, nearly all great guitarist and rock stars who were popular at the time would be clad in machismo leather and jeans, conveying a hard-male image. Prince was in a frilly blouse, wearing lace and high heels but playing guitar in the style of Hendrix and Santana and singing about sex and god. It was an interesting and, to some, confusing mix. He seemed to be a disconcerting mix of masculinity and femininity all rolled into one. He wanted to make things clear at this interview. Interestingly, he also stated that he was not Jamie Starr. The interview with Hilburn would be Prince's last interview until 1985. He would become the biggest musician on the planet, but speak less.

As the tour continued, the Prince show was scheduled for a performance at Detroit. It turned out that Detroit was fast becoming a Prince stronghold, so much so that he played a full 6 concerts there at the Masonic Temple Auditorium, selling in excess of 30,000 tickets, including 2 matinee performances to fit in with demand. Also, around a week later, Prince held a benefit concert when the tour reached Chicago. Marva Collins was founder and director of a charity for children with learning difficulties, and Prince's show raised over $10,000 for the cause. Prince also sat in on some of Collins' classes and this began a long association between Marva Collins and Prince. She had lots of success in her

teaching methods and was seen as a revolutionary figure in reaching children with Autism and those with learning difficulties - she was ahead of her time in her methods. A year after her first meeting with Prince it was reported that President Ronald Reagan wanted to nominate Collins as Secretary of Education, but Collins took herself out of the running for the position. Also in 1983, Reagan cited Collins during an unveiling of a national program to combat adult illiteracy. In 1994, Prince featured Collins in his music video for *'The Most Beautiful Girl in the World.'* He also donated $500,000 to the Westside Preparatory School Teacher Training Institute, which was created to teach her methodology.

On the 16th December 1982, a major change happened in the career of Prince that would finally make his crossover dream possible. Until this point Prince was, despite his efforts, seen as a black artist. Prince did not want to be seen in any specific category; understandable considering the depth and versatility in his music. He was, in nearly all publications written about him, described as a fusion of many styles - rock, funk, soul and pop. More than any other artist, he didn't fit into any specific genre.

Music Television, or *MTV*, was a joint venture between American Express and Warner Communications. It made its first appearance a year earlier in August 1981. By 1983 it had an audience of around 15 million and was growing rapidly. Music videos were becoming a vital part of any artist's repertoire and were beginning to be seen as an essential part of promotion. MTV targeted the mid 20s generation who were being abandoned by radio stations; it was also, until this point, a rock and roll medium leaning toward white acts with black artists very much the minority. It was only the crossover of Prince and Michael Jackson that paved the way for Whitney Houston, Lionel Richie, Tina Turner and Janet Jackson. This crossover held its own until mainstream rap acts emerged in the late 80s and became a regular feature for black artists. On 16th December 1982 MTV added the video for *'1999'* to its playlist. This immediately gave Prince a new audience and opened up a significant amount of exposure he would not otherwise have had. Before this point, Prince was essentially a cult artist. Although he had a rapidly growing fanbase the exposure of the *'1999'* video catapulted him into the mainstream. Without this it is fair to say it may have taken years of continuous touring to reach this level of exposure, especially with his resistance to interviews on radio or TV. The album shortly after this point started to accelerate up the charts, and the audiences on the second leg of the tour started to change to a more mixed race crowd as opposed to being predominantly black as before.

During Christmas 1982 Prince shot a cover photo for *Rolling Stone* magazine with Vanity alongside him. He was offered $10,000 for an interview to go alongside the photo. Prince agreed to the shoot but refused the interview, and the money. A week later during the break Prince, in typical style, checked back into Sunset Sound to work on some extended versions of some tracks. He recorded an extended version of *'Little Red Corvette'* and met Stevie Nicks, who was working on her follow up album after the success of her debut *Bella Donna*. Nicks was a huge Prince admirer and the two struck up a great working relationship that lasted for years to come. She was recording a song for the album called *'Stand Back'* and was having trouble with it; Prince offered to help and added keyboards to the track. She also showed Prince some of her recording set ups, in particular how she set up her microphone to get the vocal sound she wanted. Prince replicated this on many tracks going forward.

As 1983 rolled in Prince, on the back of the *'1999'* video success, recorded the video for *'Little Red Corvette'* after rehearsals. The video featured the full band, this time with Dez Dickerson in attendance, and showcased Prince dancing and using the stage to maximum effect. It would be lined up for MTV to add it to the playlist as a natural follow on from the *'1999'* video that had such commercial success. This proved to be another winning decision as, on February 9th 1983, *'Little Red Corvette'* was released and the video hit the MTV playlist at the start of the second phase of the tour, a perfect storm for reaching maximum exposure. The second leg of the tour now commenced with a concert at Lakeland.

Prince's management team, now frantic to keep hold of him, set about approaching various Hollywood studios in the hope of convincing them that this musical sensation was also a bankable movie star. As expected there was widespread refusal as many hadn't heard of Prince. Although they were impressed with what they heard, raising any sort of finance to cover a major feature film would be too much of a commercial risk. Even Warner Bros film division were too nervous to commit, especially when they realized that Prince only had 'ideas' for a film and not even a concise script.

Warner Bros Records Chairman was Mo Austin. He had, and still has to this day, maintained an exceptional career. He became well known not only as a hugely successful record executive but also for backing artists that needed assistance: he saw the artist first with the commercial aspect second, and believed that if the artistic nature worked then the commercial success would follow. This

made him widely trusted as well as commercially respected in the music industry. He encouraged creativity. Prince's management approached him for help and seeing the potential he loaned Prince and his team the finance to start the production of the movie.

It wasn't long before Prince's team realized that they needed an experienced writer to translate Prince's ideas to a script. They approached William Blinn. As a writer Blinn had had an impressive career to date: starting in the 1960s he had worked his way through the 1970s on various TV and film projects, winning many awards. He had recently written the screenplay for the hit TV show *Fame* and he also served as executive producer. *Fame* had just started and was not yet commissioned for a repeat series; it was yet to be the huge success it turned out to be. Blinn was free to take up the challenge as he waited to hear if Fame would be continuing. The brief was a simple one: Blinn had to translate Prince's ideas to a cohesive script and find an audience beyond the current following Prince had gained. They had a meeting and Blinn, although impressed with Prince and his intelligence, found it difficult to get him to expand his ideas. Despite this Prince did convey very well the feeling of the film and he knew each character and what he wanted and didn't want. Blinn went away and started to work on the script while Prince continued the second phase of the *1999* tour, this time with the help of *'Little Red Corvette'* which flew up the charts reaching the pop top 10, giving Prince his first major hit. It peaked at number 6 and was the first time a single had got higher in the pop charts than the black charts for Prince. The music video was now also being played continually on MTV and the audiences attending the concerts were now mixed completely, in some cities 60% white and 40% black, a complete reversal from the start of the tour. Midway through the second phase of the tour Prince was voted artist of the year by *Rolling Stone* magazine.

William Blinn caught up with Prince again to offer updates on the screenplay, this time in Minneapolis, when the tour reached the Twin Cities for a homecoming concert at the Met Centre, a complete sell out at the 13,500-seat venue. After the show Blinn continued discussions with Prince on the new script for the planned feature film, and Prince also met up with Stevie Nicks again, now recently married. Blinn discovered more about Prince's relationship with his father, which gave him more direction in developing the main characters in the screenplay.

The Time did not perform when the tour reached New York, with no explanation given, but it was clear that the relationship between Prince and his creation was not getting any better. Alan Leeds, brother of soon-to-be-saxophonist Eric Leeds, took over, and was appointed as the new road manager for Prince while in New York - an interesting time to be a road manager with such activity going on around the tour. Both Eric and Alan would stay with Prince for many years. Alan Leeds already had a back story and music career that would have been interesting to Prince. He began as a music writer before going on to become involved with James Brown as his publicity director in 1969. He continued to work with Brown and became his tour manager from 1970 to 1973. It's an incredible CV to have been a manager to the two biggest funk legends in the history of popular music. Alan Leeds would go on to stay with Prince for many years and eventually, in 1989, become president of Prince's *Paisley Park* label.

Two days after the New York concert Prince had more problems

Shutterstock

with The Time when, in San Antonio, Jimmy Jam and Terry Lewis failed to show up for the concert. Prince was forced to play bass behind a curtain while Jerome Benton strapped on a bass guitar and pretended to play throughout the set. Lisa Coleman stepped up to play the keyboards. Despite this Prince was keen to continue with the success of The Time and once again, between concerts, checked himself into Sunset Sound in March 1983 to record some songs for a planned third album.

He wrote and recorded 'Jungle Love' at this session, which would go on to be one of the signature tunes for The Time. The next day at a concert in Los Angeles the show was littered with stars who were keen to see the new rising star that everyone was talking about: guests included Quincy Jones, Stevie Wonder and Bruce Springsteen amongst others. Interestingly at this show The Time once again did not perform.

The 1999 tour concluded in Chicago on 10th April 1983. It had been an incredible five months. From when the tour started to this point Prince, still only 24, had worked his way from a seemingly cult figure and underground genius to a famous pop star whose reputation for songwriting and performing was getting stronger by the minute. In addition, the tour was hugely lucrative for him. It grossed around $10 million, the highest in 1983, and being 1983 that was a significant amount of money. As ever with Prince though the money was nothing to ponder over, it was simply a means to help him create more, with less interference. His creative compulsiveness was as compelling as ever. The accolades and support for Prince within the entertainment industry were evident all around the media establishment, and comedians and other pop and rock stars were eager to be associated with him now the transition from cult hero to mainstream rock star was complete.

Four days after the tour ended Prince continued at Sunset Sound on additional tracks with Morris Day for The Time's third album, as before with Morris singing over Prince's original vocals to complete the tracks. While at Sunset Sound Prince called Jimmy Jam and Terry Lewis in to fire them from The Time. The combination of the pair working on their own projects as well as missing the concert for The Time a month earlier was something Prince could not allow to continue. They did however go on to have a lucrative career of their own and stayed in close contact with Prince over the years.

The photo shoot for *Rolling Stone* magazine Prince participated in at Christmas was now featured in the May edition of the magazine. The headline title is *'Prince's hot rock, the secret life of America's sexiest one-man band'* and Prince is dressed in a purple trench coat with open blouse and bare chest; behind him is Vanity with matching eyes looking seductively into the camera. The article is well researched and examines Prince's career to date, quoting interviews with Steve Fargnoli, Chris Moon, Owen Husney and Bernadette Anderson. Interestingly it also reveals that Prince is in fact Jamie Starr and blows the cover on his involvement with The Time.

May 1983 was a month of significant movement towards the starting of the movie and subsequent soundtrack that would eventually be one of biggest selling albums of all time. At the start of the month William Blinn relocated to Minneapolis to work closer with Prince and to develop the screenplay further. Things didn't go well for Blinn, as he found he was constantly being stood up by Prince: he had various appointments scheduled where Prince simply did not turn up, without explanation. The final straw came when they went to see a movie and halfway through Prince got up and left without comment. After this Blinn decided he could not work with someone so unpredictable and flew back to Los Angeles with the script still incomplete. He threatened to cancel the project altogether unless Prince was willing to cooperate with him. Prince called Blinn a few days later and they talked at length. Blinn joined Prince back in Minneapolis shortly afterwards and this time Prince did fully cooperate, giving Blinn ideas and character developments for the script. It wasn't long before Blinn was able, now with the help of Prince, to develop the screenplay and get it to a cohesive conclusion to take forward to production.

Also in May, Dez Dickerson decided to leave the band; he was naturally replaced by Wendy Melvoin who was waiting in the wings, having been stepping into rehearsals and starting to become more confident around Prince and the rest of the band. The duo of *'Wendy & Lisa'* had started and would become synonymous with Prince and beyond as they furthered their own respectable careers.

Wendy was born in Los Angeles and came from a musical family: she was the daughter of jazz pianist Mike Melvoin who, in the 1960s, was part of the Los Angeles session musician collective The Wrecking Crew. She got her first guitar aged 6 and was always surrounded by musicians as she grew up. She was a competent guitarist but lacked the confidence to play in front of a crowd. Wendy's brother, Jonathan Melvoin, was the *Smashing Pumpkins'* touring keyboardist, and her twin sister is singer and composer Susannah Melvoin who would later be Prince's primary girlfriend. Susannah met Prince while visiting Minneapolis to see her sister; Prince fell for her and cared for her deeply, and she would be the inspiration for some of Prince's most heartfelt songs during the coming years. Wendy provided the band with a more relaxed and balanced feeling. There were, for now anyway, no issues and the band seemed to be becoming a cohesive machine. *The Revolution* was complete.

Continuing in May, Prince hired an unused warehouse in preparation for the film project. The remaining members of *The Time, Vanity 6* and Prince's new look *Revolution* settled in for dancing, acting and drama classes. They were scheduled in this space for three days a week for three months, which proved a little too much in the way of discipline for some, especially Vanity who didn't take too kindly to early starts and a strict schedule. Although Prince didn't need the dancing part he did nevertheless participate in acting and drama and gave the classes his full attention and devotion. They had designers also set up in the warehouse facility to design a new wardrobe for *Prince and The Revolution*. They expanded on Prince's own look and added a more flamboyant dress scene to The Revolution for the film.

Towards the end of May William Blinn completed the finished script, still titled *'Dreams'*, and handed it to Prince. It was significantly different to the story we know today and much darker that the released film. One major difference was that both Prince's parents were dead and Wendy & Lisa were in a relationship, which was true in real life but not so obvious in the finished film. Prince, having read the script, wanted to make a few changes, one being that he wanted the word purple in the title. Blinn set about reviewing the changes and started working on a second draft only to be called back to Los Angeles as the second series of *Fame* had been commissioned. As he was contractually obliged to this he had to return. He left Prince with the original screenplay but now there was no director.

August 3rd 1983 was a significant night for Prince and a historical night for anyone who is a fan, a night when he would record live the songs that would go on to appear in the soundtrack to *Purple Rain*. It was a benefit concert held at First Avenue in aid of the Minnesota Dance Theatre. The concert was set up by Loyce Houlton who had met Prince during the dance classes previously and asked him if he would provide a fundraising show for the Theatre. The Dance Theatre, up until this point, was having severe financial difficulties and was in desperate need of funding. The Prince concert held that night raised over $23,000 for the cause.

At the last minute, Prince decided he wanted to record the concert; he had recently started to record his concerts so he could watch them back and study the shows for improvements. This was one of the reasons his concerts were frequently changing as a tour progressed. A mobile recording unit was quickly brought in from New York and set up in First Avenue ahead of the show. This was Wendy Melvoin's debut with the band and although she had been in rehearsals she had not, as yet, played in front of a crowd. Many believe, considering what was recorded and how the live songs were used on the finished soundtrack, that it was the one of the most important and significant concerts he ever did.

The show started with the Minnesota Dance Theatre performing some dances, the last dance to Prince's *'DMSR'*. Prince and The Revolution then opened with new song *'Let's Go Crazy'*. It would be one of six new songs he would play that evening to the capacity sell-out crowd in the packed hot venue. *'When U Were Mine'* followed from 1981's *Dirty Mind* but this time a more guitar led version. Slowing things down it was followed by a brilliant version of Joni Mitchell's *'A Case of U'*. Lisa had recently introduced Prince to Joni Mitchell and he loved the *Blue* album from 1971 featuring this track. It featured just Prince on guitar and Lisa on keyboards and is a perfect showcase of Prince's versatility as he smiled and showed complete musical emotion throughout the track. He next played *'Computer Blue'* which he shredded the guitar to and moved effortlessly around the stage - this version was so raw it was rarely topped in any subsequent performances. Next was *'Delirious'* which was the next single scheduled for release from the *1999* album, before Prince sat at the piano and gave a jaw-dropping version of the unreleased track *'Electric Intercourse'*.

The encore was the exact version of *'Purple Rain'* that finished the album. Prince, covered in sweat, performed the song for the first time to the amazed crowd showing great emotion throughout, the blistering guitar solo and audience participation at the end finishing off a staggering performance. He left the stage only to return for one final encore of *'DMSR'*. These live recordings *'Baby I'm A star'*, *'I Would Die 4 U'* and *'Purple Rain'* would make the soundtrack in their live format as performed this night. Prince knew these recordings were special and immediately booked time into his home studio and Sunset Sound to work on them and write additional songs around them.

During August 1983, as preparations continued for the forthcoming production, Vanity decided she had finally had

enough and quit the film project altogether. The relationship was already volatile, with Prince reportedly having many girlfriends at the time including Vanity. She also was demanding more money for her role in *Purple Rain* and her ambitious nature was driving her to look at other projects and film roles. Prince had just written and completed the Purple Rain track *'Darling Nikki'* as well as the majority of the second *Vanity 6* album. They were also heavily into rehearsals for the movie and Prince was booked into Sunset Sound to complete other songs for the project through September, which included recording new tracks such as *'The Beautiful Ones'* which Prince was so pleased with he replaced *'Electric Intercourse'* with it for the album. He also finished overdubs from the First Avenue live recordings for inclusion and rerecorded *'Computer Blue'* with Wendy and Lisa, turning it into a longer version that was subsequently edited down before it appeared on the record. Prince continued the success of *'1999'* with a third top 20 pop chart hit *'Delirious'* which peaked at number 8 in September, again making the crossover complete to the mainstream pop charts.

<hr />

Patricia Kotero was born in Santa Monica, California, the daughter of immigrants from Mexico and the eldest of six children. Always ambitious from an early age Patricia dropped out of high school at age 16 to pursue her dream of becoming a model. Relocating to Los Angeles, she began entering various beauty competitions with high aspirations for a breakthrough of some sort. She won the *Miss San Pedro* Beauty Competition and shortly afterwards became a cheerleader for the Los Angeles Rams. Like Vanity, Patricia was driven and determined to find her big break. Her personal story reflected the role she would eventually land with Prince. The part in the film portrayed a young woman moving to Minneapolis to find work as a dancer and singer, chasing her dream. She then started working on various small modeling jobs and some acting parts.

Kotero appeared in several popular TV shows at the start of the 1980s including *C.H.I.P.S* and *Knight Rider*. In 1982 she appeared in the music videos for *'The Other Woman'* by Ray Parker Jr and *'Shakin''* by Eddie Money. She then appeared in the 1984 movie *The Mystic Warrior* before turning up in New York to audition, alongside several hundred other women, for the lead role in a new feature film starring alongside a new rock star named Prince. She got the role and on meeting Prince he decided to rename her *Apollonia* after a character in The Godfather.

Now the replacement lead was secured, the film needed a director as William Blinn was back working on *Fame*. The position was eventually filled by 30-year-old Albert Magnoli. Although Magnoli had limited experience in directing, Prince's management team were highly impressed with his ideas and vision for the movie. They immediately wanted him to meet with Prince and for the two of them to discuss the movie in detail. Magnoli wanted to make changes and he and Prince set about tweaking aspects of the script that they weren't happy with and developing the characters.

Although the screenplay is attributed to both Blinn and Magnoli it is fair to say that the majority of the script was in fact written by Magnoli; it went through significant changes that Prince wanted

Shutterstock

to make, making the transition from *'Dreams'* to *'Purple Rain'*. The name change was a spontaneous decision, as was often the case with Prince. Magnoli was watching rehearsals with Prince and The Revolution when Prince performed *'Purple Rain,'* a recently written song. Magnoli asked Prince afterwards what the song was called, Prince answered *'Purple Rain'* and Magnoli asked if he could put it somewhere in the movie, suggesting some scenes where he thought it would work. Prince asked if the movie could be called *Purple Rain* and base the whole thing around it. Magnoli agreed and from that point *'Dreams'* became *'Purple Rain'*.

With this now completed, pre-production started in Minneapolis with the cast of *Purple Rain*. Prince, as well as joining in the shooting of *Purple Rain*, took time out to record and re-record several songs for the film, including background and incidental music that could be used throughout various scenes.

Shooting began on November 1st 1983 at 32 separate locations in and around Minneapolis. The main issue was weather, with the shooting having to be complete at the outside locations before the Minnesota winter came and snowed everyone in, a frequent and common occurrence in the state. Unfortunately, the winter weather won the race and several outside scenes had to be completed in Los Angeles. The relationship between Prince and Morris Day was getting more fractured as filming progressed but Morris was not in a position to quit: the new album was in progress and he was in the middle of a major feature film where he was playing a lead role.

Prince completed the movie in November and December 1983 but also completed two brand new albums: the new third album for *The Time* now to be titled *Ice Cream Castles* and a debut album he had written for his new co-star Apollonia. With Vanity now gone, so had *Vanity 6* as a band. Prince decided on keeping the same two

backing singers and he moved his new co-star into the role, the new band to be called *Apollonia 6*, naturally. Prince also, as well as all the above, started to write for a new singer recently joining the camp called Jill Jones.

Jill Jones was first introduced a few years earlier, in 1980 at age 18. She was the backing singer for Teena Marie who was, for a while, the opening act during the *Dirty Mind* tour. Prince loved her voice, and the pair stayed in touch on and off over the years. She became a backup vocalist for Prince when he invited her to Sunset Sound in 1982 to sing backing vocals for several tracks on 1999. Prince also asked her to appear in some music videos, notably *'1999'* and *'Little Red Corvette'* where she can be seen assisting Lisa Coleman on keyboards. She now was singing backing vocals for *Apollonia 6* when Prince, as usual, had a surge of creativity and started writing material for her. She would eventually move to Minneapolis and become one of Prince's on/off girlfriends and remain close to him for many years. She had a small part in *Purple Rain* as a waitress yearning to gain the attention of Prince who, in the film anyway, was indifferent to her interest. Her debut album wasn't actually released until 1987 on Prince's *Paisley Park* Records.

Between these recordings some scenes at First Avenue had to be re-shot due to the crowd getting overexcited at the spectacle. Once these scenes were finished Prince and his team attended a wrap party. Amazingly even at this stage, despite all the filming and work that had gone in to the project over the past year or so, Prince's management team had not yet secured distribution. They saw this party as their chance, and they presented the scenes and work they had done so far to Warner Bros film division, who agreed to distribute the movie with a 6-million-dollar deal. The film was financed and ready to go.

CHAPTER FIVE

BABY I'M A STAR

In January 1984, five months before the *Purple Rain* album release and a full six months before the movie release, Prince started to record his next album, *Around the World in A Day.*

Even before the album was actually completed and officially finalized, Prince was moving on to the next project and writing and recording songs at an incredible rate. During these sessions, Prince also recorded *'Take Me With U'* while working with Apollonia but took it back for himself and included it on the *Purple Rain* album. Early in 1984 Prince also started to work with Sheila Escovado, a Latin percussionist who he had met early in his career.

During these sessions, she provided vocals on the soon to be released B-side to *'Let's Go Crazy'*, *'Erotic City'*. She was taken under Prince's wing and went on to be successful in her own right; the two struck up a friendship that lasted many years. Sheila was one of the first artists that Prince worked with that had an established and critically acclaimed career before working with him. This was an interesting direction for Prince. When we look at the artists he had developed beforehand - Vanity, Apollonia, Jill Jones and Morris Day - these artists were moulded by Prince. They were at best singers and performers, and at worst puppets on the Prince machine. Sheila was not a singer and was not a natural performer but she was an incredibly talented drummer and percussionist.

Prince, by instilling the confidence in her to sing and perform, had unlocked a potential star who could sing like those before her but equally gain respect for her musical skills. Sheila was unique to Prince at this time in the fact she had worked alongside some of the greats in the business: jazz bassist Alphonso Johnson, George Duke, Lionel Richie, Marvin Gaye, Herbie Hancock, and Diana Ross. Her jazz tinged Latino style brought a whole new element to Prince's own sound. He quickly signed her and she became a Prince act, beginning a successful solo career with her critically acclaimed debut album which included the career-defining song *'The Glamorous Life'* which Prince wrote for her. She became a mainstream solo star in 1985 following the success of several follow up singles. *'A Love Bazaar'* and *'The Glamorous Life'* became her signature tunes. She is commonly referred to as the *Queen of Percussion*.

Paisley Park Studios is forever ingrained in the music of Prince. It was his sanctuary of creativity, somewhere he could, unrestricted by time, create and produce music whenever he wanted. At this moment in time, May 1984, Paisley Park was still a distant dream for Prince. The foundations for it started here when Prince returned to Minneapolis having completed the final bits and pieces for the *Purple Rain* movie and album out in LA. The original building the band were rehearsing in at St Louis Park was now abandoned as work was completed; a new building needed to be found.

Eventually a new location was chosen in Eden Prairie, on Flying Cloud Drive, for the band's rehearsals and recordings. Prince liked the new location and instructed for all his home studio equipment to be set up there. Initially he rented the building but Prince had a feeling about the space and purchased it for just under $500,000. In 1984, this was a significant sum of money and shows just the level of ambition and business acumen Prince had. He was still only 25 years old, but saw the potential for future development of his musical empire by purchasing this warehouse facility. This building would eventually end up being *Paisley Park*.

During May this year Prince showcased *'When Doves Cry'* to Warner Bros as his preferred choice for the first single. He had recorded it completely alone but something bothered him on the track that he couldn't quite work out and at the last minute he punched out the bass. Warners were, as before, hesitant about the track, arguing that it was too different to the mainstream pop songs that filled the charts. And of course, everyone around Prince was convinced that a song without a bass line would never take off. Those he played it to immediately commented on the lack of bass - some even thought it was unfinished or the speakers were faulty - it was simply unheard of to have a pop song without a bass line.

Despite Warners' tribulation Prince insisted. He added *'17 Days'* as a B-Side, an older track he had recorded alone in 1983 which he rerecorded with Wendy Lisa and Matt Fink. It fits in perfectly with the film both in content and feeling. The music video showcased the forthcoming movie and the combination of the song itself, the B-side and the music video proved too much of a combination to refuse - and so it was released.

The single became a massive worldwide hit. It was a monster, shooting up the charts and hitting the number one spot for over 5 weeks. It was certified platinum with sales exceeding 2 million copies, the accompanying video serving as the perfect trailer and a stylish commercial endorsement.

FOR NOW, WHETHER PRINCE LIKED IT OR NOT, THE MUSIC OF PURPLE RAIN WOULD BE ALL THAT THE CROWDS WANTED TO SEE.

Shutterstock

As these various recording sessions continued, Prince was starting to favor more live drums on his recordings. Engineers at this time were amazed with what they described as Prince's internal clock, a phrase to describe the way Prince would record his drums in one take without the use of a click track, the ability to start playing, stop playing and come back in for an 8-bar break or equivalent.

The click track was used as a synchronization tool and quickly became part of standard recording technology, used for films, radio and other sound recordings. It was applied to one of the tracks on a multi-track tape recorder and by the 1980s, when Prince was recording albums such as *Purple Rain* and others using synthesizers and digital recordings, the click track became computerized and synchronizing different instruments became more complex. Click tracks became very important in the creation of accurately timed music for radio/TV spots, commercials, and other timed production music. In this type of use a rhythm section or ensemble would play all instruments to a click track. With the use of MIDI sequencing in the 80s and 90s it became possible to build an entire music track that was accurately timed. With modern day studio engineers fully used to this latest technology, it was seen as something extremely musical to watch a modern-day pop star record without this assistance. It was almost primitive and showed an incredible musicality and internal timing to create a complete drum part with no other instruments as a guide for an entire song with all the gaps and fills throughout.

Sheila Escovedo, now Sheila E, released her debut album *The Glamorous Life* on June 4th 1984. The album was directed by Sheila E and The Starr Company giving anyone in the know no doubt as to who was behind it. Prince plays most instruments on the album, which was mostly recorded at Sunset Sound in early 1984. Jill Jones added some background vocals and interestingly it's the first album in which Prince used a saxophonist, a clear nod to Sheila's past work. The first single from the album 'The Glamorous Life' became a smash hit, shooting Sheila into the mainstream. Her appearance and live show fitted with *Prince and the Revolution* at the time; even the choreography on stage had Prince's approach and direction. This meant that Sheila, although a respected musician in her own right, struggled to brush off the Prince involvement on her album. She repeatedly denied any involvement with Prince but to anyone in the know and indeed anyone listening to the album or watching Sheila perform, it was obvious that the whole album was a Prince project, and he was pulling the strings.

Shortly after the release of the album Prince, now number one on the singles chart and the most talked about pop star of the moment, played again at First Avenue on his 26th birthday, 7th June 1984. Sheila E attended the gig alongside Prince's management team. Prince showcased some new tracks and before the concert was finished the audience sang a version of 'Happy Birthday'. Afterwards the party continued in Uptown with a private party where Prince was joined by his mother and stepfather, his old school friend Andre, and his mother Bernadette Anderson.

On 25th June 1984 *Purple Rain* was released. Immediately it became Prince's bestselling record so far, riding high on the back of 'When Doves Cry' and the momentum Prince had gained in the past few years. It was no surprise that this album would become the perfect record at the perfect time for him. It sold over a million

31

copies in its first few days of release alone, and it went on, in this first year, to sell 11 million copies and 5 outside of the US. It would stay in the number one spot on the album charts for an incredible 24 weeks. It launched Prince immediately into the mainstream and it's fair to say that whatever life Prince had before 25th June 1984, it would never be the same again.

The musical feel within the album captured perfectly the Prince sound at the time, and made everyone who for whatever reason was not aware of Prince suddenly sit up and take notice. The album showcases all his incredible talents but also it creates a movement, a trend of sorts. It's also a collaboration with *The Revolution* who now had their own identity and would, in the months to come, be even more in the spotlight with the soon-to-be-released movie. It's the first album that Prince actually credits the band with *'Produced, arranged, composed and performed by Prince and The Revolution'*. The Revolution in band form actually appear on four of the tracks, *'I Would Die 4 U'*, *'Baby I'm a Star'*, *'Let's Go Crazy'* and *'Purple Rain'*. *'Computer Blue'* is a solo effort by Prince but Wendy and Lisa added pieces and vocals to the track when it was revisited. All other tracks are essentially solo efforts by Prince with Apollonia adding vocals to *'Take Me With U'*. Prince added string sections to some of the tracks and worked with Wendy and Lisa on the arrangements.

What works with *Purple Rain* is the movement toward more mainstream melodies. There are still experimental sounds testing the listener but it all fits together in a major push forward inviting the listener into his world. Lyrically *Purple Rain* is less graphic than its predecessors, less explicit and more accessible to fit in with the forthcoming movie. It does run through the similar themes, there is a nod to God, there are the sexual and predatory women who want to use men for their own pleasure, there is partying and of course there is enlightenment. They all though have a more accessible nature than previously and the songs themselves have more structure and discipline.

Albums that sell in the numbers that *Purple Rain* eventually did don't just rely on the music; there has to be a perfect storm of other factors, and timing is essential. *Purple Rain* is one of the biggest selling albums of all time but it's not just the brilliance of the music that keeps it selling. Cultural movements, political aspects, rebellious protest against the current establishment and general public feeling waiting for the next new thing all have to land together, the music encapsulating the feeling at the time. If this is in place correctly, as time goes on, these factors then become nostalgic and people revisit the music to take them back to that time, which is why albums such as *Purple Rain* continue to sell in mass quantities in the years ahead. All these elements were in place, the stars were aligned and it all landed perfectly.

What also added to this incredible success was Prince himself. He didn't speak publicly, a rare thing in a commercially publicized media. For anyone other than Prince this could be commercial suicide, even more so today in an environment when celebrity and musical success rarely has anything to do with musicianship or talent. Prince hadn't done an interview in years, and this added to the explosion of *Purple Rain*. He was just about the music and the performance, which drew the audience in to listen more. It made people more interested to check out the shows and pay more attention to what Prince was doing and saying. The contrast

between Prince on stage and Prince in person was becoming fascinating and something that the mainstream press found difficult. They wanted a piece of him, wanted him to talk but instead they got his band members, Shelia E, Morris Day etc. to talk on his behalf. This in turn made interviewers ask repeatedly *'about'* Prince, which in turn led to more mystery around him. What is also significant is that this was Prince's sixth studio album, meaning that anyone who was discovering this extraordinary talent for the first time had the added bonus of another five albums to indulge in. Furthermore, with a little investigating there was also *Shelia E, The Time, Vanity 6, Apolonia 6* and other albums to unearth in the growing back catalog.

Prince knew *Purple Rain* had made him a star. He was also keen, as Prince always was, to not dwell on it and to move quickly to the next project. He had already started recording tracks for his next album *Around the World in a Day*. Unfortunately for Prince though this particular album would be difficult to shake off. There was the impending movie to come which would shoot the album and Prince himself even further into the mainstream. And of course, there was the tour, which would be the biggest and most lucrative of his life. For now, whether Prince liked it or not, the music of *Purple Rain* would be all that the crowds wanted to see. In reaction to this and with an ever-increasing output of material Prince now created another band to release albums through. He now assembled *The Family*.

Morris Day was now estranged from *The Time*. He had moved permanently to Los Angeles and had separated himself from Prince and his management company. It was interesting timing as the movie was months away and would turn Morris into a recognizable figure, which could have been lucrative. He had left Prince and the team within a month of the breakthrough movie showcasing him on cinema screens all over the world. With Morris gone, Prince now reconvened the remaining members of *The Time* to create the new band. *The Time*'s core members were essentially gone but the outer core sidemen still remained. At a meeting at Prince's house Jerome Benson, Paul Peterson and Jellybean Johnson were all informed of Prince's plan for *The Family*. Prince asked Peterson to front the new band - he was already known to Prince and could sing - and they were finally joined by *Revolution* guitarist Wendy Melvoin's twin sister Susannah Melvoin.

The Family were different to *The Time* in many ways. Prince changed his songwriting to adapt to Peterson's style. Morris Day would not have had the vocal range to cope with the songs Prince recorded for *The Family* and equally Paul Peterson would not have had the swagger and humor to pull off songs for *The Time*. Prince, as ever, charged on into the recording studio at the Flying Cloud Warehouse and recorded songs for *The Family*'s debut album. *The Family* has, on four of the album tracks, significant saxophone embellishments scattered across them - a new addition to Prince's sound. Prince had seen Bruce Springsteen at The St Paul Civic Theatre on his *Born In the USA* tour and in particular Clarence Clemmons on saxophone and decided to add his own saxophonist to his current ensemble. Prince's road manager Alan Leeds introduced Prince to his saxophonist brother Eric, who played on the tracks. Prince was absolutely thrilled with the sound and results and decided that Eric Leeds should stay. He became a major musical collaborator within Prince's sound and stayed with him for many years to come.

Eric Leeds was born in Milwaukee, Wisconsin and at the age of 7 moved to Richmond, Virginia. He lived in Richmond until 1966 when he then moved to Pittsburgh, Pennsylvania and, at the age of 14, attended junior high school and college. It was here that his musical career started. He studied saxophone with mentor Eric Kloss and attended Duquesne University where he played in a band during the 1970s and played on the jazz scene through the 70s and 80s often with his friend Matt Blistan who was an old classmate. Blistan would also join Prince's band forming a tight jazz section element to Prince's sound. Leeds would go on to have an established and respected career, recording his own solo albums on Prince's *Paisley Park* label as well as collaborations with Prince on his own albums. Leeds would work with Prince off and on for over 10 years.

Despite Morris Day's departure and Prince's focus on *The Family* as his new ghost band, the next album recorded for *The Time* was scheduled for release. *Ice Cream Castle* was released on 2nd June 1984 and immediately became another hit for the now dismantled *The Time*. Amazingly even on tour Prince managed to dive into recording studios in the early hours to record songs; the album itself was recorded while Prince was actually on the *1999* tour at Sunset Sound between March 1983 and January 1984.

As before it's a complete solo effort by Prince with a few *Time* members adding bass, keyboards and other vocals here and there. As before Morris added his own vocals over the top of Prince's scratch vocals previously recorded. Of course, to the general public this was still a fully-fledged funk band, and the upcoming movie release was going to fuel the fire on the band even more; but for now there was no band as such behind the album. The album reached platinum status hitting over 1 million copies, and singles *'The Bird'* and *'Jungle Love'* became signature tunes for the band. These two songs would be featured on the *Purple Rain* movie and push *The Time* and these two songs in particular to the mainstream.

On the 14th July 1984 Prince recorded some more tracks for *The Family*. He recorded many songs during this session and worked with Paul Peterson and Susannah Melvoin who were adding vocals over his own scratch vocals. One of the songs Prince recorded on this day was *'Nothing Compares 2 U'*, a seemingly ordinary track that Prince wrote very quickly and got Susannah and Paul Peterson to sing over. The track was never released as a single and sat idle on the debut album by *The Family* waiting for Prince to decide a release date. On 8th January 1990, the song was covered by Sinead O'Connor and it became a massive worldwide hit. It topped the charts in O'Connor's native Ireland, Australia, Austria, Canada, Germany, Mexico, Netherlands, New Zealand, Norway, Sweden, Switzerland, the United Kingdom and the United States. It also became a top-five single in France and a top-twenty in Denmark.

The single was certified platinum in Austria and the United Kingdom, and gold in Germany and Sweden. In the United States, it spent four weeks at the top of the Billboard Hot 100. It became the third best-selling single of 1990, the 82nd best-selling single of the 1990s, and was certified platinum by the Recording Industry Association of America in April 1990. Naturally this was extremely lucrative for Prince.

Shortly afterwards more success for Prince followed with the release

of *'Let's Go Crazy'* following on from *'When Doves Cry'*. It hit the number one spot yet again adding more success to the *Purple Rain* album. It quickly hit the 1 million mark and came with the brilliant B-Side *'Erotic City'*. *'Erotic City'* is significant as it's the first song in which Prince used his speeded up vocal, often referred to as *'Camille'*. It's a song he recorded with Sheila E who joins him for the chorus. Prince performs all the instruments on the song, which was recorded in March 1984. This vocal technique was used many times going forward for Prince, giving him a sort of alter ego, often referred to as Prince singing from the perspective of a woman.

Prince's vocals are one of the most interesting and fascinating aspects to his genius. He had in his locker any type of voice he wished to switch to. He had a soft falsetto, a pure rock voice, gospel screams and the rap/singing swagger in perfect time to the beat. His overall vocal register was quite phenomenal. Most musicians and singers have a distinctive voice that the listener can identify immediately; Prince is an artist that can be just as easily identified, with a whole host of different voices but still sounding distinctive to the listener. There is simply no other artist that can sound so vocally different and yet still remain completely and uniquely distinctive. In addition to these natural aspects he now added technology to transform the sound of his voice with unique studio techniques. For songs such as *'Erotic City'* and others that would follow, the tape machine for recording was deliberately turned down using a variable speed control, then returned to normal for playback resulting in a high-speed sound. Prince around this time started experimenting with microphones, with a preference for a Sennheiser 441 Dynamique which was recommended by Stevie Nicks.

Prince was now, without question, the biggest star on the planet and still refusing to speak to press or tabloids. He was still working at an incredible rate already recording most of his next album as well as recording songs for others he was developing. For now though it was time for him to pause and step back as he attended the *Purple Rain* premiere at Hollywood's Graumans Theatre on the historic Hollywood walk of fame, a day before the official opening in theaters across the US. The venue, as you would expect, was crammed full of celebrities with a scattering of competition winners in attendance. The theater was covered in purple balloons and streamers and Prince entered, after everyone else, holding a purple flower with a cloak over him, looking the complete mysterious package that fitted the event perfectly. *Prince and The Revolution* performed a short set to the mesmerized crowd. Morris Day was in attendance but didn't acknowledge the other members of *The Time* or *Prince*. The whole event was broadcast live on MTV.

A day later, on 27th June 1984, *Purple Rain* opened in 917 packed out theaters across the US. Another 100 venues needed to be added after just 7 days due to demand. Many critics hailed it as the greatest rock movie ever made, and still do to this day. It was clear that the success of the singles, the album and now the movie would be something that Prince himself would probably never top.

After just 3 days *Purple Rain* had taken nearly 8 million more than it actually cost to make. It went on to be one of the biggest films of 1984 in any division and grossed nearly 170 million. As previously mentioned the perfect storm of contributing factors played heavily on the success of *Purple Rain*. In addition to this there was, behind the scenes, another factor that helped. There was now a blending of TV, film and records, which previously had been completely separate entities. This allowed Warners to advertise aspects of the film on TV, MTV to broadcast the premiere and the singles previously released served as mini adverts for the forthcoming movie. Everything in these three mediums crossed over beautifully with each one selling the other: singles promoting the album and movie, the album promoting the movie, the movie promoting both the singles and the album and all crossing over to form a perfect cross promotion. This was of course not the first movie and soundtrack ever released, far from it, but it was the first that utilized all three to sell each other to such incomparable success.

On 4th August 1984 *Purple Rain* replaced Bruce Springsteen's *Born In the USA* on the top spot on the US charts and would remain there for another 24 weeks. It also hit number 1 spots all over the world turning Prince into a truly global star. His back catalog of albums also raced up the charts as the realization hit new fans that there was an entire collectable amount of material already amassed by this unique performer and musician.

As always, before a major tour Prince played a warm up at First Avenue. This time though it was different as the police had to be drafted in to deal with the fan hysteria. Just after midnight *Prince and The Revolution* played a session that would form the backdrop of the set for the forthcoming tour.

Prince hit the studio again in mid-August 1984 to record more songs for *The Family*. As well as incorporating saxophone into the sound with Eric Leeds, Prince wanted to add some strings to the music. This would be his first work with Clare Fischer, who was recommended to Prince by David Rivkin. Prince was aware of Clare's previous work and sent him a tape. He was delighted with what came back and this began a long and established relationship between Prince and Clare. Prince never met him in person and preferred to just send tapes across for Clare to work on; he even became superstitious about the relationship and didn't even want to see a photo of Clare to see what he looked like. Clare became a regular collaborator from here on and Prince would be his biggest exposure to pop music.

> ON THE 9TH FEBRUARY, MADONNA'S LIKE A VIRGIN ALBUM REPLACED PURPLE RAIN AFTER NEARLY 6 MONTHS AT THE TOP OF THE CHARTS.

Douglas Clare Fischer was born on October 22nd 1928. He was an American keyboardist, composer, arranger and bandleader. Fischer graduated from Michigan State University, from which five decades later he would receive an honorary doctorate, and became a pianist and arranger in the 1950s. Fischer went on to work with some big names at the time, notably Donald Byrd and Dizzy Gillespie, and became known and respected for his Latin and bossa

nova recordings in the 1960s. He composed the Latin jazz standard *'Morning'* and the jazz standard *'Pensativa'*. Fischer was consistently cited as a major collaborator with Herbie Hancock and would go on to be nominated for eleven Grammy Awards during his lifetime; he won in 1981 for *Clare Fischer & Salsa Picante Present 2 + 2.*

On the back of this success Fischer embarked on a parallel, and far more lucrative career, adding his orchestral talents to pop hits. His technique was referred to as *'String Sweeteners'*. Prince became a regular client from 1984 onwards, and he also added arrangements and orchestral embellishments to songs by Robert Palmer, Paul McCartney, Michael Jackson, Celine Dion, and many others. Prince would send Clare his songs with instructions as to where he wanted the orchestration to be. Unlike other musicians Clare had worked with Prince had no budget restrictions for his songs, so Clare could use full orchestras to compose his pieces for Prince's songs. The results were always impressive with Prince rarely rejecting anything Clare did; the orchestration often strokes sideways over the music Prince previously recorded. A great example of this appeared on *'Pink Cashmere'* released on August 31st 1993 and appearing on *The Hits/The B Sides* compilation; it demonstrates Clare's orchestral composition technique beautifully slicing through at the end of the song playing alongside Prince's guitar solo.

A month later as plans and rehearsals for the mammoth tour lay ahead *Apollonia 6* released their debut album. The tracks are attributed to *Apollonia 6, The Revolution* and *Sheila E.* In reality though it was a Prince solo album with a little help from Lisa Coleman and Brenda Bennet. Prince essentially plays all the instruments with the same format as before, Apollonia and the girls singing exactly over his scratch vocals. The album reached number 62 on the pop charts with the single reaching number 85; after this point the project faded away and Prince lost interest, focusing instead on his other projects, one being *The Family*, which Prince finally completed tracks for in October 1984. The album was to be held until the Purple Rain tour was completed. He recorded *'Yes'* on the 8th October which became the last song for the album, which was now completed and ready to be mixed.

On 4th November, the *Purple Rain* tour was launched in front of 20,000 people at the Joe Louis Arena in Detroit, chosen as it was Prince's strongest city to date. Many stars attended the opening night including Stevie Nicks and most of the original *Time* members. The show itself was, as expected, Prince's most lavish to date and was awash with special effects and visual spectacles. The set itself cost over $300,000 and featured lasers, hydraulic lifts and a rising bathtub for Prince to relax in as the crowd screamed. He played guitar on lengthy solos resembling Hendrix and Santana, he danced like James Brown on extended jams, commanding the band at will to stop and start again, putting the tight ensemble through its paces. He interacted with the crowd and played the showman throughout; he even had a bizarre conversation with God during the piano interlude when he slowed things down. Prince played at the Joe Louis Arena in Detroit for 7 shows and sold over 133 thousand tickets in the city alone before moving on with the rest of the frenzied tour.

With hardly a night off from a sell-out concert *Prince and The Revolution* continued around the US playing in arenas and stadiums through November, often playing more than one night due to demand. In December, the tour reached the Twin Cities for a five-night stop at the civic centre in St Paul selling a record breaking 90,000 tickets. Remarkably Prince finished off his next album *Around the World in a Day* while he was in his home town before moving on with the rest of the tour. It continued through to the end of 1984 with multiple stops in Dallas and Houston where he also played a free concert for handicapped children.

The 28th January 1985 would be a bittersweet night for Prince. As he blazed around the States, Prince took time out from the record-breaking tour to attend the American Music Awards in Los Angeles. He won three awards, Favorite Album *Purple Rain* in the pop rock category, Favorite Single for *'When Doves Cry'* and again for *'Purple Rain'* in the black category. Prince and the Revolution performed *'Purple Rain'* on the night, changing at the last minute as Prince originally wanted to perform *'Paisley Park'* from his new album, until it was highlighted that only nominated songs could be performed.

After the awards around 50 of the biggest names in American music, and indeed the biggest names in the world at the time, gathered at A&M recording studios in LA to record a single named *'We Are the World'*.

⟐

The *USA for Africa* appeal featured artists such as Michael Jackson, Bruce Springsteen, Bob Dylan, Stevie Wonder, Tina Turner, Diana Ross and Lionel Richie who all willingly spilled into the studios to record the song. *USA for Africa* was a blatant attempt to replicate the 1984 Bob Geldof charity single dubbed *'Band Aid'* with the song *'Do They Know It's Christmas'* which featured British stars and raised a large amount of money for African Famine on the back of Geldof's demanding pressure and exasperation for the cause. It went on to be the biggest ever single in British chart history and word across the pond was for America to record their own song; and where better than in LA where all the biggest stars would be congregated after the American Music Awards.

The project was a collaboration that started with the *"King of Calypso"* and veteran performer Harry Belafonte, who contacted Quincy Jones to produce the record. Jones, who to this point had produced both Michael Jackson's albums *Off the Wall* and *Thriller*, started, through his management, to enlist artists for the recording. Jones had invited Prince to attend and left a spot next to Michael Jackson in the studio. Whether Prince did not get the memo through his inner circle or decided to attend the event the following day or even simply misjudged the enormity of the event is up for debate. Either way the recording continued all night and Prince failed to show. To make matters worse, Prince was spotted by photographers in the early hours of the morning at a restaurant in town with Jill Jones and some friends. On his exit the photographers became impatient and tried to get into Prince's car for pictures; a struggle ensued and two of Prince's bodyguards forcibly removed the photographers. One of them was arrested for battery and the other for robbery after taking and smashing a camera. In the early hours of the morning Prince's management team, now aware of the situation, called Prince who agreed to go to the studio to put down a guitar part. With the song wrapped

up, Quincy Jones told Prince it wasn't required, as recording had been completed and the song finished. It was agreed that Prince instead would contribute a full song that would appear on the album.

Prince was heavily criticized in the press for his no-show, many raising the point that it would be a small sacrifice to make in light of the cause. It does though seem unlikely, especially considering Prince's personality and shyness at this time, that he would be at all comfortable in such surroundings - singing next to Michael Jackson "and co" on a Quincy Jones produced song co-written by Lionel Richie. It's also hard to picture Prince anywhere on the record when watching the full cheese and overdone theatrics of the music video with each performer doing their utmost to outperform the rest with a single line.

On reflection Prince's own quiet contribution, the song *'4 the Tears in Your Eyes'*, was a beautiful heartfelt stripped down acoustic song befitting the project perfectly. Prince recorded it using just a mobile recording unit which was parked outside the Super Dome in New Orleans. in one take. Sadly, with the media frenzy that ensued this was overlooked.

The *We are The World* album was released on 12 April 1985. It reached the top of the charts very quickly and generated around $50 million for the cause.

A day after the recording for *We are The World* the *Purple Rain* tour continued into January and February 1985 when, on the 9th February, Madonna's *Like A Virgin* album replaced *Purple Rain* after nearly 6 months at the top of the charts. The commercial peak, as far as official album sales goes, was over. Prince, in the years ahead, would never try to 'officially' replicate *Purple Rain* in any way. He instead always moved in different directions and never tried to repeat himself. A record company would have the opposite view of course - they ultimately want more of the same: if it worked and was successful then they wanted a carbon copy, sticking to the winning formula.

Unfortunately for them they were dealing not only with a songwriting machine but also someone who was never satisfied musically and was always striving and pursuing a new direction. Prince held a listening party for Warner Bros executives at their main offices in Los Angeles on 21 February 1985 to preview his next album *Around the World in a Day*. The reaction was one of surprise, as the guys at the top were expecting another *Purple Rain*. What they got was a completely different sounding record and also one that would undoubtedly take the wheels off the *Purple Rain* monster driving forward any further. Prince was moving on and fast: there would be no *Thriller* style long pause and sitting back on the album to milk it.

The *Purple Rain* tour was one of the most successful rock tours of all time. By the end of it Prince had performed for nearly 2 million people in over 31 cities. He played over 89 scheduled concerts with more added as the tour continued. It generated, by April 1985, over $30 million, and also had a huge charitable side to it. Unfortunately for Prince this side of the tour wasn't well documented as the tabloids were more interested in his relationships with Madonna and others and his no-show for the evening of the *'We are the World'* charity song. The charity events Prince performed at during the tour raised thousands for various causes with most having food drives and clothing donations on entrance. He also raised over $500,000 for *The Marva Collins Teacher Training Organization* in Chicago.

Ten days after the mammoth *Purple Rain* tour was completed Prince returned to the studio to start work on his next album *Parade*. Remarkably he had already completed *Around the World in a Day*, which wasn't even released yet, and now he was working on the next album as well as a feature film. He worked through until mid-May and wanted this album to be a soundtrack for another movie after *Around the World in a Day*. The film was to be called *Under the Cherry Moon* and *Parade* would be the accompanying soundtrack. During these recordings, Wendy and Lisa were more collaborative than ever with Prince, giving them incomplete songs and compositions for them to work on. Another Minneapolis band *Mazarati* were recording in the same studio at the time and Prince gave them a song *'100mph'* as well as working through some of *The Time*'s songs he had written but not used.

Prince completed the first half of the *Parade* album during these sessions. He also started working on the movie itself, formulating ideas and a basic script. The first songs recorded on *Parade* were actually recorded as they appear on the record. Prince as usual recorded them all at a blistering pace, this time having several studios on the go at the same time. Drums were played first in one take, then he added the bass and guitars and so on. These first sessions again show a completely different musical direction for the next album.

Prince now was one of the biggest, if not the biggest, pop star on the planet. He had achieved everything he had ever hoped for; all the hard work and all the dreams and aspirations he had growing up in Minneapolis had come to fruition. He was regarded as a musical genius at the top of the game: there was no one out there who could match his performances, his creativeness and his overall pop icon status. The tabloid press, often confused by his silence and unwillingness to cooperate in mundane interviews and basic promotional nonsense, looked for scandal, rumor and gossip to fill column pages, while musicians and collaborators sang his praises. For Warner Bros the investment and belief in him had paid off more than they could have ever imagined and now they could not say no to anything that he wanted creatively or musically.

So, when Prince said he wanted to make another film they had no reservations. He then told them it was to be a sort of romantic comedy, it was to be filmed in the south of France, and one other thing: it would be in black and white.

CHAPTER SIX

EVERYBODY'S LOOKING FOR THE LADDER

Prince continued his plans for his new feature film and the accompanying soundtrack. **He was now determined to try and move away from *Purple Rain* and quickly onto the next album; he didn't want to be forever labelled with *Purple Rain*.**

With such a ferocious output of different styles of music, he wanted his next album out quickly, allowing him to move forward. On 22nd April 1985 Prince released *Around the World in a Day*, his seventh studio album. Again attributed to Prince and The Revolution, it was a complete and deliberate departure from the commercial sound of *Purple Rain*, with more experimentation with psychedelic styles and opulent textures.

Prince requested that the record company release the album with minimal publicity and purposely withheld accompanying singles until at least a month after the album's release, thus creating concentration on the full album itself as opposed to individual singles. Prince originally wanted *'Paisley Park'* as the first single but opted instead to have the album received as a whole. Prince instructed Warners to let radio stations choose which track they wanted to play, a bold move and one that was ahead of its time. Radio stations were confused as to which song they should be playing; of course, the perfect picture would have been for different radio stations to play different songs, thereby creating perfect promotion for the album as a whole package. This strategy makes sense for Prince, particularly on the back of *Purple Rain*, with its overplayed singles repeated all over the radio. Prince's management, in trying to avoid radio confusion, tried to convince him to make a couple of videos and at least commit to one single for the record. Prince agreed that *'Raspberry Beret'* could be highlighted as the first single, at least giving radio something consistent to play.

Not surprisingly *Around the World in a Day* was released to a mixed reception: after the success of *Purple Rain* many expected 'more of the same' to come. It nonetheless succeeded in eventually going

platinum and becoming Prince and the Revolution's second number one album on the Billboard 200. Of course, critics and musical journalists commented immediately on the album's difference in sound to its predecessor, but from Prince's point of view that was the whole point. It was different because it was different. If you didn't get it then you missed it.

It was recorded at Sunset Sound, The Flying Cloud Warehouse and Capitol in Los Angeles between January and December 1984. The album's biggest hit single *'Raspberry Beret'* was a Prince song originally recorded in 1982 but he chose to re-record it from scratch for inclusion on the album. Although the album is a deliberate departure from *Purple Rain* there is still continuity in the sound with Prince using the LM-1 drum machine on tracks, giving the similar back beat to the songs and structure. Guitars mainly take a back seat leaving synths and the trademark Oberheim to be prominent in the sound. There are also touches of difference in flute-like instruments, splashes of darbouka, a hand-held drum, and finger cymbals. Most of the album is mid-tempo and compared to previous Prince albums, it is slightly sombre and lethargic in its overall feel; it certainly lacks the power and electric energy of *Purple Rain* but nevertheless has outstanding and beautifully experimental songs. What was achieved brilliantly was that although it was a completely different sounding record to *Purple Rain* it still, without question, sounded like a Prince and The Revolution record, and this of course was the ultimate objective.

Prince continued work on his next album *Parade* and his new film project *Under the Cherry Moon* immediately after the release of *Around the World in a Day*. A first arrangement of the album was completed in May 1985 but would go through significant changes as he worked through the film, the album itself going through several re-workings to make it a consistent fit with his vision of the movie.

In mid May 1985 Prince agreed to the planning of a new state-of-the-art recording facility in the city of Chanhassen not far from his home. It was within walking distance of the offices of PRN productions and would serve as a base for all activity Prince would be involved in. It would also allow him to create all day every day without restriction. It would be a groundbreaking studio complex and serve as his recording empire with everything Prince could possibly want at hand 24 hours a day. Prince started to draw up plans for how he wanted the studio complex to be.

The conception of Paisley Park was now in production but for now rehearsals continued at the Washington Avenue warehouse. Prince worked through his ghost band *The Family* with a proposed tour planned for the band at the end of the year. *The Family* now consisted of Paul Peterson, who formerly played keyboards with *The Time*, twin sister of *Revolution* guitarist Wendy Melvoin Susannah Melvoin, Eric Leeds, Jerome Benton and Jellybean Johnson. The tour was to also feature Sheila E and Mazarati showcasing a Prince force similar to the support acts on the *1999* tour that featured *Apollonia 6* and *The Time*. Prince also assembled a couple of backing dancers who were former bodyguards on the *Purple Rain* tour, Wally Safford and Greg Brooks. Both Safford and Brooks would hold their place on stage through the *Parade* tour alongside Jerome Benton and onto the 1987 *Sign o the Times* tour. Unfortunately, despite big plans The Family only ended up playing one performance, which was at First Avenue on 13th August 1985.

Prince also entered the charts again in May with the release of 'Raspberry Beret', which shot to the top of the charts. The song was chosen for the simple reason that when radio had the freedom to choose to play what they wanted, it became the most played track. It became Prince's seventh top ten hit in recent years keeping him high in the charts again and getting more attention for the album. The B-side 'She's Always in my Hair' was recorded at Sunset Sound in January 1984 and was inspired by Jill Jones. The song has a very distinctive drum beat which was a technique Prince first used on the Apollonia 6 song 'Sex Shooter'. He programmed the LM-1 through a time delay processor which gave a shift variation and produced an almost chugging sound to the beat. The song became a personal favorite of Prince's and was often played live through the years giving him free rein to play out a lengthy and impressive guitar solo at the end of the song.

⇐◆⇒

Shortly after the release of 'Raspberry Beret' *Around the World in a Day* became the number one album in America, ironically replacing *We are the World* in the top position. It stayed there for a further 3 weeks.

Prince released a further single from *Around the World in a Day*, 'Pop Life', on 10th July 1985, featuring the B-side 'Hello'. 'Hello' is an autographical song recalling the events of the recent confrontation with photographers on the night of the 'We are the World' recording session. The song lyrics highlight Prince's argument that he didn't want to originally sing but contribute a song instead and that this was pre-arranged without any issue. The song features Jill Jones on backing vocals and Prince playing all the instruments as well as live drumming. The song reached number 7 on the pop charts giving Prince another top 10 hit.

With most of the *Parade* album completed and Prince happy that the film was to his liking, he flew to France with Susannah to spend time in Paris prior to shooting *Under the Cherry Moon*. While in Paris Prince, along with Martin Scorsese, had a private tour of the palace of Versailles. After the tour the two had dinner and Prince asked if Scorsese would direct the movie, but Scorsese politely declined, reportedly saying two geniuses working together would not be a good idea. It's interesting to think how *Under the Cherry Moon* would have looked if it had been directed by Scorsese.

Susannah was originally scheduled for the lead role: Prince had written her in from the start and she had gone through rehearsals and script development; but as conversations over casting continued, it was agreed that Susannah should not play the lead role of Mary as she had no previous acting experience. It was decided it should be played by a professional actress. After auditions took place at Prince's hotel in Paris a young British unknown actress called Kristen Scott-Thomas was offered the part.

Upon leaving school Kristen moved to Hampstead in London and worked in a department store. She then began training to be a drama teacher at the Central School of Speech and Drama. On being told she would never be a good enough actress she left at the age of 19 to work as an au pair in Paris. Speaking French fluently she studied acting at the École Nationale Supérieure des Arts et Techniques du Théâtre in Paris and at the age 25 she graduated. Shortly afterwards she auditioned for the role opposite Prince as Mary Sharon, a French heiress in *Under the Cherry Moon* and was offered the part.

While Prince and his team were in France the debut album by *The Family* was released on Paisley Park Records. Prince played everything on the entire album but, as before, he tried to distance himself from it, instead only taking credits on 'Nothing Compares 2 U'. The lead singer Paul Peterson was sent to LA for acting classes for a future role in a film project; however on hearing that the album was only at number 63 on the pop charts he became despondent and lost interest in the whole project. It wouldn't be long before Peterson quit the band and, in a telephone conversation with Prince while he was in France, explained his frustration at the lack of promotion on the record and his desire to quit. This conversation spelled the end of the band and although there were threats by Prince's management team and attorneys of legal implications towards Peterson he was, in effect, left to walk away.

A week later another Prince record was released, Sheila E's second album *Romance 1600* on Paisley Park records. Most songs on the album have Prince's input with the whole thing being recorded during the *Purple Rain* tour between December 1984 and February 1985. Of all the albums Prince was involved with around this time *Romance 1600* feels like a substandard one. Sheila simply didn't get enough of Prince's time to produce an accomplished follow up to *The Glamorous Life*. 'A Love Bazaar' as a single did well reaching number 11 on the pop charts, with the album itself eventually going gold and peaking at number 50 on the pop charts.

IN DECEMBER 1985 WHEN PRINCE WAS WORKING ON ADDITIONAL AUDIO WORK FOR *UNDER THE CHERRY MOON* HE RECEIVED A VISIT FROM MICHAEL JACKSON.

Filmed primarily in Studios de la Victorine in Nice and on location in the French Riviera, *Under the Cherry Moon* tells a story of a gigolo played by Prince and his friend, played by Jerome Benton, whose main aim is deceiving and defrauding rich women. When Prince's character Christopher Tracy targets 21-year-old heiress Mary, things get complicated. It was a story that could not have been further from *Purple Rain*. The issues with the film's script became apparent almost immediately. Prince, now one of the biggest stars in the world, had pretty much carte-blanche when developing ideas and the studio green-lit the project without even having seen a script, confident in the belief that they would be gaining another success like *Purple Rain*.

Prince wanted the film to be a romantic comedy with a 1930s vibe set in an exotic location like Palm Beach, Miami or Capri. He wanted Jean-Baptiste Mondino to direct, but when he was unavailable, video director Mary Lambert was recruited and German cinematographer Michael Ballhaus was hired as director of photography. Seasoned actors Terrance Stamp and Francesca Annis were cast as Mary's parents. On initial filming Warner did raise concerns about the film being shot in black and white, which was something that Prince had his heart set on from the outset, but since Prince was at the top of his fame he got his way and shooting proceeded.

Once shooting commenced the production was marred by problems. A few weeks into shooting Terrance Stamp retracted himself from the film, citing it was not the role he was led to believe. Steven Berkoff was quickly hired as his replacement. Prince and the crew were also dissatisfied with Mary Lambert's directing and she was fired; and Prince, who was already co-directing many scenes, took on the directing of the film by himself. Prince, despite having little experience in directing, won the respect of his fellow

actors and crew, working quickly and quietly on the scenes for the movie. Prince also changed the script somewhat once he was at the director's helm; he changed certain scenes and added additional ones he thought would enhance the film.

On a day off from shooting the movie *Prince and the Revolution* played a brilliant and captivating impromptu video performance live for the released single 'America', the third single to be released from *Around the World in a Day*. Eric Leeds joined the Revolution for the extended jam which was watched by 200 fans who won tickets for the mini concert through local radio stations. They also played 'Paisley Park', 'Delirious' and 'Little Red Corvette'. After the concert, Wendy and Lisa flew to London to continue work on several tracks on *Parade* with Prince flying in to join them at weekends as filming continued. Prince also conducted another interview, this time on MTV, to counter criticism of himself in the press. He spoke for around 25 minutes and the interview was broadcast on 15th November. He did come across as someone who was quite withdrawn and uneasy at the line of questioning.

During filming Prince held a party in Nice. Several others flew in for the party including Susannah and the rest of *The Family*, obviously without Paul Peterson. This would be the start of what would be dubbed 'The Expanded Revolution'. Prince, on the back of the 'America' mini live session recently played, liked the idea of Eric Leeds' saxophone and the additional dancers and musicians giving a new element to the band. Obviously, the original Revolution were not happy with the additional members suddenly drafted in and sharing the stage. The video for 'Girls and Boys' was shot shortly afterwards and Prince decided the Expanded Revolution should appear in the video itself. It was the first time the members of The Family were shown as an addition to The Revolution and incorporated into Prince's backing band.

Back home Prince now had a 30-acre new home completed just a mile away from the proposed site for his studio under construction, 'Paisley Park', and Prince gifted his father his old home on Kiowa Trail.

In December 1985 when Prince was working on additional audio work for *Under the Cherry Moon* he received a visit from Michael Jackson. The pair played table tennis together and spoke of a future collaboration. Prince shortly afterwards visited Michael who was preparing songs with Quincy Jones for the *Bad* album. Jackson wanted Prince to appear in the video for 'Bad' - the Wesley Snipes character in the video would have been Prince. Unsurprisingly Prince declined but did feed a pizza to Jackson's chimp Bubbles who was in the studio with him. The National Enquirer reported that Prince used 'mind power' on the Chimp to drive him crazy. Another great piece of journalism.

⎯⎯◈⎯⎯

Around this time, Prince started work on several projects that would ultimately funnel themselves into *Sign o' the Times*, his next studio album. Before this though the ideas were flowing into different ventures, often starting and stopping. The first of these stemmed from a recording on 16th December 1985 during sessions at Sunset Sound when Prince recorded *The Dream Factory*. *The Dream Factory* early on was going to be the next album and it seemed, over the following months, to flow into other albums he was working on such as *Roadhouse Garden, Camille, Crystal Ball, Rebirth of the Flesh, Madhouse* and other names. It was a time of frantic output flowing out of Prince at an incredible rate. He was literally working on six albums at the same time. In addition, he was playing more live drums, a direct influence from having Sheila E around, and becoming more accomplished, pushing himself to play more on his recordings. He started recording tracks for jazz legend Miles Davis, who he had recently connected with and who Prince's management were keen for him to work with.

> IT'S FAIR TO SAY AT THIS JUNCTURE THAT THINGS DIDN'T GO AS PLANNED ON THE MOVIE SET FOR UNDER THE CHERRY MOON.

Miles was a huge fan of Prince and had been following him since around 1982. Eric Leeds in particular was pushing heavily for the two to work together and intervened as a sort of musical messenger between the two. Prince submitted *'Can I Play With U'* and sent it to Davis for him to add trumpet to. Davis signed to Warners in 1985 and in turn sold his publishing rights to the label as part of the package. The pair stayed in touch and did meet but no official releases were ever brought to fruition between the two legends.

Inspired by Davis, Prince began jamming with a new makeshift band: Sheila E on drums, Eric Leeds on saxophone and Levi Seacer Jr on guitars. The band was a tight jazz ensemble taking Prince in a completely new direction; it was becoming clear that Prince was moving away from *The Revolution* in favor of this more jazz tinged sound. So pleased was Prince with the results of the tracks they recorded he returned with Eric Leeds two days later and they worked on overdubs for a possible release. The session was to be tagged as *The Paisley Jam* and produced the songs *'A Question of U', 'Madrid', 'Breathless', 'High Colonic', '12 Keys', 'U Just Can't Stop', 'Slaughterhouse'* and many more.

As 1986 rolled in, the hits for Prince continued with the release of The Bangles album *Different Light*. It contained *'Manic Monday'* which went on to be a huge worldwide hit for the band. Prince recorded it in February 1984 at Sunset Sound when working with Apollonia 6. The credits again note the word *'Christopher'* as writer. The song reached number 2 in the US and became the breakthrough track for the band.

On 5th January 1986 construction of Paisley Park Studios began with all plans now finalized. It was built by architect Bret Thoeny. It was something he had never constructed before and completely unique at the time; it was an unusual and extraordinary request for an architect to work on. In the mid 1980s artists simply did not build their own state-of-the-art fully functional compounds, let alone live in them. Prince had a vision of having everything under one roof, decades before it was common for any individual to do that. It would be a self-contained 55,000 square foot $10 million creative-complex - a vast amount of money in 1985 but for Prince this simply was not an issue: the creative freedom and opportunity

to have everything to hand under one roof was everything he wanted. As far as recording songs and producing was concerned this unique artist warranted his own creative place.

It's fair to say at this juncture that things didn't go as planned on the movie set for *Under the Cherry Moon*. Despite Prince's workaholic nature and his ability to direct the entire movie himself as well as the music and the script, it was a major concern for those with financial obligations as it sat waiting for a release. Prince meanwhile was moving on as ever: with the movie finished he continued jamming and recording with his new expanded line up throughout January 1986 recording songs at will, many for no particular project.

As February began the *Parade* and *Under the Cherry Moon* venture launched into action. The first single for the project was released, *'Kiss'*. It was a fantastic start to the project, as *'Kiss'* became a smash worldwide hit hitting number one in the US - Prince's third American number one single. It came with the B-side *'Love or Money'* which was a theme better suited for the movie, a raw funk number with Wendy and Lisa adding vocals to Prince's speeded up voice. The single also came with a delightful video showcasing

Prince's new look. The stripped-down video suited the song perfectly, with Prince as showman, advertising the new live theme perfectly as he prepared to take the new entourage on to the road.

Prince's mood was dampened however as it emerged that Pepe Willie had released his own album of early recordings with Prince entitled *Minneapolis Genius -The Historic 1977 Recordings*. It was released just when Prince was enjoying a major hit around the world to maximize its publicity. The album incorporated six songs recorded between 1975 and 1979 which all featured Prince as a studio musician. Willie released the record on Hot Pink which was a small independent label. He was seen by some as cashing in on Prince and was asked by him not to release the record. Pepe felt that as he had assisted Prince in the early days he should now be rewarded. He argued that he and Prince had had some kind of mutual agreement. Prince however strongly disagreed and the two had a heated discussion. The album does showcase the early Prince but it is substandard, particularly in light of the albums and music Prince was now releasing and recording; the production also sounds amateurish and it's easy to understand why Prince would be upset at this release from these early collaborations with the then teenager.

Showcasing the new line up Prince again played at First Avenue on 3rd March 1986. The show was an incredible spectacle and Prince had family members watching in the balconies. The new line up freed Prince to now become the ultimate frontman and showman. He danced and displayed an incredible number of moves with all kind of theatrics and stagecraft. The expanded *Revolution* now consisted of Wendy on guitar, joined by Miko Weaver, Brown Mark on bass, Matt Fink and Lisa on keyboards, Eric Leeds on saxophone and flute and Matt Bliston on trumpet. Bobby Z remained on drums despite Prince regularly jamming with Sheila E who was waiting for her opportunity in the background. Susannah Melvoin provided backing vocals alongside Wally Salford and Jerome Benton who also acted as dancers alongside Prince on certain well-rehearsed sections in between Prince's own spontaneous moves. Prince was able to cue in the band at ease, using many of his established hits in new ways and fusing one song into another.

Prince now had, in addition to his Paisley Park development now under construction, a brand-new state-of-the-art studio fitted in his new home. It was designed by Westlake Audio and provided Prince for the first time the ability to complete full band recording there. This meant that even when Prince was finished at the studio he was still able to work at home and produce music. Prince started in earnest on *The Dream Factory* project once the studio was completed. It was mainly a solo project but he was assisted by Wendy, Lisa and Susannah. He recorded several songs for it, the first being *'The Ballad of Dorothy Parker'* which later appeared on *Sign o' the Times*.

On 31st March 1986, a good three months before the movie was scheduled, the *Parade* album was released. It covers an amazing variety of musical styles, encompassing tight arrangements and sounds. The jazz element of Prince's past jamming and unreleased music is evident within many of the tracks and it takes the music away from the earlier albums he released. *Parade* was a new sound and new venture. It is a lot more focused on the melodic element of Prince's sound and takes a step away from blistering guitar solos

> THE REVIEWS OF PARADE WERE EXCELLENT. PRINCE'S EUROPEAN AUDIENCE WAS ALSO GROWING AND MANY CRITICS IN EUROPE PRAISED HIM HEAVILY.

and rock heavy formats. It also demonstrates Prince having an interest more in creative momentum than pure chart hits, which he could write, produce and record at ease if he decided to.

As before, Clare Fischer added orchestration on a lot of tracks, more evident here than on any previous Prince release. Prince recorded the first four tracks in sequence all alone starting on drums in the studio. One aspect of *Parade*, if you take it in the context of a soundtrack, is its disconnection from the movie itself. Whereas *Purple Rain* was clearly a soundtrack and fitted snugly into the narrative of the film, *Parade* is essentially a standalone album that nods towards the movie, once you have seen it. The only connection in some cases is the themes of the songs which fit with certain themes of the movie. It could be seen as Prince purposely making this the case as he must have had a feeling the movie wasn't going to be the smash hit follow up to *Purple Rain* he first hoped for. Therefore, the music would not, and did not, suffer.

The reviews of *Parade* were excellent. Prince's European audience was also growing and many critics in Europe praised him heavily. The album also received great momentum from the *'Kiss'* single and video which became a massive global hit. It reached number 3 on the pop charts and 2 on the black charts. Interestingly for the first time he outsold the US sales with a stronger following from European audiences and the rest of the world: Prince was becoming more popular around the globe than in the US.

This would form the start of a love affair with European audiences and global admiration for the decades ahead. It meant that, at the very least, if his star ever faded in the US he could hit the road around the world and play to sell-out crowds in arenas and stadiums on very lucrative tours.

His plans however would be halted as, maybe for the first time in his career, he would have to deal with negativity and criticism over a piece of work he had created. He had had his fair share of criticism in the tabloid press but this was mainly gossip to sell papers and magazines in relation to his personal life, and was mostly exaggerated.

This, however, was criticism over a piece of work he had created and spent time over. Although the hardcore fans loved it, the movie he was so proud of would be perceived as nothing more than an egotistical self-centered flop.

CHAPTER SEVEN

TIMES...

For many musically minded people and casual critics, this period of Prince's career was his peak. **Of course, this needs a closer look - and as ever with Prince, things are** not quite what they appear to be.

The notion that Prince spent time in the recording studio and came out a few months later with an album called *Sign o' the Times* would be impressive to say the least. It's one of the greatest albums of all time, certainly by a single individual, and if this was the case then countless documentaries could have been produced from fellow musicians and collaborators telling us all how he managed to do it. Prince though didn't stop, so there is no cut off from one album to the next. He simply recorded every day, wrote every day, performed every day. There was no stopping at the end of anything to start again, therefore the album that became *Sign o' the Times* was a mass fusion of other projects and work he was creating at an incredible pace.

Prince continued with the *Dream Factory* album into June 1986 and put together an incredible 19-track double album, the listing as follows: *'Visions', 'It's a Wonderful Day', 'The Ballad of Dorothy Parker', 'It', 'Strange Relationship', 'Teacher Teacher', 'Starfish & Coffee', 'In a Large Room with no Light', 'Sexual Suicide', 'Crystal Ball', 'Power Fantastic', 'Last Heart', 'Witness 4 the Prosecution', 'Movie Star', 'A Place in Heaven'* and *'All my Dreams'*. There were also several interludes of music in-between certain tracks. It's an astonishing collection of quality material which Prince submitted to be mastered - however he still saw it as 'work in progress' and refused to give it the complete green light as he continued to work on other songs for the album.

It's one of many *'what if?'* albums that Prince could have released during this period. Maybe one of the reasons why he was stalling was the fact he had so much music ready to go of such quality that it was difficult to choose what should go and what should stay for later use. A 19-track album would be a heavy piece of work for most artists and would take a long time to produce. It would keep them going afterwards for years. For Prince however this was nothing and he knew the record company would want a period to milk it and make the most of anything he released, therefore slowing down any future projects.

On 1st July 1986, the *Under the Cherry Moon* premiere was held. It was at an unlikely venue: normally premieres for such high-profile stars would be in LA, New York or London. In keeping with the issues Prince had with the movie, the location was the sleepy town of Sheridan, Wyoming. MTV had run a competition with Warner Bros for the winner to receive the premiere at their hometown and also to be Prince's 'date' for the evening. The winner also got to invite 200 of his/her friends to the party. It was won by Lisa Barber who was a 20-year-old hotel worker, the 10,000th caller to a radio station. The event was covered by MTV, which showcased a 50-minute special, as well as *Good Morning America* and other programs and news publications. Prince and the Revolution performed at the event and played a blistering show of which MTV broadcast around ten minutes. The next day the film opened in cinemas across America.

Prince's vision for the film was to have the message that true love cannot be separated no matter what was thrown at it, even death. Unfortunately, the message was somewhat lost in the characterization of the leading roles: they appeared selfish and money obsessed. The film was written off almost immediately and it was apparent that this was not going to be another movie success in any way. It cost around $12 million to make and earned around $3 million in its first week. During its very limited box office run it ended up grossing around $10 million. The press panned it in every way. Prince had absolutely no regrets over the movie, but he did cancel any plans for a US tour, opting instead to head to Europe and Japan to tie in with the release of the film in these areas. Prince planned concerts in Belgium, Holland, UK, France, Sweden and Japan as he continued with some *'Hit & Run'* concerts in the US and further work with Eric Leeds on the *Dream Factory* project.

More problems and disappointment lay ahead however when Wendy and Lisa told Prince they wanted to go their separate ways. They both felt that they were not given enough credit for their contributions and that they were not involved enough in the key decisions of songs that they had contributed to. They also were unhappy with the *Revolution* expansion, which went from a tight 5-piece band to encompassing the members of the disbanded *Family*. Sheila E was still sitting in the wings waiting for a permanent drum place and Prince was continuing with his jazz/funk fueled sessions with Eric Leeds, Atlanta Bliss, Sheila E and Levi Seacer. Wendy and Lisa didn't take too well to the introduction of the three male dancers Prince had brought in and the overall machismo banter that surrounded it.

Prince was undoubtedly having a lot of fun with the expanded band but sometimes it felt at the expense of the original members. Wendy, on a personal level, was not happy with Prince's relationship with her sister; the two were still together but the relationship was still very much stop start. Bass player Mark Brown also decided he had had enough, citing that he felt pushed out on stage by others now in the fold. It took Prince and Eric Leeds to convince them to stay until at least the *Parade* tour was over. It was for this reason that, despite a final listing being completed, *The Dream Factory* album was again shelved.

Some of the songs would end up on Prince's next project, dubbed *Camille*, which was Prince singing solely in his speeded-up voice. Camille was an alter ego he had created and is often described as Prince singing from the point of view of a woman, although this isn't really clear in many of the songs using this vocal technique. It was slated for release without mention of Prince and would contain eight funk tracks sporting Prince's sped-up vocals. Prince wanted to slide this into release without his name anywhere and have the public discover that 'Camille' was in fact Prince. He clearly wanted *'Camille'* to have a separate identity to Prince and was playing around with gender and identity - a funk twist and nod to Bowie's *'Ziggy Stardust'*.

'Ziggy Stardust' was written and recorded by David Bowie for his 1972 concept album *The Rise and Fall of Ziggy Stardust and the Spiders from Mars*. The song describes Bowie's alter ego Ziggy Stardust, a rock star who acts as a messenger for extra-terrestrial beings. It was a character based on British rock 'n' roll singer Vince Taylor. Bowie met Taylor when Taylor suffered a breakdown and believed himself to be a cross between a god and an alien. This formed the basis of the character as Bowie, who was fascinated with the encounter, drew inspiration. In contrast Prince's *'Camille'* character was probably more an evolution than any outside inspiration and grew from studio techniques which formed the style with funk led songs.

Prince did not pursue the character on stage like Bowie did; he instead kept 'Camille' on record and it remained a musical alter ego and direction not a visual character. He did play with it a little on his European tour in 1988. Many of the *'Camille'* tracks were reworked and resurfaced at a later date mingling in with other albums where the original pure identity of 'Camille' was lost. This wasn't a bad thing in itself as it demonstrated Prince with different vocals on albums. What's remarkable is you can listen to *Sign o' the Times* for example and hear all these different vocals and yet there is still a continuity that is identifiable as Prince. The Camille tracks which ended up on *Sign o' the Times* were *'Strange Relationship'*, *'If I Was Your Girlfriend'* and *'Housequake'*. The songs *'Shockadelica'* and *'Feel U Up'* would go on to be B-sides. In the movie *Bright Lights Big City* soundtrack, released on April 1 1988, *'Good Love'* was contributed, which was also used on *Camille*. Another Camille track, *'Rockhard in a Funky Place'* popped up on Prince's shelved *Black Album*, while a studio version of *Camille* opener *'Rebirth of the Flesh'* at the time of writing has never officially been released.

So, at the time of the release of *Parade* Prince had two albums scheduled to be released as well as all the writing he was doing and recording for other artists, and in mid tour. *The Dream Factory* was a 19-track album, now shelved, and *Camille* was in the making forming an alter ego of pure funk driven songs, now scheduled at 9 tracks.

Before the European tour began, Prince played two sold out concerts at Madison Square Garden. Many celebrities attended the shows and after-show parties including Mick Jagger, Eddie Murphy, Andy Warhol, Debbie Harry, Keith Richards and Vanity.

The European tour itself began on 12 August 1986 with 3 sell-out shows at Wembley Stadium. The British press and critics raved about the shows with many stating it was the greatest show they had ever seen. Many were surprised at Prince's seemingly relaxed attitude, a huge difference to the perceived megalomaniac often reported. Again, many celebrities crammed into royal boxes for the shows including Phil Collins, George Michael, Duran Duran, The Pet Shop Boys and Spandau Ballet. Ronnie Wood joined Prince onstage for the after-show at a London nightclub playing *'Miss You'* into the early hours. Prince also, while in London, played with Eric Clapton during a post-concert party at the Kensington Roof Gardens for a short set with Eric Leeds on sax.

At the final concert in France at Le Zenith a mobile recording truck was actioned in to record the show, which was performed on 25th August 1986. Prince took the recording of the encore, *'It's Gonna Be a Beautiful Night'*, back to the studio and added in additional vocals including a rap by Sheila E; this would be the actual recording to appear on *Sign o' the Times*. While in Paris, and before he moved on with the tour, Prince found a large apartment in an exclusive area close to Champs Elysees which he decided to rent indefinitely and use as a base whenever he was in the city. This would be a long-term home of his and he had it tastefully decorated

and installed a pool table, a personal favorite of Prince. The tour then moved on to Germany and Belgium and a show in Hamburg concluded the European leg of the 15-date tour. It was a huge success, seen in Europe by around 120,000 thousand fans, and it left the fans and critics alike shouting from the rooftops in praise of Prince and his performances. The mood however was a sombre one as, at the start of September, Prince arrived in Japan for the final leg of the tour, which would to be his final few shows with the *Revolution*.

The Japanese leg of the tour started with two concerts at Osaka with two additional concerts at the 30,000 capacity Yokohama stadium. Sheila E was the opening act on this section of the tour and it was no surprise that she was waiting in the wings to replace Bobby Z on drums. With Wendy, Lisa and Brown Mark set to leave at the end of the Japanese leg it made sense for Prince to put in place a completely new band for touring. On 9th September 1986 he played the final concert at the Yokahama stadium, which was the last show he performed with *The Revolution*. Prince broke all the strings on his guitar during the encore.

Through September 1986 Prince started work on a project entitled *The Dawn*. It was to be a film project based around a musical featuring two rival bands. The songs recorded from these sessions would ultimately end up on future albums and projects but the focus on *The Dawn* saw Prince casting his attention again towards film. The project was never fully developed, but the core theme of two rival bands would ultimately manifest itself into *Graffiti Bridge* in 1990. One of the reasons *The Dawn* was not fully developed was a simple one and one that is a common theme: Prince was simply working on numerous projects at the same time, his nonstop workaholic nature taking so much of his time that he couldn't fully commit to one single project without downing tools and jumping on the next. When he returned to work on a project his ideas had often changed, so whatever he was working on was in constant motion. While working on *The Dawn* for example, Prince also started on the *'Madhouse'* project which was a jazz/funk ensemble featuring Eric Leeds on saxophone and flute, Matt Blistan on trumpet with Matt Fink assisting on keyboards. The *Madhouse* album was to be called simply 8 and feature eight songs.

Prince had been wanting to expand on the ideas of an instrumental jazz–funk album ever since he recorded his first tracks alongside the introduction of Eric Leeds with *The Family*. Leeds provided Prince for the first time with a live horn sound, where Prince before had preferred keyboards for any horn style grooves, forming a backbone for the Minneapolis Sound. With the additional loose jam sessions that followed, which he loved and was delighted with, he really wanted to get an album out which would showcase this style of music but not be credited as a Prince album as such.

The concept which came from 'The Flesh' sessions at the end of 1985 would be an eponymous pseudo-band. This project, like many, was abandoned, but its concept would be lightly modified to become *Madhouse*. After the album was recorded in Prince's own home recording studio it was mixed and edited at Sunset Sound. Prince received all songwriting royalties for the album but didn't want his name attributed, choosing instead for the music to stand on its own merit. The songs themselves are a tight harmonically complex arrangement with a heavy lean towards jazz and funk, and there is a spontaneous feel to the whole album. It also showcases

Prince's versatility on a number of instruments: he played acoustic drums, keyboards and bass. Despite the lack of Prince's name on the record and any marketing type publicity it did well, especially on the black chart where it reached number 25, '6' as a single reaching number 5.

In October Prince and his publicists in New York formally announced the disbanding of *The Revolution*. Prince a few days before had gone for dinner with Wendy, Lisa and drummer Bobby Z to announce to them he was replacing Bobby with Sheila E. Sheila had been successful as a solo act, albeit a Prince act, but she was getting frustrated at being just another Prince spin off. Going back behind him on the drums would at least give her some kudos as a musician again and she wanted this respect. She also added a new sound to Prince's recordings, a more Latin/jazz style that fitted in well with the direction Prince was going in. Even though she would now be his touring drummer Prince still continued to write and record for her and they set out working on her third solo album. Wendy did appear with Prince a few days later when he guested with The Bangles at a show they were performing in Los Angeles.

> ## INCREDIBLY PRINCE WANTED, AT THE SAME TIME AS THE PSEUDONYM CAMILLE ALBUM RELEASE, TO ALSO RELEASE AN ALBUM UNDER HIS OWN NAME, CRYSTAL BALL.

Through November Prince spent much of his time working on the aforementioned *Camille* album. He got the horn duo of Eric Leeds and Matt Bliston to add saxophone and trumpet. He also recorded many more songs for the project during a frenzied ten-day recording session; many of these songs would morph into other avenues including *Crystal Ball* which Prince started to work on at the end of November.

Incredibly Prince wanted, at the same time as the pseudonym *Camille* album release, to also release an album under his own name, *Crystal Ball*. It was obvious that this would be too much for the record company to justify so instead Prince blended songs from *Camille* onto *Crystal Ball*, which made it into a 22-track triple album. He spent more time at Sunset Sound and now turned his attention solely to *Crystal Ball*, recording more songs for the album and going through final preparations. On 30th November, the completed 22 tracks were ready. **Side 1:** *Rebirth of the Flesh, Play in the Sunshine, Housequake, The Ballad of Dorothy Parker;* **Side 2:** *It, Starfish and Coffee, Slow Love, Hot Thing;* **Side 3:** *Crystal Ball, If I was your Girlfriend, Rockhard in a Funky Place;* **Side 4:** *The Ball, Joy in Repetition, Strange Relationship, I Could Never Take the Place of Your Man;* **Side 5:** *Shockadelica, Good Love, Forever in my Life, Sign O Times;* **Side 6:** *The Cross, Adore, It's Gonna be a Beautiful Night.* In total seven songs were lifted from the scheduled *Camille* album and re-assigned to *Crystal Ball*.

Crystal Ball is an astonishing array of musicianship and talent, a one-man force frankly unmatched in the world of modern day musicians. It covered all aspects of Prince's musical genius ranging from the studio techniques of the pseudonym style *Camille* to pure funk and hard rock. There were gospel tinges and soothing ballads, there was soul, funk and dance. It had modern distortion techniques and diversity and innovation throughout. Prince as ever plays everything on the album displaying an unmatched ability to enter a recording studio alone and create an incredible amount of quality material to a level unseen before in its quantity, quality, speed and variety of style.

However, despite the brilliance of the album and the excitement of Prince, his management and Warner Bros were concerned: they again had reservations over the commercial aspects of such a large body of work. There would have to be a higher price, something Prince would not have considered, and if he had it wouldn't have been seen as an issue. Many years later when Prince was finally free from Warners and not under any contractual obligations the first thing he did was write, record and release the triple album *Emancipation* - this time of course he could release as much as he wanted.

> ## AT THE LAST SHOW HE PERFORMED WITH THE REVOLUTION, PRINCE BROKE ALL THE STRINGS ON HIS GUITAR DURING THE ENCORE.

Crystal Ball was eventually released on January 29 1998 by NPG Records. The only similarity between this album and the one shelved in 1986 was the title. This album, which became a three-disc set containing previously bootlegged material, came together with a fourth disc containing an album of 12 new acoustic songs titled *The Truth*. The box set was initially only available through direct orders by phone through Prince's 1-800-NEW-FUNK and the Internet. The direct order edition included a fifth disc which was an instrumental studio album by The NPG Orchestra titled *Kamasutra*. Shipment of this edition started in January 1998 approximately two months before its official release. *Crystal Ball* became the second triple album in succession following *Emancipation* - what better way for Prince to celebrate his freedom than to release two triple albums in quick succession? Each of this version of *Crystal Ball* contained three CDs containing 10 tracks and lasting almost exactly 50 minutes, mirroring *Emancipation*'s 12-song, 60-minute disc lengths. The album released in 1998 though was nothing like the original scheduled album of 1986: it contained completely different songs and was incoherent as an album narrative.

Crystal Ball was the first significant bust up between Prince and the record company; there were disagreements before but nothing on this scale. From this point on the relationship between Prince and Warner would be in slow decline. Prince's artistic vision and work didn't fit with record companies' commercial aspirations. Warners had invested a lot of money in Prince and they expected, whether he liked it or not, results. They felt that they had the right to refuse something presented to them that they perceived to be commercially risky. Prince, on the other hand, didn't see risk. He trusted his artistic vision and followed it regardless. It was about the creative process and above all not repeating yourself and always going to the next level with something new and creative - which of course was the last thing a record company wanted.

Reluctantly Prince accepted the decision to reduce the album and started to record songs for a new double album. He recorded *'U Got the Look'* and decided that one of the songs on the original album, *'Sign o' Times'*, would be its new name. This made it a focal point and gave Prince a sense of direction under its new theme. Prince eventually discarded seven songs for the new album as he re-worked it into a coherent arrangement.

His relationship with Susannah had also ended in December. He recorded the song *'Wally'* which was about the break up. The song is a significant one as Susan Rogers, who engineered the session, and most of Prince's work during this period, watched Prince create this beautiful heartfelt song and then purposely and permanently erase it. After completion when Prince looked up and asked Rogers to erase it, she declined, saying it was a beautiful piece and should remain. Prince reached over and deleted the whole song. It was gone, just like the relationship itself.

As January 1987 came around, Prince started rehearsals again with plans to hit the road for a tour to commence in May. Paisley Park was still in construction so rehearsals remained at this time at the warehouse on Washington Avenue. All of the former band members had now gone with the only remaining member being keyboardist Matt Fink. Backing dancers Greg Brookes and Wally Safford remained and he also kept his horn section of Eric Leeds and Matt Blistan. Miko Weaver retained guitar with Sheila E now taking the drums. She also introduced two of her former friends and musical associates Levi Seacer Jr and Boni Boyer to Prince. The last significant member of the new band was Cathy Glover who was brought in as a dancer and choreographer. She had previously worked for years as a club dancer in Chicago, which is where Steve Fargnoli had met her. She moved eventually to LA and got her big break on the TV show *Star Search*. She met Prince several times in the clubs of LA and eventually was hired as a dancer.

Prince completed *Sign o' the Times* at the start of 1987. He also worked with Sheena Easton, recording several songs for her. She wanted Prince to produce her next album *The Lover In Me* but he couldn't commit to fully producing her album as he was working on his own album. Eventually Prince completed the reworking and on February 18th *'Sign o' the Times'* the single was released. It reached number 3 on the Billboard chart and number 1 on the black chart. The B-side was *'la, la, la, he, he, he'* which he recorded in his home studio in January 1987, a lighthearted tune in complete contrast to the main track. The song *'Sign o' the Times'* was constructed by Prince almost entirely on the Fairlight sampling synthesizer. This provides the primary keyboard riff, and also gives the sampled electronic bass sounds heard on the track. Unlike some artists using the Fairlight around this time, Prince did not program new sounds for this song, but used the standard sounds the Fairlight offered.

The single marked a shift from those pulled from the albums

Parade and *Around the World in a Day* again with Prince showing diversity and a different sound to his music. It has a sparse electronic-based arrangement, a simple drum machine hits with minimal stacked synth patterns, and he adds a bluesy, funk-rock guitar part over this, giving a moodiness to the feel that fits in perfectly with the lyrical content. The record was noticeably bluesier and more downcast, melodically and lyrically, than any of Prince's previous singles. It addressed various socio-political problems including AIDS, gang violence, natural disasters, poverty, drug abuse, the *Space Shuttle Challenger* disaster and impending nuclear holocaust - a much deeper and more meaningful single than anything he had previously released. It set the stall beautifully for the new album.

> ## IF PURPLE RAIN WAS PRINCE AT HIS COMMERCIAL PEAK THEN IT COULD BE ARGUED THAT SIGN O' THE TIMES WAS HIS CRITICAL PEAK.

Sheila E was Prince's drummer and was sitting in rehearsals going through the paces with Prince as he worked the band through his new ideas leading towards the forthcoming tour. She still though had her third album ready and this was released on 19th February, entitled *Sheila E*. The album was co-written by Prince as expected with five of the ten songs from sessions that took place between December 1985 and September 1986. As before, Prince showcased his new show at an unannounced stop at First Avenue in Minneapolis. He performed a one hour set testing songs and the new band. It was basically a mini version of the forthcoming tour and Prince made it clear at the start that it was a rehearsal and the band were trying new things out. With the exception of *'Girls and Boys'* and *'Kiss'* the set was comprised of new material from the forthcoming album with a lengthy jam on *'It's Gonna be a Beautiful Night'* to close the show.

On March 30th 1987 Prince released *Sign o' the Times*. It was seen as his greatest achievement to date, the 16-track album consolidating all his versatility and musical styles. Although the album is a collection of songs from the abandoned albums from 1986, *The Dream Factory, Camille* and *Crystal Ball*, it still stands together as a cohesive album. The tracks were recorded in the main from March 1986 to December 1986 at Sunset Sound and Prince's home studio. Two songs survived from as far back as 1982: *'I Could Never Take the Place of Your Man'* and *'Strange Relationship'* were re-worked for inclusion. *'It's Gonna be a Beautiful Night'* was taken from the live recording in Paris from August 1986 on the *Parade* tour and reworked by Prince in the studio.

The album, although a Prince solo effort, also features guest appearances: Sheena Easton duets on *'U Got The Look'* and Susannah sings backing vocals on both *'Play in The Sunshine'* and *'Starfish and Coffee'*. There are also backing vocals by Lisa Coleman on *'Slow Love'* and of course Eric Leeds adds saxophone on a variety of tracks, *'Housequake'*, *'Slow Love'* and *'Hot Thing'*. Drum

programming is evident too on many tracks with Prince using it more inventively than ever before, in particular the sparse way he uses the trusted LM-1 and Fairlight.

Prince uses the speeded-up vocal which was primarily set aside for the Camille album in several songs, notably *'If I was your Girlfriend'* and *'Housequake'*. The effect is also used, but not as strongly, on *'Strange Relationship'* and *'U Got the Look'*. Interestingly on all on these four songs Prince credited 'Camille' on the lead vocal. Many critics noted the album's ability to blend all traditional elements of music together from soul, funk, jazz, rock and pop, and compared Prince to a huge variety of artists; including Smokey Robinson in relation to Prince's slow songs featuring his falsetto; Marvin Gaye on the sexier tunes and also the social commentary, likened to *'What's Going On'*; James Brown, Jimi Hendrix, Kate Bush, Maceo Parker, Sly Stone, Parliament, Robert Palmer and songs from the past British Invasion - all used to describe an album written and performed by one man. And all this on an album that had to be chopped and changed from three originals.

The themes ranged from hedonism, partying, sexual desire, infatuation, love and hate, devotion, intimacy and jealousy. Two songs on the album venture out of this realm, with *'Sign o' the Times'* and *'The Cross'* displaying themes outside of what can be controlled, both painting pictures of troubled times ahead.

Understandably *Sign o' the Times* was voted album of the year; in one poll of critics in *The Village Voice* it became the biggest winner in the poll's history. It sold very well. One issue the record company kept coming back to however was Prince's output. He had released 3 albums and a film in the past 3 years - other artists in his global category were releasing an album of around 9 songs every 2-4 years or so. Prince's musical output was seen as dangerously close to saturating a market that needed time to commercially strategize a release to obtain the maximum return. Prince prepared to unleash the *Sign o' the Times* tour on the road, regardless of what the record company thought; he was at a critical high and his popularity was growing in Europe and the rest of the world.

The European leg of the tour was scheduled to play stadiums of around 10,000 capacities with plans to move the tour to the US once Europe was completed. The concerts themselves lasted for around 90 to 110 minutes and although they followed the album roughly through the set it still felt spontaneous as Prince worked and cued the band from the front. The tour continued through Europe to amazing reviews, and Prince played some after-shows along the way while in Germany and Sweden, mainly loose jams incorporating James Brown and Jimi Hendrix songs. The UK leg of the tour encountered problems. Prince originally planned two concerts at Wembley Stadium, both of which were sold out, but due to weather issues he had to reschedule to another venue, Earls Court, on three days' notice. However, Kensington and Chelsea Council needed 28 days to acquire a license, and as a result, the UK leg of the tour was cancelled, with additional dates added to in Holland and Belgium. In response Prince decided to film the remaining shows around Europe to release a concert film; he also decided not to continue the tour around the US, using the concert film to showcase the tour to the US market and to those who had had their tickets cancelled. Many in the camp tried to convince Prince to continue to the US, but Prince had his mind made up.

Prince's engineer Susan Rogers was flown in and mobile recording trucks were assembled for the remaining concerts. The tour closed in Antwerp, Belgium on 29 June 1987. It was without question another huge success: the 34 date European tour was seen by over 350,000 fans, almost three times that of the *Parade* tour. Prince completed the *Sign o' the Times* film back in Minneapolis in late August 1987 at a cost of around $2.5 million.

Even though many songs were performed on the tour from his back-catalog Prince decided that the video would only showcase *Sign o' the Times* material, the exception being a brief interlude of *'Little Red Corvette'*. The band were seen in the film but the largest spotlight went to dancer Cat, who was perpetually at the centre of the action and the story that loosely connects the songs.

If *Purple Rain* was Prince at his commercial peak then it could be argued that *Sign o' the Times* was his critical peak. It managed to be uniquely different to the mainstream albums of the time, but also have the distribution of a major label. It meant that he was on the edge of what was commercially acceptable and what was creatively zealous.

Despite the critical acclaim, Prince was feeling artistically restricted. He had produced in the past year or so some outstanding albums and they had been rejected for commercial purposes - he was forced to slash them down. He was also essentially working alone again, with Wendy Lisa and Susannah gone, the people he shared so much creativity with over the past years. This meant that his work now entered a darker phase in his recordings, and this darker element would ultimately change. To Black.

CHAPTER EIGHT

RAIN IS WET AND SUGAR IS SWEET

From dark to the light **would be a good way of describing Prince's next phase in his career. He was held in constant high esteem by critics and fans alike - there was no one to match him - but even he was getting bored with his own genius; it's no surprise then that he was heading to some sort of epiphany as he tried to make sense of his life to this point.**

It's usually at this juncture in a pop/rock star's career that things start heading away from the music and into other avenues of distraction, whether that be drugs, alcohol or such like escapism. In reality Prince only had music and that was what he turned to and expressed himself through. Prince was music: he lived it, he breathed it, there was not a day passed when he wasn't writing, recording or performing. It wasn't work, it was simply what he did all day, all night. And with the ability to create everything himself, on all instruments without relying on anyone else, it was his existence.

Prince released *'U Got the Look'* on July 14th 1987, and it became his biggest chart hit since *'Kiss'*. It shot up the charts and hit number 2 on Billboard, staying in the charts for a further 25 weeks. This made not touring the US even more of an issue because in hindsight, when he would have toured, this single would have been high in the charts and would have served as a great promotional tool for both the album and tour. On 11th September he played a short set at the MTV Music Awards in Los Angeles. He played *'Sign o' the Times'* and *'Play in the Sunshine'*. *'Sign o' the Times'* just saw Prince centre stage alone, with Cat highlighted above in silhouette. The rest of the band joined the stage for *'Play in the Sunshine'*. A star studded after-show was performed with Huey Lewis joining Prince on stage for *'Forever in my Life'*.

On the same day, 11th September 1987, *Paisley Park Studios* was officially opened at 7801 Audubon Road, Chanhassen, Minnesota.

It was everything Prince wanted: he had until this point flitted between various locations to conduct his recording, rehearsing and performing, but now he had it all under one roof in a place that he could call his own. Paisley Park would become as much a part of Prince and his legacy as the music, a place that would be forever associated with him and become part of who he was as an artist, performer and musician.

Costing at the time around 10 million, Prince invested heavily in the complex, renegotiating some terms with Warners as part of the deal. Studio A was a 1,500-square foot state-of-the-art studio; Prince had a granite walled isolation room installed to create reverberation techniques without any echo. It also had a 48-track recording console. Studio B was slightly smaller at 1000 square foot but also had a 48-track console installed. Studio C was designed for audio recordings, photography, rehearsals and stage productions. The largest section of the building was a 12,400-square foot soundstage the height of an arena which would be used for full on concert rehearsals; it had been designed to have incredible acoustics despite its size. The whole complex was based on Prince's concepts and was very much in his image. As time went on he would take complete ownership of it and have an apartment installed inside, as well as various relaxation and communal rooms, a reading room, clothing designers and a nightclub.

The writing for others continued with *Jill Jones* releasing her debut album on Paisley Park records. Prince is credited as co-writer but he was in fact the sole writer on all tracks. Unlike previous albums Prince wrote for others Jill Jones's debut contains some of the strongest material outside his own releases from 1982-1986, with the exception of *'With You'* which was a cover of the Prince track from 1979. All the tracks were recorded in Prince's home studio and contain again the orchestral additions of Clare Fischer. *Taja Sevelle* also released her self-titled debut album on Paisley Park records containing two Prince songs *'If I Could Get Your Attention'* and *'Wouldn't You Love to Love Me'*. The album did well mainly due to the first single *'Love is Contagious'* which became a big hit in Europe.

Despite the lack of commercial success for *Under the Cherry Moon*, which even by this point in 1987 had more or less been forgotten, Prince was still planning another movie. He started writing a script for *Graffiti Bridge* while in Paris in September 1987 before finishing a basic draft back in Minneapolis. Interestingly Prince wanted the lead role to be played by Madonna and he sent a copy of the script to her directly. While waiting for Madonna's answer Prince attended two concerts by David Bowie at the Civic Centre in St Paul, and afterwards Bowie and his group attended a private screening of *Sign o' the Times* and a party with Prince at Paisley Park.

> # HIS IDEA WAS TO PUT AN ALBUM OUT AND HAVE THE PUBIC SLOWLY DISCOVER IT WAS IN FACT A PRINCE ALBUM

Prince now started work on *'The Black Album'* although it never really had a name, and never was intended to have one either: the concept was unique and a great example of how Prince's mind worked with his music and art. There would be no promotion, no singles, no videos, no name. In 1987 this was unheard of. Prince wanted simply to release an album with no cover and no connection to him at all. His idea was to put an album out and have the pubic slowly discover it was in fact a Prince album. Again, record company people would hold meetings, confused at the briefing by one of their biggest global stars that he wanted to release his next album without any public announcement or marketing activity at all. The irony of this is that *The Black Album*, as it would be known, would become one of the biggest bootlegs in music history. Record companies however don't make money from bootlegs, and Prince knew this.

Madonna arrived in Minneapolis to discuss the *Graffiti Bridge* movie with Prince, but she declined the role and only stayed in Minneapolis for a day. Prince put the idea on hold and continued work on *The Black Album*, which he finished in November 1987. A second *Madhouse* album was also completed and released in November keeping up with the numbered titles: it was named *16*. As with the previous Madhouse album *8* the credits named the usual musicians as writers although it is a full-on Prince project - in fact 5 of the 9 songs are Prince completely solo, and as a result it leans towards funk more than jazz.

A week before the scheduled release of *The Black Album* Prince cancelled the whole project. It is true that Warners were concerned that the album was scheduled to be released so soon after *Sign o' the Times*, and concerned also about the nature of the release, with no marketing whatsoever, but the decision to cancel it was driven by Prince alone. There is a lot of speculation surrounding the reason for the last-minute cancellation. Prince later described the evening of his decision as *'Blue Tuesday'*, which was Tuesday

December 1st 1987. He visited a nightclub in downtown Minneapolis where he met Ingrid Chavez, a local poet and singer, and she claimed that they then when back to Paisley Park, Prince had some kind of nervous religious experience at some point during the evening and suddenly became very concerned about the dark nature of his new album and what impact the subject matter and tone may have on others, especially the young. He had a moral dilemma.

He described the dark side of this theory to be *'Spooky Electric'*, the opposing light to emerge as *'Lovesexy'*. The *Lovesexy* tour program explained this and the concert itself was based around dark and light, good and evil, temptation and positivity. The speculation though was that Prince had taken Ecstasy and had a bad reaction, or trip, to the drug, which he took as a sign or signal to move from the dark to the light. His next album *Lovesexy* was to counter the dark nature and satanic influence of *The Black Album*. The word Ecstasy is one of the floating words in the *'Alphabet Street'* video, as is *'Love God'* and *'Don't buy the Black album, I'm sorry'*. This gives this theory some kudos; however Prince was never known to take recreational drugs so if this was the case it was a complete one-off.

Another theory is that Prince wanted to take the album to another level: only people who really searched for it could actually get it. This fits in with Prince's practices, especially regarding concerts, where he would, over the years, favor hit and run style events where people searching for him, who had the patience and will, would always get a ticket to a performance.

Prince wanted the album to be released without any fanfare, no marketing, no singles, no photos on the cover, no words or lettering, just a plain black cover and a plain black record. Word of mouth would spread out that this was in fact a Prince album. By cancelling it at the last minute, and after 500,000 had actually been pressed, he made it even more searched for by fans. If you were lucky enough to have an original factory pressed album with an official number it became instantly valuable. Could it be that it wasn't Prince wrestling with his conscience, but rather a brilliant piece of strategy to make this album a legendary underground record that bypassed the record companies completely?

The songs on *The Black Album* are pure funk, the type of music that Prince did in his spare time, the style of music that came very easily to him and which he could record and play with ease. The songs were written, pressed and played in various clubs so Prince could see the reaction of people to the songs. Some were written for Sheila E's birthday party and played for the first time after Prince had recorded them the night before. Prince often recorded dance/funk numbers, had them pressed and then would get a DJ to play them while he watched the dance floor for audience reactions. Whatever the motivation behind the decision to pull *The Black Album* it would remain a legendary album to own in any form, and Prince's own announcement that fans should not listen to it only fueled the fire to seek it out. Critics that had heard it praised it as one of funkiest and darkest albums they had ever heard. The album also represented a dark period in Prince's life. He was missing the collaborative company of Wendy and Lisa, his relationship with Susannah and now his relationship with his closest manager Steve Fargnoli was starting to deteriorate. Fargnoli didn't really back the *Graffiti Bridge* project and also as manager gave Prince commercial advice about previous releases.

Many songs on the album are very negative so it's no surprise that Prince didn't feel any warmth towards it.

Around 500,000 copies had been pressed before Prince pulled the plug on *The Black Album* and naturally destroying them was extremely difficult, so many were leaked onto the market, culminating in it becoming the most bootlegged album of all time. It had an early estimated vinyl and CD copy rate of around 250-500,000 albums very quickly, and of course this would be copied again and again on cassette duplications around the world. It would sit forever as the Prince album to get to complete a back catalog and would continue to be searched out by record collectors and fans alike for decades to come.

The rumors of Prince's epiphany regarding *The Black Album* were centered around Ingrid Chavez, who he named *The Spiritual Child*.

Prince had met her in a nightclub in Minneapolis and she was said to have asked to ask him to smile more. She appears in the notes of his next album *Lovesexy* as The Spiritual Child. Chavez had moved to Minneapolis in 1986 and had been writing poetry for years. Prince started working with her at the end of December at Paisley Park putting music to her poetry. Her album was eventually released in 1991 and featured new backing music. It's a weak album by any stretch and features mainly mood style music over Ingrid's spoken poetry. However, these sessions clearly had a positive effect on Prince and he started to lean towards spirituality as a core theme in his life and work; the results were extremely positive and his outlook became happier and focused as moved away from what he saw as the darkness of *The Black Album* and that period in his life.

In mid-December 1987 Prince assembled his *Sign o' the Times* touring band at Paisley Park, dropping dancers Greg Brookes and

Wally Safford. Paisley Park would naturally be his home for recording, tour rehearsals and creativity. On 11th December, Prince and his new ensemble recorded two tracks that would appear on *Lovesexy*, 'Eye No' and 'Positivity'. 'Eye No' was a live band recording and 'Positivity' a solo song with Prince on his own. Both songs show Prince's new outlook and pave the way for the new album's themes of positivity, openness and spirituality.

Prince also continued work with Sheila E on her new album, which took them through to the start of 1988. One track recorded for her was 'Scarlet Pussy' which became a Prince B-side. The other songs recorded were never released and stayed in the vault. Throughout January 1988 Prince, at furious pace, continued with *Lovesexy*, adding layers and layers of overdubs, horn sections and montages to the album. His new state-of-the-art studio allowed him to layer sounds and add to songs at will. Many thought that the album's brilliance was being diluted with the process of continuing to add instruments to each song, but Prince was undeterred and carried on with his new recording.

> IT'S QUITE AMAZING THAT MADONNA AND PRINCE WERE HAPPY TO LET THIS COLLABORATION SLIDE ONTO THE ALBUM WITHOUT FANFARE

One aspect of *Lovesexy* that is different to his previous albums is that it was a complete album written from start to finish with a theme in mind. With Paisley Park Prince didn't have to juggle recording studio time, and could work 20 hours a day. The whole studio was running 24/7 with no breaks and it was clear even in these early days of Paisley Park that the operational costs would be very expensive. For Prince though, as ever, this kind of thought was secondary to the creativity he was producing.

On New Year's Eve 1987 Prince and his new look band played at Paisley Park in front of around 400 people. It was a charity concert in aid of the homeless with each ticket for the cause costing $200. Miles Davis joined Prince on stage, and the concert naturally turned into an impromptu jam session that saw in the new year.

This was one of the few recorded moments between Prince and Davis with Prince commanding the band with his hand gestures as he allowed Davis to improvise during the set. Prince also played a large guitar solo of *Auld Lang Syne* which blended through the 'Purple Rain' backbeat. There were also covers of 'Chain of Fools', 'Cold Sweat' and 'Take the A Train'. It was basically a very funky revised version of the *Sign o' the times* set with a blistering 35-minute version of 'Its Gonna Be a Beautiful Night' at the end. In the crowd were Prince's parents as well as his stepfather Hayward Baker.

At the start of 1988 Prince put the final touches to *Lovesexy* alongside continual rehearsals through January with the band. Originally, he planned to not produce any music videos for the record at all but was persuaded otherwise and subsequently recorded a video for 'Alphabet Street', which was scheduled to be the first single from the album. The video was recorded at Paisley Park and it's clear that it's an in-house piece of work, certainly in comparison to Prince's previous videos. Paisley Park allowed Prince to take ownership and complete control over everything in his career without the need to book or schedule time anywhere; if he decided at the last minute to produce, direct and perform a music video like 'Alphabet Street' it was a case of simply setting it up and shooting it. The only control he didn't have at this stage was the ability to release what he wanted and when, but this would in the coming years be rectified.

Prince worked on a song for Madonna in March 1988 for her album *Like a Prayer*, eventually released on March 21 1989. Prince worked with her on certain tracks including 'Love Song', which was recorded by Prince and sent to Madonna who worked on it with her own musicians before returning it to Prince to continue. Prince also worked on many other tracks on her album adding guitar work here and there. The album is a personal one for Madonna that she dedicated to her mother who died when she was young. From a marketing viewpoint, this particular duo in 1988/89 was star power at its most extreme but despite this 'Love Song' was not released as a single. It's a funky tune and has a radio friendly hook throughout but Prince and Madonna chose for it to take a quiet backseat behind five singles including the title track, which topped the Billboard Hot 100 for three weeks. They also spoke about touring together but Prince decided against it, stating that the world wasn't ready. So the song that could have been one of the biggest collaborations in popular music remained a quiet afterthought. When you consider a similar situation with Paul McCartney and Michael Jackson a few years earlier it's quite amazing that Madonna and Prince were happy to let this collaboration slide onto the album without fanfare, and Prince's work scattered throughout this album again went quietly unnoticed.

Prince recorded a second video from Lovesexy for the single 'Glam Slam' at Paisley park. Many extras were drafted in with Prince and his band performing a set for them all. Quincy Jones attended the recording and songs were played that were to be performed on the tour. The stage itself was a constant work in progress with ramps and elevated sections which meant that the band, as well as playing to the standard Prince demanded, also had to cope with moving sections and various additional choreography.

May 10th 1988 saw the release of *Lovesexy*, an album that stood as personal sermonizing from Prince and found him justifying his newfound enlightenment in the dark wake of *The Black Album*. It was recorded amazingly in seven weeks from start to finish. Prince said of the album that he saw *The Black Album* as not really him but the devil's work whereas *Lovesexy* was a record made for God. The record marked a change in Prince's attitude to his writing and everyday persona; colleagues noticed that he was happy most of the time and became easier to work with.

The one aspect of *Lovesexy* that caused major concern was the cover photo. Many confused it as pornographic when in essence it was designed to show a rebirth of spirituality for Prince and his sound. Many retail outlets refused to have it on display and kept it behind the counter. Prince was very upset with this misinterpretation and felt the cover reflected the content of the record. The cover shows a semi-naked Prince relaxing in a peaceful, almost serene way amidst the petals of flowers. It was shot by fashion photographer and video director Jean-Baptiste Mondino and shows a distinctly phallic stamen pointed at his chest. Some retailers even covered it completely, selling it, ironically, in just a plain black cover.

The entire *Lovesexy* album was recorded from mid December 1987 to January 1988 and unlike other Prince albums was conceived as an entire album without the need to chop and change or bring in unreleased pieces of work from his huge back catalog. The critics loved *Lovesexy*, with many feeling it was his strongest album to date. It sold initially just under 2 million outside the US putting it alongside *Parade* and *Around the World in a Day* and it peaked at number 11 on the pop charts in the US. Prince chose on the strength of the European sales and positive reviews to tour Europe before the US, to allow time for it to gain momentum stateside.

Despite the positive reviews Prince's relationship with Steve Fargnoli was coming to an end. He was increasingly frustrated with his management team, especially in what he felt was the lack of commitment to his record label Paisley Park records. He felt that they didn't promote his releases sufficiently and therefore sales were lost on his projects. He also changed his PR team in the light of these recent frustrations; he had worked for over eight years with the Howard Bloom Organization based in New York but decided to switch over to Warner Bros. Of course, it could be argued that Prince released so much material it was difficult to promote everything that he put out, but Prince was oblivious to this and his opinion was that he made the music and paid others to put it out, promote it and distribute it accordingly. In the years ahead he would take control of this himself, setting the tone for others to follow in the wake of his eventual success in complete self-management around music and distribution. For now though this wasn't an option so Warner Bros were tasked with the promotional side of Prince and his label's releases.

Rehearsals continued in May 1988 with the tour kicking off on July 8th at the 20 thousand capacity Palais Omnisport de Bercy which was renamed in October 2015 the Accor Hotels Arena. Shows over Europe sold out within minutes of announcements and demand was incredible. Prince's team were stretched heavily: his decision to tour Europe first with the US to follow made it very difficult to sort out venues and logistics in such a short window.

The stage show itself cost, in 1988 money, around 2 million dollars, with the design again falling to Roy Bennet. The stage was circular with rises and ramps throughout. It had a miniature basketball court, a hydraulic brass bed, a swing and curtains. It also had the speaker system elevated high above the set, enabling the band members to move around freely on stage. It was visually spectacular with lighting changes, costume changes and a variety of props and effects that kept constantly moving with the shifting music. It had the ability to feel like a small show and retained intimacy even though it was a full-scale production. Prince even entered the stage in a Thunderbird car that circled around before he climbed out the back to start the show with *'Erotic City'*. As with all Prince concerts there were constant changes to the set as the tour continued, with some covers thrown in from time to time during the heavy jam sessions.

During this tour Prince gave many after-show concerts, often

IN GENERAL HE HAD A FEW HOURS' SLEEP FROM AROUND 5-6AM BEFORE STARTING OVER AGAIN.

jamming with the band until dawn. Many of the after-show concerts were played for over 2 hours and often started around 1am after Prince had finished his main concert and had returned to his hotel and changed. The first, in London, was at Camden Palace where many celebrities attended including Eric Clapton, Terence Trent D'Arby, Bananarama and Ron Wood, who joined Prince onstage for a rendition of The Rolling Stones' *'Miss You'*. Prince's routine at this stage was quite breathtaking: he survived on little or no sleep at all. The mornings were generally put aside for conducting business meetings, the afternoons for rehearsing his band or recording various ghost bands he was writing for, and the evenings for shows or studio recording or both. In general he had a few hours' sleep from around 5-6am before starting over again. This made working with him very difficult as engineers and fellow musicians were put through marathon recording sessions and rehearsals on a daily basis; this is one of the reasons why his band and engineers changed frequently as they struggled to keep up with his total non-stop dedication and constant recording, writing and performing.

The tour continued through August moving from Wembley to Birmingham in the UK before heading to Sweden and Norway. The Dutch leg was witnessed by over 100,000 fans before it progressed to Denmark, Italy and Germany finally concluding on 9th September at Dortmund where it was filmed and became the 2-part video *Lovesexy 1* and *Lovesexy 2*. The 32-date tour sold in excess of 500,000 tickets in Europe alone. It was both a personal and commercial success and proved Prince was indeed correct to abandon the US and tour Europe first.

The US leg of the tour could not have been more different. Prince and his entourage returned to Minneapolis with Prince heading straight into the studio to work on a few songs before heading in to the US leg. Most performances on this side of the pond though were not sold out, even in Minneapolis, mainly down to the poor US sales of *Lovesexy*. The tour concluded in Dallas on 29th November and although the 38 concerts in the US were not completely sold out, in some venues they were seen by over 600,000 fans. The US leg, despite this incredible number, actually lost money due to the elaborate stage show.

In typical Prince fashion, straight after the tour it was back into the studio to continue various musical projects. At Paisley Park Prince worked on the next *Madhouse* album titled *24*. It was a mix of free-flowing jazz funk in the same style as the previous albums, but Prince worked mainly alone on this one with added touches of saxophone and flute from Eric Leeds. Although it went through mixing and Prince continued working on the tracks he soon drifted away from it and subsequently it never was released as a complete album. Eric Leeds did revive some of the tracks for his own album later in 1991. Sheena Easton released her third album to have Prince input in December 1988 with *The Lover in Me* featuring co-written Prince tracks, attributed to Joey Coco as a Prince pseudonym. The title track as a single reached number 2 on the Billboard pop charts with the album itself going on to be certified gold in the US.

Prince's finances at this point were becoming an issue to those around him; he had now a full-on state-of-the-art recording complex running 24 hours a day, with numerous staff running it. He had offices, he had a clothing department making his clothes from his designs every day, he had a full-on sound stage for rehearsals that enabled him to perform full shows as if he was in concert with all the lighting and state-of-the-art effects to hand, he had movie and film projects on the go, he had private chefs, musicians, producers and engineers on the payroll, every instrument available and a full-on management team as well as all the outgoing projects he was working on.

Paisley Park wasn't just a single studio, it was a full complex operating 24 hours a day. Put plainly at this stage in his career he had more going out than he had coming in. Prince was oblivious and carried on with his projects regardless and simply recorded, wrote, rehearsed and jammed, leaving those he employed to run such trivial matters. His output was an ongoing issue: his record company desperately needed him to slow down so they could milk

to the max his latest offering. George Michael, in comparison, had the previous year released *Faith*, and it would be three years before his next album *Listen without Prejudice Volume 1* and a further six for the next *Older*. Michael Jackson had a similar output: *Off the Wall* was released in 1979 with *Thriller* three years later, *Bad* five years later and *Dangerous* after another gap of four years.

It's no surprise looking at this that Prince would be the first to use the Internet as a direct form of distribution in the years ahead, the first to visualize *itunes* and the equivalent platforms for instant access to music long before it was ever created. Direct access to new music without restrictions was what he was always working towards.

What the record company wanted now was a huge hit album, and to be fair Prince needed this too. The US album sales were poor, by his standards, and a big return to chart success would be welcome both for Prince's status in the charts and also his finances to secure his lavish lifestyle of creativity.

It's almost as if he needed a superhero to come knocking on his door at Paisley Park...

CHAPTER NINE

PARTYMAN

In mid December 1988 Prince's management were contacted by the team behind the forthcoming blockbuster movie *Batman*. *Batman* was a huge success as a TV program in the 1960s but when cancelled the superhero became just another comic book character from the past. Tim Burton's film was to change all that and on a rough draft script a couple of Prince songs were included, *'1999'* and *'Baby I'm a Star'*, which Burton's team thought worked really well. The cast were also huge Prince fans so from the start they wanted Prince in some aspect to be part of the movie.

Tim Burton was born August 25, 1958 and as a film director is known for his dark gothic and eccentric fantasy-style films. This mysterious dark edge was very much Prince's style so it's no surprise that, on seeing a later script and pieces of the forthcoming movie, the general mood of the film would be of interest to Prince and get his creativity flowing. Burton had previously been known for working on the hugely successful adventure comedy *Pee-wee's Big Adventure* in 1985 before taking on the *Batman* film project.

Prince's team were approached for Prince to be involved in the music for the film at the same time many actors were being considered for the role of Batman himself, which eventually and controversially went to Michael Keaton. Jack Nicholson accepted the role of the Joker under strict conditions that dictated a high salary including a portion of the box office profits, and this would prove to be very lucrative to him. Warner Bros were of course very excited about the project; it would be for the first time since *Purple Rain* that they could combine a Warners film and music together in one huge marketing package, and it was looking like it could be financially good for all parties involved. Despite this, Prince was skeptical about the project and took some early convincing as negotiations took shape.

Despite the excitement in Prince's team around the forthcoming project, and the lucrative nature of what lay ahead, Prince still couldn't let his perceptions of the *Lovesexy* failings go; it was a very important time for him both spiritually and commercially, and there had been many projects over the past year or so that he felt were not handled well, with opportunities missed. He fired the entire management team on January 3rd 1989. It was a ruthless cull of his entire management and staff, including Bob Cavallo, Joe Ruffalo and Steve Fargnoli. He also fired his business lawyers who had been with him for eleven years. Alan Leeds was promoted

to General Manager of Paisley Park Records and Albert Magnoli was appointed as Prince's manager, his first job being to bring in a new legal team to handle entertainment and law matters. Despite this, on a personal level Prince had his new girlfriend Anna Garcia move in with him in Minneapolis as this relationship had become quite serious and the two were very close. She was 18 when she moved in with him.

Prince and his new manager flew to London to meet with Tim Burton to discuss the new movie. They visited Pinewood Studios and saw elements of the set. Prince was absolutely blown away with it and was full of excitement over the project; he agreed to write new songs for it and immediately cancelled a planned break in Paris to begin work. He even tried to cancel a final Japanese leg of the *Lovesexy* tour but it was too close to do so. He had to commit to the Japanese leg first and then proceed straight in to *Batman*.

The Japanese leg of the *Lovesexy* tour saw 8 dates across Japan, all sold out and hugely successful. It was so commercially successful that it made up for the shortfall incurred during the American leg of the tour. The tour itself had little change from the previous *Lovesexy* shows. Prince's focus was now strictly on his next project, and he immediately ended any contractual obligations with his band as he didn't intend to tour for the duration of 1989. He flew back to Paisley Park to start work on *Batman* as a solo project.

Initially Prince was scheduled to write just a few songs for *Batman*, but Prince asked if he could provide a full soundtrack for the movie. He had already, in a matter of weeks, completed over eleven songs. Prince continued working alone through songs based on the themes around the movie; he also had collaborations with Sheena Easton again, who duetted with him on *'Arms of Orion'*, and he also worked with Kim Basinger and Tim Burton himself who visited the studio to watch Prince work.

Two albums involving Prince were released prior to the *Batman* project in early 1989. Madonna released her *Like A Prayer* album featuring Prince throughout and in particular the duet on *'Love Song'*, and it was a huge success, hitting number 1 in most countries around the world and in particular the UK and USA.

In addition, Mavis Staples released her own album on Paisley Park Records *Time Waits for No One* in May 1989. This was Mavis Staples' first album on Paisley Park Records, and critically it was a success as many thought it was one of the best Paisley Park records so far; commercially however it wasn't a huge hit and languished around the edge of the charts.

Three days before the release of the *Batman* movie the Prince soundtrack was released on 20th June 1989. It was a huge success and catapulted Prince back to the top of the charts. The Warners machine was heavily in action now they had an album soundtrack and a film shortly to be released: they promoted heavily and made it the must-buy album and must-see movie of the year. The album itself is a Prince album first and foremost, but he captures the mood of the film perfectly with the songs he wrote. The album cover is also a perfect piece of marketing showing the familiar bat sign that stood out in record stores and on T-shirts all over the world. It doesn't sound like a standard Prince album but its sparse drum beats and moody dark feel fits perfectly with Burton's gothic shadowy vision of Gotham City. With the added pieces of dialogue the record is an outstanding complement to the movie, and the movie would soon be the perfect complement to the soundtrack.

> THE SOUNDTRACK, IN THE WAKE OF THE FILM, WAS A HIT ALL OVER THE WORLD AND BECAME PRINCE'S BIGGEST ALBUM SINCE PURPLE RAIN.

The album was recorded in just a few weeks at Paisley Park and the overall feel is that of a prolonged bout of recording. The drum beats are the main ingredient, with backing synths; the guitar work is held back for embellishments as opposed to solos or structure for the songs. The only exception is on *'Batdance'* which includes a guitar solo. It's easy to look at this album as a substandard collection of songs alongside Sign o' the Times or Lovesexy but the album was constructed to fit in with the mood of the movie and Tim Burton's vision of Gotham city, and if you look at it from that perspective Prince had the concept absolutely spot on. Of course, Prince managed to put his own spiritual themes into the album by playing with Batman and the Joker, Good and Evil, Darkness and Light. He even manages to play with both these characters within himself for the album and sings each of the songs as a different character from the movie.

As expected the soundtrack, in the wake of the film, was a hit all over the world and became Prince's biggest album since *Purple Rain*. In fact, since *Purple Rain* Prince's record sales had been in slow decline, even though his critical acclaim and live draw was at its highest. *Batman* reversed the trend and put him back at the top of the charts all over the world, and of course with this came a resurgence in his back catalog once more. It proved to be another multi-platinum successful cross-media enterprise by Warner Bros much like *Purple Rain*. The album was No. 1 on the Billboard albums chart for six consecutive weeks and sold over eleven million copies worldwide.

Prince's music videos were also captivating for the singles released, showcasing a brilliant understanding of the movie characters, with Prince playing and dancing in character perfectly. All were directed by Albert Magnoli and saw Prince at his mischievous best. The singles were also massive hits hitting number 1 all over the world:

'Batdance' hit the top spot in the US on 9th June 1989 with *'Partyman'* following shortly after.

Again, the crossover was perfect, the videos advertising the album and movie and the movie advertising the singles and album. As this was a structure of album/film and various copyright ownerships the franchise itself became very complicated. Prince had to agree to sign the publishing rights to the songs used in the film over to Warner Bros, something he had never done in the past. This is one reason why future greatest hits collections fail to feature any of the singles from the album.

Prince attended the opening night of the *Batman* movie in Los Angeles on 19th June 1989 before it opened in the US on 23rd June 1989. It was an incredible success. It returned in its first weekend alone over $40 million, which was the biggest in motion picture history. It would go on to be one of the biggest grossing films of all time, clearing over $250 million in the US alone. It would go on further to earn over $400 million in box office totals. The film received a Golden Globe nomination and won an Academy Award. It also inspired the equally successful *Batman - The Animated Series*, paving the way for the DC animated universe and leading the way for future modern marketing and development of the superhero film genre. When the film opened it was backed by the biggest marketing and merchandising campaign in film history at the time. The success of the film helped establish Burton as a profitable director and it also proved to be a huge influence on future superhero films, which became much darker and less comic book after the achievements of *Batman*.

Batman actress Kim Basinger was now in Minneapolis and rumors of a romance were circulating amongst the tabloids. Prince was now heavily driving forward with his next movie and album project *Graffiti Bridge*, a loose follow up to *Purple Rain*. They started working through a script together and eventually she moved in with Prince at his home. Prince had recently ended his relationship with Anna Garcia early in the year.

Dutch saxophonist Candy Dulfer also joined Prince at Paisley to work through songs and jams. She also guested on the video shoot at Paisley Park for *'Partyman'* where Prince added a line in the song as a mention for his new saxophonist. Prince had met Dulfer while in Europe and asked her to play with him onstage; he was impressed with her and subsequently invited her to Paisley Park to work on some ideas he had formulated. Eric Leeds was still heading up the *Madhouse* project with Prince and was assembling a sequence of instrumentals for a third album which were to be numbered *17-26* in keeping with the previous song titles. Prince however on this occasion didn't feel the album was worthy of his involvement, feeling it was more in keeping with jazz, something that was more in Eric Leeds' and Matt Blistan's field. An agreement was reached that this album would be released as an Eric Leeds solo effort. In addition to the above, Prince started work on a second Jill Jones album, and even cut some videos for the project, although it would never come to fruition.

Prince released *'Partyman'* as a second single from the album on 15th September 1989, and it was another huge worldwide hit. It failed to hit the number one spot however and sold less than the first single *'Batdance'*. The video for *'Partyman'* is one of Prince's best to date, his role perfectly fitting with the movie. Prince also started working on another album for The Time, *Corporate World*. He wrote and recorded songs directly for the project, but Warners requested he put the album on hold as they wanted to bring the original Time members back to the ghost band and to get them involved in it. Prince agreed, and leaving them to continue where he had left off he now turned his attention to his next project.

Prince continued with plans for *Graffiti Bridge*. *Graffiti Bridge* would be unusual in that Prince would heavily use songs pre-written from his past, selecting and updating them for the project instead of writing completely new material. He updated songs taken from the vault with a few exceptions notably *'New Power Generation', 'Melody Cool'* and *'Round and Round'*, with *'Thieves in the Temple'* being added at the last minute through a sudden rush of creativity for the project. It would also be a largely collaborative album with Prince moving far away from the *Batman* solo project and bringing in guests and musical friends to join on vocals and songs. Of course, Prince controlled everything, playing 99% of the music, writing all the songs and directing and writing the movie, but he wanted the album to have a sense of joint venture that would be in keeping with his vision of his film.

On paper the movie idea was perfect: it looked like another *Purple Rain* or even *Purple Rain 2*. As recordings progressed Prince took time to perform *'Electric Chair'* on the 15th anniversary special of *Saturday Night Live*. A couple of days later on the 27th September 1989 a documentary was aired in the UK entitled *Prince: a Musical Portrait*, providing a brilliant insight into his recording process and featuring unseen footage of rehearsals and recordings. It was directed by Albert Magnoli and although it was only a nine-minute documentary it captured the feeling around Prince and his inner world beautifully. It featured comments from Eric Clapton, Little Richard, Miles Davis and George Clinton.

On the wave of all of the recent success Prince decided to hit the road again and head out for a major tour, again heading out to Europe and Japan. A press release was issued and almost immediately all venues were completely sold out; almost 20 additional dates needed to be added to meet demand. Prince was determined to put on a less extravagant show: the *Lovesexy* tour was an incredible spectacle but it proved to be expensive and if the venues were not sold out could even make a loss, so on this tour Prince wanted to step away from that and focus more on the performance and the music and less on props and visual additions. In essence, it would be a more stripped down show than before, and it would be a greatest hits tour with songs from *Batman* in the mix.

As before, with Prince managing the *Graffiti Bridge* project and writing the script, certain doubts from those around him started to creep in. Albert Magnoli was one of those who raised concerns about the direction of the movie. He made suggestions to Prince about where he thought changes should be made. Prince was adamant however about what he was doing and refused to make any changes away from his initial vision for the film. It resulted in Magnoli walking away from the project altogether after the pair could not reach a compromise. With Magnoli now gone Prince was forced to look for a new team, and he wanted a team that would fully back *Graffiti Bridge* and stay true to Prince's script and direction. At first Warners showed little interest in the movie but became interested once it was pitched by the new team as a sequel

to *Purple Rain*; this was exactly what they wanted to hear.

As 1989 ended Prince continued with writing *Graffiti Bridge*, working on the soundtrack and completing a third draft. This one would include both Kim Basinger and Jill Jones in the leading roles.

In December 1989, another future member of Prince's band arrived in Minneapolis. Rosie Gaines from California had previously had some connections with Prince's bass player Levi Seacer jr and had sung on a couple of tracks he was producing. Prince heard her voice and immediately invited her to Paisley Park. Rosie had been performing from an early age and had sung and played keyboards in a variety of bands, mainly jazz and funk outfits. Prince drafted Rosie into his new band for the forthcoming *'Nude Tour'* and rehearsals began. The band now consisted of Levi Seacer, Matt Fink, Miko Weaver and now new addition Rosie Gaines who added vocals and keyboards. Young drummer Michael Bland was appointed after jamming with Prince several times over the past few months; he was previously scouted after Prince saw him play at a Minneapolis club. In addition, he also added three goofy dancers named *'The Game Boyz'* who were Damon Dickson, Tony Mosley and Kirk Johnson. The three dancers appeared in a small cameo while dancing on a balcony in the *Purple Rain* movie. Kirk Johnson would stay alongside Prince for many years in a variety of roles.

> **PRINCE WAS CONTROLLING EVERYTHING; HE HAD LITTLE EXPERIENCE AND HIS PASSION FOR CREATING WAS BLURRING THE PICTURE.**

Prince moved into 1990 with continued rehearsals for his *Nude* Tour, putting his new band through their paces and working through another script which now became the fourth version of the script for the movie. The main reason for this was the break up of his short relationship with Kim Basinger. Prince quickly re-wrote the script and drafted in poet Ingrid Chavez to play the lead role alongside him. Chavez would eventually have some success of her own when, while filming *Graffiti Bridge*, she went into the studio with Lenny Kravitz and Andre Betts and co-wrote and recorded what became Madonna's sultry 1990 hit *'Justify My Love'*. She would eventually receive a large out-of-court settlement for not being credited on the single.

In April 1990 Prince delivered the first cut of *Graffiti Bridge* at a screening for Warner Bros. The reaction wasn't what Prince was hoping for. They recommended changes as it was clear that the one-man-band approach to making a movie was showing signs of fracture. Prince was controlling everything; he had little experience and his passion for creating was blurring the picture. It was true he was highly efficient at creating and directing music videos but a full-on movie was looking like a step too far. They recommended the appointment of an editor, which Prince reluctantly agreed to. He was so determined to get it perfect that he suggested postponing

the *Nude* Tour to concentrate on finishing the movie. Tickets sales had been so high though, with many venues selling out, that financially it wouldn't make sense to postpone. Instead dates were re-arranged to allow Prince to make the recommended changes before the tour started. Steve Rivkin, the brother of David Rivkin, was drafted in to help Prince with the editing process.

As work continued Prince still needed to prepare the tour. He played a couple of warm up concerts around Minneapolis in preparation. One of these shows was a benefit show for his former bodyguard Chick Huntsberry. Chick passed away earlier in the year without life insurance. The money Prince raised went straight to his widow and family. Prince also played an incredible full show at the St Paul Civic Centre to around 17 thousand fans with all the proceeds going to the homeless in Minneapolis.

As Prince was practically nocturnal he now turned his attention to owning a nightclub. He was always giving songs to DJs around the city to play at clubs and enjoyed seeing the reaction to the new tunes. The club would be his second construction project after Paisley Park. Prince spent around $2million of his own money on the club, situated in Minneapolis, to be called *'Glam Slam'*. It was

initially designed by the same company that was involved in the set-up of Paisley Park. Prince's plan was to have a chain of clubs around the US over the coming years. The budget raised concerns: Prince only initially planned to finance the first club to around half a million but it very quickly ballooned as updated sound equipment was required. *Glam Slam* eventually opened in October 1990, a two-story building around 20,000 square feet in size. New keyboardist and singer Rosie Gaines played a live set to celebrate the club's opening on the first couple of nights.

On 2 June 1990 the *Nude* Tour began with a three-month trip around Europe, the first concert being at Stadion Feijenoord in Rotterdam. In the past Prince had always toured after an album release but this time he toured before the release: he wanted to get the hundreds and thousands of fans excited about the new music and the new movie. As expected, the title of the tour made the press hungry for what was to come, and many tabloids wrote articles suggesting the tour would be some kind of live sex show. The opposite was of course the case. The name purely related to the stripped back music that was to be played: no fuss, just real music and real musicians.

The show itself was far less extravagant than previous tours and relied less on props and effects: it was basically good lighting, a stage with musicians, and of course Prince front and centre showcasing his usual brilliance in performance. For the first time, it incorporated the male/female symbol which would be used on many future tours; it later had pride of place suspended in the air holding the lighting, before moving on to being the actual stage shape itself. The lighting was mainly black and gold and there were the usual props like side ramps, fireman's pole and stairs. The show was again designed by Roy Bennett. The two opening concerts at Rotterdam alone were seen by nearly 100,000 fans, although the second one had to be cut short due to a severe thunderstorm and lightning strikes.

The *Nude* Tour was not alone in the summer of 1990; other big stars were also heading around Europe with their own tours, notably Madonna, Tina Turner, The Rolling Stones and David Bowie. This meant that there was not only competition for tickets but also comparisons all over Europe as to who gave the best live performance and show. The tour continued to Denmark before hitting Germany for 9 concerts before Prince landed in England for an incredible 16 nights at Wembley arena.

The statistics for previous Prince tours are quite incredible on their own, particularly for a solo artist, but the London 16-night stay broke records for Prince. He would of course smash his own records in the years to come. In England alone in 1986, Prince was seen by around 37,000 fans; in 1988 he was seen by around 77,000. On this tour he sold, just in England, 300,000 tickets. Prince broke the record at Wembley for tickets sold. The European leg of the tour continued with 900,000 tickets sold. It was even more impressive given that Prince did not have an album out before the tour itself: when it came down to pure performance Prince was first and foremost an incredible live performer of unique standing who could simply sell tickets all over the world.

The album *Graffiti Bridge* was eventually released just towards the end of the European leg of the tour and just before Prince continued onto Japan. The album itself, unlike previous Prince albums, contained many songs going back nearly 10 years in some cases. Even though there is a considerable guest list on *Graffiti Bridge* it was, as usual, a solo album by Prince with most of the songs featuring him on his own. The 17-track album is a mix of styles and genres throughout. It's awash with a variety of sounds but all uniquely Prince. Funk and rock are heavily cast with layers of harmony and texture built up in each track. During the recording of *Graffiti Bridge* for the most part Prince locked himself away and worked tirelessly, the engineers around him taking shifts to keep up with his insatiable routine of recording, often 3 or 4 songs per night in their entirety.

The sales for *Graffiti Bridge* were, as expected, less than that of *Batman*. As with *Around the World in a Day* which followed *Purple Rain*, it followed an album that had a massive marketing budget and a full cross-media strategy; against this you couldn't expect similar sales. It did however do very well and landed in the top ten on both sides of the pond. The *Nude* Tour also helped with the recognition of the album with Prince concluding the tour, now with the album released, with the Japanese leg. This started at the 100,000-seater Tokyo Dome which was broadcast live and became the Prince in Tokyo concert video.

With the highly successful and lucrative tour completed, Prince jetted back to the US to put the finishing touches to a film that had now changed considerably since its first draft. The premiere was launched on November 1st 1990. Prince attended the premiere but didn't attend the after-party, which was broadcast by MTV.

The changes Prince had been requested to make changed the whole movie. There was so much taken out that it resembles a collection of music videos intertwined together by a loose narrative, roughly following a sequel to *Purple Rain*. The basic story is of two clubs that are bitter rivals, Prince playing *'The Kid'* and Morris as himself.

Morris wants to close down The Kid's club as it no longer makes money, mainly because of the spiritual music that The Kid is playing. Obsessed with women and money, Morris cannot let this happen. The Kid though is searching for a higher, more spiritual goal than his materialistic rival. The Kid is visited by a guardian angel who steers him towards the light and tries to keep his spirits high and fight for what is right. She appears every time he is on the verge of losing everything, and even spends time with Morris to try and appease the situation. The final outcome of this situation is the death of the angel which unites them all together. The message is that love, understanding, tolerance, harmony and togetherness will make the world a better place. Visually the movie is a triumph and showcases Prince's brilliance in capturing mood, color and atmosphere on the screen. The music videos are also very impressive and link well with the what the movie is trying to achieve. What is very obvious though are the weaker points of the film: the overall acting and story line.

The changes imposed on the movie obviously had an effect as the message that Prince was trying to convey was eroded by the poor acting and heavily edited story. This was a great disappointment as it could have been an outstanding solo project if left to its own devices in accordance with the vision Prince had. The movie went on cinema release on 2 November across the US on 688 screens. It grossed around $4.5million in its first month.

Regardless, Prince was back in the studio and his next project *Diamonds and Pearls* was underway. He was moving towards introducing more collaborations into his studio time and starting to involve other musicians. For this project, he would adopt a big band approach. Over the past few years Prince had been a one-man-band, the only regular exceptions being horn sections and orchestral pieces that were added on once Prince had completed his own recording.

In the winter of 1990 Prince locked himself away recording at Paisley Park and reinvented himself, with a new look. Gone was the long hair that dominated the *Batman* and *Graffiti Bridge* look. Prince now sported a 'Typhoon' hairdo and his clothes became full of color and unique designs. His clothing department were kept busy with his new imagery and designs as Prince typically wore a different outfit every day. He tweaked his new band and was rehearsing them hard: there would be some changes made as he went forward from the *Nude* Tour and significantly, for the first time since *The Revolution*, the new band would be named alongside him, and ultimately they would have an identity of their own.

From now on it would now be Prince and The New Power Generation.

CHAPTER TEN

WILLING AND ABLE

Rehearsals at Paisley Park were always fluid because Prince loved to jam. Often ideas would be formalized through this kind of extensive session. He gave the band members time to develop and often when a groove was hit he signaled to the engineer to quickly record that particular piece. Many of Prince's sounds and melodies were found because free flowing music could lead to something that Prince could latch onto and develop further.

Prince had a rough new band in place as he worked through the winter of 1990. He retained Rosie Gaines on vocals and keyboards and Michael Bland on drums. Newly drafted in were Tommy Elm who Prince renamed Tommy Barbarella, playing keyboards and replacing Matt Fink. Prince chose the name because of the hairbands Tommy wore to keep his hair tied back which happened to be called Barbarellas. Tommy had sat in for Matt Fink during some earlier rehearsals when Matt couldn't make it, and since Prince was impressed and looking to freshen everything up he decided to keep him permanently, and thus Matt Fink, who indecently was the longest of all Prince's band members to reach this point, was replaced. The dancer trio of *The Game Boyz* were kept in place and Sonny Thompson, who had been on the Minneapolis scene since Prince was a teenager, came in on bass. In typical Prince style, he renamed him Sonny T.

Prince named his new band *The New Power Generation*, often abbreviated to *N.P.G.* To highlight the collaborative nature, he also decided it would be *Prince and The New Power Generation* on the next album and tour, giving them their own identity and emphasizing the joint venture in the recordings. This next stage in his career would push Prince to the mainstream once again; he now wanted a hit album that would ride high in the charts. Warners were also looking for this and Prince now concentrated on just a single album. As with all Prince projects he had moved on quickly. *Graffiti Bridge* was done, the *Nude* Tour was over, and it was now time to again start something new: he had a new band, a funky new look and a new energy.

He recorded many songs that would end up on the album in December. He recorded *'Live for Love'*, *'Cream'*, *'Push'* and many more. The collaborations also continued as Prince wrote and recorded so much material that he could just work it through other side projects he had on the go at the time. Martika was one such artist that Prince began working with. She was on her second album and recorded *'Love Thy Will Be Done'* as well as *'Don't Say You Love Me'* and *'Spirit'*. He also gave her *'Martika's Kitchen'* which became the name of the album. It was eventually released in August 1991 as Martika took the songs away to work on them with her own musicians. From the songs Prince recorded for her four of them eventually made the album. The single *'Love Thy Will Be Done'* made the Billboard top 10 and from that the album was certified gold. The singles were also hits in the UK with the album reaching number 15.

With the *Glam Slam* nightclub now fully opened Prince used it as a venue to turn up and jam as and when he wanted. It was a showcase for any up and coming live bands around but partygoers were always expecting and anticipating an appearance by Prince. He turned up in January 1991 unannounced to showcase his new band, *The New Power Generation*. Prince was scheduled to play the *Rock in Rio 2* festival and this performance was a sort of rehearsal for that concert. *Rock in Rio* is one of the largest music festivals in the world, with a staggering 1.5 million people attending the first event alone in 1985. The concert was held at the Estadio Maracanã in Rio De Janeiro. In 1991 the festival was attended by 800,000 people, and Prince performed in front of around 60,000 during his headline dates.

Three days after the *Rock in Rio* appearance Prince continued in South America with a concert at Estadio de River Plate in Buenos Aires, playing a shortened set lasting around 75 minutes. Many in the crowd were disappointed as Prince didn't appear for an encore, something which he was renowned for. He played his second concert at *Rock in Rio* shortly after completing his South America visit.

The new show was an extension of the *Nude* Tour but had more of the rap element involved. Many tracks featured Tony Mosley as the lead vocal rapping along with the two dancers either side. This was something Prince was happy to let happen and was a move to bring in an edge to the sound and a darker mood. In 1987 on the pulled *Black Album* Prince clearly let his opinions on rap be known - the song *'Dead On It'* pulls no punches - here in 1991 he was embracing it, controlling it, and using it as a clear positive message to his songs and performances. The movement on stage never stopped and the band could move seamlessly from one musical genre to another; versatility as well as musicianship were in abundance. It did though at times sound overbearing as Mosley was the weakest link in an otherwise exceptional bunch of musicians. It brought with it a new dimension to Prince's sound and updated him, increasing his current chart appeal. Prince's unique blend of rock and funk was beginning to fall behind with the new movement of dance, hip hop and rap, and his new show addressed this.

Overall the show was extremely varied; much like Prince as a musician it covered all aspects of showmanship and musical styles. Prince was quite happy to jump from full on rap with the three dancers and rappers to full on blues. He would push in the crowd favorites and surround them with the new sound and visual he had created. The difference this time, as he moved towards the release of *Diamonds and Pearls*, was that the band itself had a clear identity within it.

> ## THIS WAS WHEN PRINCE STARTED TO WONDER ABOUT THE WHOLE INDUSTRY, AND THIS WOULD RESULT IN THE YEARS AHEAD IN A VERY PUBLIC BATTLE.

Some past work made chart hits during early 1991, notably Mica Paris using *'If I Love u 2 Nite'* on her album *Contribution*, which Prince originally recorded way back in 1979 during the *Rebel* sessions. He re-visited the track again in 1987 and Paris put her own version on her album. The original guide vocal Prince recorded for use on the song appeared by mistake and was included on the rare Mica Paris *'Stand for Love'* EP; only a handful of this version are in existence. Saxophonist Eric Leeds released his first solo album *Times Squared* in February 1991 and featured many contributions by Prince, as well as the *Madhouse* members Sheila E and Matt Blistan. The songs were all previous recordings from the past few years and some were from the *Madhouse* sessions. Nine of the eleven tracks were written or co-written by Prince and he played most instruments, with Eric Leeds playing saxophone and small parts played by other musicians. *Times Squared* was an evolution from the planned third *Madhouse* album *26* put together in September 1989 from instrumental tracks recorded between 1985-1988. The album was recorded at various favorite locations and studios for Prince and his bands including Sunset Sound in California, Prince's home Studio in Chanhassen, Paisley Park Studios, Townhouse Studios and Medley Studios in Copenhagen. In keeping with previous *Madhouse* releases, tracks were given simple numerical titles of *17* to *26*. When Prince suggested the album should be released as a solo album by Eric Leeds, Leeds came up with titles for each track and recorded a new track called *'Lines'* in Spring 1990. *'Lines'* became the new opening track. The songs on *Times Squared* are more accessible and easier on the ear than the more complex *Madhouse* albums; melody replaces hard funk/jazz fusion and Eric adds a more laid-back feel to the music.

There is also a subtle Latin feel to the album hinting at an influence by Shelia E.

Business and contractual conflicts now started to become more prominent. Prince was often challenged because of his output and frequently had to scale down projects or completely change things: there are many examples of this type of intervention over the years from albums to movies to videos and all sorts of other projects. His two movies since *Purple Rain*, *Under the Cherry Moon* and *Graffiti Bridge*, were loved by his huge army of fans but were in the main panned by critics. Both these movies however were significantly changed from the initial vision Prince had, from changes of actors to complete changes in script and editing. It's true that costs of a project were simply not on his radar, and sometimes understandable that a record company would look at spiraling costs and question if they would see a return. For Prince and his fans however it was still a disappointment to see a cancelled album, or a cancelled or dramatically changed movie, or indeed three albums scheduled for a release only to find them depleted down to a single double album, the remaining songs locked away in an ever-increasing vault.

This was when Prince started to wonder about the whole industry, and this would result in the years ahead in a very public battle. For now, there was a lawsuit against him from his old management team of Cavallo, Ruffallo and Fargnoli. They were suing him for breach of contract, claiming that Prince had made marketing and financial decisions against their advice. Mo Austin of Warners also had a lengthy 3-hour meeting with Prince and tried to convince him that it was time for a greatest hits package, something he absolutely was against.

For Prince, a greatest hits package signified the end of a career. Prince always said his greatest song was the next one, the one about to be written. He had written so many songs to this point that he had hundreds if not thousands in his vault at Paisley Park, and to choose a 'greatest' selection from this vast amount of quality material seemed insane. Warners were just after commercial gains. It was sold to him as a way to bring him back into the charts and into the mainstream.

Graffiti Bridge was deemed by Warners to be a weak selling album, at least by Prince standards. Prince though had always flirted with charts: he didn't want to be in there all the time and he was beginning more and more to question the viability of a chart. In the 1980s there was really only one chart, calculated on sales of raw product that you bought from a shop that linked and registered the product to a large database that counted and collated the sales. There were some breakaway sections of charts for defined groups but the Billboard was the main one and it was this that would determine where your music was positioned and therefore how successful you were. Prince was starting now to wonder what this measure of success was. For him success was producing an album which was true to yourself, not repeating yourself, and then touring and performing. He was selling out stadiums all over the world - his tours were always sold out within hours of announcement - this was real success. But of course, the record label benefited from sales of albums.

Graffiti Bridge had ended up a confusing mix - of course not entirely Prince's fault as the record company interfered with his

BEHIND THE SCENES WARNERS STILL WANTED TO RELEASE A GREATEST HITS PACKAGE

initial vision - but despite this the record itself held some of the most endearing jams Prince has written. The movie didn't help either and ended up being a very loose story held together by a series of music videos. Loyal fans would of course look past this and enjoy it, but Prince's management and Warner Bros were both in agreement that the world had had too much material from Prince and thought the market was suffering from Prince fatigue.

Behind the scenes Warners still wanted to release a greatest hits package to give the public a break from new Prince projects and highlight all of the great things he had made since his debut in 1978. Prince however was now full on into planning *Diamonds and Pearls* and was completely focused on delivering a hit record. Warners now had a chance to listen to the album and see the music videos and whole concept behind it, and they realized the commercial promise it held. They put the greatest hits idea on hold and focused on the new album, but they still wanted to return to it after *Diamonds and Pearls*. As before, Prince was not interested. The prolific nature of his recordings meant that he was starting to focus on the next album even before *Diamonds and Pearls* was released.

There were several different versions of singles scheduled for release, but in total there were seven commercially sold singles planned to promote the album. Prince had the hunger for a commercially viable hit record with *Diamonds and Pearls*. Prince had heard the critics and was intent on showing them that he could, at the drop of a hat, produce a commercial hit record… if of course he wanted to. The flip side of this was that he wasn't creating self-satisfying art but yielding somewhat to chasing popular trends. It could be argued that he was bowing to pressure from Warners and his management. He did however get to produce a new album and not a greatest hits collection, so in this respect Prince had musically won this battle, and everyone was a winner.

Prince was so determined to make *Diamonds and Pearls* a success that he did all of the usual promotional activities that other artists do. For the first time in years he carried out promotional videos, industry showcases, television appearances and mini concerts prior to the album's release. He was committed to the commercial aspect of *Diamonds and Pearls* as much as the artistic concept of his past albums, and of course this wasn't a concept album, just a collection of songs that had been recorded with his new muse, *The New Power Generation*, and he was determined to showcase them. Rosie Gaines would be an iconic piece of this early line-up of *The New Power Generation*, and even though she was truly only around for one album, she set the precedent for the women working with Prince going forward. It can be argued that there hasn't really been any female duetting with Prince since Rosie Gaines that has a voice so distinctive. *Diamonds and Pearls* put a spotlight on the members of the band in a way that hadn't happened since *The Revolution*.

While the draft version of the album was being assembled Prince

was able to free some time to develop other musical projects he had ongoing. He spent the early part of 1991 working on former *Graffiti Bridge* colleague Ingrid Chavez's debut album. The relationship went sour however and Prince withdrew from the project leaving it to be finished by an engineer. He also started working at this time with a female rapper called Tara Patrick. Prince would soon rename her Carmen Elektra. Prince worked with her and recorded songs throughout the year for her debut album. The album would go through several changes as Prince revisited it, and would eventually be released in February 1993. She would later go on to find fame in the hit series *Baywatch* and as a model, in various forms.

Dancer Robia LaMorte had appeared in more than thirty music videos and had recently toured as a dancer with the Pet Shop Boys. Prince picked her to be the lead dancer for the *'Gett Off'* video. Prince had originally had the idea to have identical twins, something he returned to around 2006, but choose LaMorte along with another dancer Lori Elle because of their similar appearance and the dance chemistry they had. Elle quickly became *'Diamond'* and LaMorte *'Pearl'*. They would go on to appear in the *'Cream'* and *'Strollin'* videos as well as the title track. Prince also added them on the album's holographic cover and they were drafted in to join the European tour. Prince from here decided to temporarily refuse to do any public speaking, something he was never comfortable with anyway. LaMorte and Elle served as his spokespersons and conducted the main promotional efforts for *Diamonds and Pearls*, as Diamond and Pearl. It was a stroke of genius and served perfectly the mystique surrounding Prince as momentum for the new single and album grew stronger.

While in LA Prince performed at two unannounced venues. One was for record company executives and the other was an evening performance with many celebrities. The performance featured many *Diamonds and Pearls* tracks as well as songs from *Graffiti Bridge* and the usual crowd pleasers through an electric set. The label knew it was on the verge of another huge hit album, which of course was what they wanted. The new band were now well established and the rehearsals and live recording sessions Prince had recently put them through were coming together. With every performance they were getting tighter. These warm up sets were showing great potential as Prince planned a major tour to showcase his new album and his new band. One such concert was planned for Blenheim Palace in England.

The Blenheim Palace Concert was dubbed *'The Summer Extravaganza'* in the grounds of Blenheim Palace, Woodstock, England. It would have been the event of the summer in England with a stunning setting, serving as a fantastic UK promotional tool for *Diamonds and Pearls*. There were many high profile warm up acts booked to perform on the all-day event including boy band Color Me Badd and C + C Music factory. Of course, with an all-day event in such a setting there were many complicating factors to consider including other vendors and contractors. The concert was marred with troubles from the initial planning with the new production company Diamond Productions.

Prince's organization was not receiving the scheduled payments that usually precede any major event or concert. Prince was in an impossible situation and it resulted in him issuing a statement and pulling out of the event entirely. Prince had no choice as the financial obligations to vendors, other companies and suppliers were simply not met. As a result, and common in such cancellations, there was a major ticket problem as many thousands had already been sold, not to mention travel plans and hotels etc from those who were traveling from all over Europe. Prince quickly issued a further statement promising anyone who had purchased a ticket that they would get tickets to his next tour. He took a large hit at his own expense to cover this.

Prince performed another warm up set with his *New Power Generation* at the *Special Olympics* opening ceremony at the 50,000-seater Metrodome in Minneapolis on 19 July 1991. The Special Olympics is the world's largest sports organization for children and adults with intellectual disabilities. Like the International Paralympic Committee, the Special Olympics organization is recognized by the International Olympic Committee; however, unlike the Paralympic Games the Special Olympics World Games are not held in the same year or in conjunction with the Olympic Games.

Prince released *'Gett Off'* as the first single at the end of July and it was an instant hit. It, along with the full-blown production of the music video, pushed him straight back into the mainstream charts. The song was an evolution from several earlier compositions starting with the song *'Glam Slam'* from *Lovesexy* a couple of years earlier. Prince created an unreleased remix in early 1991 called *'Glam Slam 91'*. In this remix Prince took the chorus of *'Glam Slam'* and added new music and lyrics that were in part from *Graffiti Bridge's 'Love Machine'*. Prince played with the song and, knowing it had potential for a hit, added a new chorus before eventually teaching it to *The New Power Generation*. Prince then used additional vocal contributions from Rosie Gaines and Tony M and flute by long-time associate Eric Leeds. Prince also added a guitar solo as the main hook to the song.

───────◆───────

On 28th September 1991 Miles Davis died. Without doubt Miles was one of the most influential figures in the history of jazz. He was also one of the most acclaimed musicians of the 20th century. As Prince was in the same bracket as Davis as far as musicianship and respect for influence in modern music was concerned, it was natural that he would be approached by Warners. They wanted to put together an album with the material Prince had worked on in collaboration with Miles. It would also include some of the *Madhouse* collaboration songs the two worked on. Prince refused, feeling that the material didn't reflect Miles at his best. He didn't want to touch up any previous unfinished material now Miles wasn't around to review and agree it. For years these two geniuses had drafted music back and forth but never actually put aside time to bring together a true collaboration project. A few days later at Paisley Park Prince recorded *'Miles is not Dead'* with Michael Bland on drums. Not surprisingly the song was never released.

On October 1st 1991 Prince released *Diamonds and Pearls*, his 13th studio album for Warner Bros. Of course, this number is highly inaccurate given the amount of material Prince had contributed and released outside of standard releases for his record label.

Diamonds and Pearls was a major departure for Prince in many ways, with the most significant being the collaborative aspect of this album: it was in the main a band recording. He allowed Rosie Gaines and rapper Tony Mosley to share the vocal spotlight in a clear commercial tactic to appeal to the mainstream and the black audience.

By now, hip hop had become a major element in popular music and had penetrated the mainstream charts. Prince started to take notice of what the movement had to offer and entwined it into his sound. MC Hammer and Vanilla Ice were commercial acts, while NWA and Public Enemy were more hardcore and interested in social issues. All were relevant, even though musically they were a universe away from Prince. The *NPG* was designed to move with these times and provide Prince with a black sound that he could effortlessly blend into his own creations. Prince featured Tony M on nearly half of the songs on *Diamonds and Pearls*, giving him free reign to put the hard edge to the feel of the songs. Prince had first heard Tony Mosley rapping while on the *Nude* Tour and subsequently asked him to put a rap on the end of one of his songs. Impressed, Prince put the idea to test and soon Tony Mosley had become Tony M and was quickly promoted from backstage dancer to front and center of the *New Power Generation*.

The album is credited to the band as a whole with Levi Seacer Jr now on guitar after previously playing bass on the *Nude* Tour, old Minneapolis friend Sonny Thompson on bass, Tommy Barberella on keyboards alongside Rosie Gaines on keyboards as well as vocals. Michael Bland remained on drums with Kirk Johnson and Damon Dickson on percussion and backing vocals. Tony M is described as lead rap and vocals. Interestingly there are no vault items on *Diamonds and Pearls*, all the songs having been written and recorded with the band for the album over 12 months with 13 tracks making the album. As with all Prince albums, there were many songs that didn't make the album and were stored away for possible use on another project or to give away to another artist. The album marked a bit of a turning point for Prince, as a harder blacker sound took over from the more familiar pop sound of the 1980s, and this trend would continue through his future albums in the 1990s.

Diamonds and Pearls proved to be a huge commercial success and did everything Prince wanted it to. It shot through the charts and went double platinum in the US and proved to be an even bigger international success around the world. It produced four huge hits around the globe and kept the album and momentum alive as Prince continued promotional activities and appearances. It was an interesting album and project as it managed to give Prince his biggest commercial hit since *Purple Rain* but left many hardcore fans slightly bewildered and frustrated with the move towards commercial trends. Either way Prince was now smack back in the mainstream and public eye.

His record company would have loved Prince to announce that now he had delivered a massive global album he was taking some time off to allow them to release a greatest hits package. This would give the public a break and let them digest everything that Prince had released over the past years. This was never going to happen of course as, without a break, he went straight back to the studio and set up a five-piece band with drummer Michael Bland and a new horn section. They jammed and recorded songs for a new

Madhouse style album. Again, Prince would mix a commercially successful album with a complete change in direction. Prince wanted enough material so that his new jazz creation could play as a support act for his new tour to support *Diamonds and Pearls*, which he was now planning.

Allowing the newly formed members of the NPG to promote *Diamonds and Pearls* allowed Prince to move on. The promotional machine could travel around various media outlets and free Prince to work on his next album, his tour planning and the other projects he had on the go. Prince wanted the new tour to feature new material from his next album and so blend the two together. It would be a seamless transition from one project to another; in fact many engineers who worked with Prince often cannot recall what they worked on and what they didn't. There was such volume and continuity in his work rate that everything just blended into one long recording.

Mayte Garcia was born on November 12 1973 at Fort Rucker Alabama army base. Both her parents are of Puerto Rican descent; her father flew aircraft in the U.S. military and her mother was a school and dance teacher who passed her dancing skills on to her daughter. Because of the military connection Mayte and her older sister grew up in both Germany and the USA with Mayte spending the summers of her childhood with her extended family in San Juan, Puerto Rico. Because of her travels she became fluent in English, German, and Spanish. Mayte began belly dancing at just three years old and when she turned eight appeared on an American television program called *That's Incredible*. She was billed as the world's youngest professional belly dancer. She came to the attention of Prince earlier in 1990 while Prince was on the *Nude* Tour when her mother Nelle submitted a video cassette of one of Mayte's performances. Prince eventually met her briefly and the two kept in touch, with Mayte sending him tapes to Minneapolis. Prince told her that when she turned 18 he would invite her to Paisley Park and they could start collaborating on a project. In November 1991, she had just turned 18 and she arrived at Paisley Park a few weeks later.

❖

Prince's next album would be completely inspired by her. The one with no name, the one with a symbol, a symbol that would form an identity of its own in the years ahead and be forever associated with Prince himself.

CHAPTER ELEVEN

THREE CHAINS OF GOLD

Prince continued with promotional activity for *Diamonds and Pearls* as the year drew to a close in 1991. **He featured in many publications including *Black Beat* which was published in January 1992 and *Vogue* which was also published in January.**

The images from the *Vogue* shoot would eventually be used on *The Hits/The B-Sides* album. There was also an excellent documentary entitled *Prince Rogers Nelson* as part of the BBC's *Omnibus* series broadcast in the UK on 13th December 1991. It's one of the most accurate and engaging documentaries on Prince and his work and captures brilliantly the mystique and musicianship of Prince in all his guises. It was made in collaboration with Paisley Park and Prince submitted archive and unseen footage.

Of all Prince documentaries this one is the most fulfilling for any fan looking for an accurate insight into the life of this musical genius at work. It should stand as a lesson for the awful Channel 5 documentary, *The Prince Story Icon Genius Slave*, broadcast in the UK in April 2017 which is by far the worst piece of television on Prince ever shown. This BBC broadcast was perfectly narrated and showed interviews with fellow musicians and credible collaborators spanning his career to date.

With Mayte now working alongside Prince and integrated into the NPG as a dancer, he moved into 1992 with more recordings and songs scheduled for the new album. Alongside this prolific writing he continued to work the band through a new show to take on tour at the start of April. In March 1992 Prince met with film director James Brookes about contributing songs for a new movie he was working on entitled *I'll Do Anything*. He also filmed the video for *'Sexy MF'* over 3 days from March 20th at Paisley Park, and shot a video for another new song *'The Continental'*. Both would go on to appear on his next album.

The band flew to Tokyo for the start of the *Diamonds and Pearls* world tour on March 27th. Prince spent a few days in Paris before eventually joining the entourage in Japan. The tour kicked off at The Tokyo Dome, and the reviews were incredible, with the show becoming the must-see tour of 1992. Prince played five concerts in Japan before the tour moved to Australia, which was the first time he had played in the country.

The *Diamonds and Pearls* tour wasn't just showing Prince the pop star, it was also showing Prince the blues, soul and jazz man, a musical historian of black spectacle whose show has elements stretching far back into the history of music. This show was Prince giving for the first time a truly black sound. It drew comparisons with Earth Wind and Fire and Funkadelic, it had elements of Sly and the Family Stone as well as the usual references to Hendrix.

His vocals on slower numbers nodded towards Smokey Robinson and Curtis Mayfield. The show had jazz analogies in Ellington and of course the raw funk and moves of James Brown. Prince had mastered all the above and littered the show with clues and references. Later in the tour Prince brought blues straight to the stage with Rosie Gaines with *Doctor Feel-good* and *Chain of Fools*, the former featuring some heaven-shredding blues guitar from the man himself. His image was new as well, sporting the jet-black Typhoon hairdo which contrasted against the yellows and greens of his various handmade unique outfits.

In Australia Prince played 15 dates and broke the record for tickets by selling 72,000 in just two hours in Sydney alone. The record was held previously by INXS and Bruce Springsteen. *'Cream'* was number one in the Australian charts at the time of arrival so the overall enthusiasm for the show and demand for tickets was incredible, with many hundreds of people camping overnight near venues for a chance of seeing Prince live. As usual with Prince, many shows featured the infamous after-show concerts in smaller venues with many celebrities in attendance. While in Australia Prince also booked studio time and wrote songs for the *I'll Do Anything* movie before the tour reached Melbourne for 5 concerts in Flanders Park. He wrote and recorded nine songs for the project and visited the studio to record after every show.

While in Australia, Alan Leeds resigned from the Vice President role at Paisley Park Records. He had run the label since 1989. It was an amicable agreement and didn't have any influence on Prince's long standing musical relationship with Eric Leeds.

The Australian section of the tour concluded on May 3rd 1992 with an additional concert at Sydney's cricket ground to alleviate demand for tickets. In Australia alone Prince had sold over 200,000 tickets and the show was an incredible success both critically and commercially. Prince flew straight to the US afterwards to continue work on the *I'll Do Anything* project and his next album before the tour relaunched in Europe.

The European section of the *Diamonds and Pearls* tour was scheduled for 32 dates over 7 weeks. It travelled to Germany, Belgium, Holland, France, England, Scotland and Ireland. Tickets for the European section had already sold over 500,000 proving that Prince had a popularity in Europe that was unmatched at the time. The final concert finished the German section in Hamburg on 10th June before a one-off concert in Ireland at the Royal Dublin Showgrounds.

> THE ENTIRE DIAMONDS AND PEARLS TOUR HAD BEEN AN INCREDIBLE SUCCESS, PUTTING PRINCE ON TOP OF THE CHARTS, UNMATCHED AS A TOURING ACT AMONGST MODERN DAY POP ACTS.

Prince next moved to London for an eight-concert residency at Earls Court, the concerts again breaking the box office records for the arena. Unfortunately, there was a bomb in London which exploded a few doors away from a scheduled after-show Prince was planning. He subsequently cancelled all other after-shows during his stay in London and only played the Earls Court arena concerts, which for any other artist would be incredible but for Prince was disappointing. During his stay in London 'Sexy MF' reached number one on the video chart. It featured model Troy Beyer, and there were unfounded rumors in the tabloid press that the two were an item giving another boost, if one was needed, to the rollercoaster of the *Diamonds and Pearls* tour.

After the 22nd June Earls Court show Prince held a lavish party at the *Tramp* in Central London. Guests included Mick Jagger, INXS, Kate Bush, Kylie Minogue, Tom Jones and Rod Stewart. The London concerts concluded on 24th June before shows in Manchester, Glasgow and then a return to Germany. 'Sexy MF' was eventually released as a single to the album ♀ but it naturally suffered in airplay due to its graphic nature. Prince's final leg of the tour hit France on 10th July with another after-show event at Les Bains Douches Club in the early hours immediately after the 11th July concert in Paris. Kylie Minogue and Michael Hutchence were again in attendance during the 75-minute set.

The entire *Diamonds and Pearls* tour had been an incredible success, putting Prince on top of the charts, unmatched as a touring act amongst modern day pop acts. His versatility on all instruments, his guitar playing, piano playing, bass playing, drumming, vocals and dancing were shown in full during the tour. His recording and appetite for non-stop performing with full concerts and after-shows only added to the popularity of this unique individual that many, including fellow musicians and stars, found fascinating. The show had been seen by over 850,000 people. The tour came to a final close with a party at Quai Quest

which is a boat on the Seine. It's also a restaurant and open to this day. Kylie Minogue was at the party again and danced with Prince during the evening.

Rosie Gaines left the band shortly after the tour, although she did continue to work with Prince throughout the summer on some songs he wrote for her. She was quickly replaced on keyboards by Morris Hayes who had been on the music scene in Minneapolis for many years. Morris Hayes was born on November 28th 1962 in Jefferson, Jefferson County. Inspired by the religious music he heard in church as a child he went on to study art at the University of Arkansas. When a rhythm and blues band on campus lost its keyboard player, Hayes, who had learned to play a bit in high school, offered to fill in. Although he was still learning to play the keyboard he played well enough to take the spot. Shortly after graduating from college Hayes moved around playing in churches and with various bands. Eventually he played in a band called *The Bizness*, which former *Revolution* bass player Mark Brown heard. Brown asked the group to come to Minneapolis and record a demo.

Hayes recorded the demo and was asked to join Brown's band *Mazarati*, which clearly had a close association to Prince. When *Mazarati* finally disbanded around 1991, Hayes remained in Minneapolis. He linked up with *The Time* for a short while, playing keyboards in the band. He went on to form another group called *G Sharp and the Edge*. This group performed as the house band at Prince's Minneapolis *Glam Slam*. As they played at *Glam Slam* Hayes and his band were asked to join Prince on some nights during the *Diamonds and Pearls* tour, and they played backing for Carmen Elektra during her initial sets before Prince had a change of heart as to the opening act. When Rosie left the NPG, Hayes was a natural replacement for the keyboards. However the vocal ability of Rosie Gaines on record and live would not be matched.

With the tour complete Prince in usual fashion hit the studio and worked on several projects throughout the summer of 1992. He finished off his new album ♀ and shot several music videos for it at Paisley Park. He also shot a film called *Act 1* and recorded a full live performance called *The Ryde Dyvine* which was scheduled for broadcast in December 1992 for ABC and their *In Concert* series. He worked on an album called *Goldnigga* with the NPG which was a continuation of songs he first started while at the Olympic Studios in London. Prince also worked with Mavis Staples, and also recorded a song for Earth Wind and Fire called 'Super hero' which featured on their 1993 album *Millennium*. The 'My Name is Prince' video was also shot on location in Minneapolis, with actress Kirstie Alley playing the part of a reporter.

On 31 August 1992, with his existing contract expiring, Prince signed a new contract with Warner Bros. It's possible that this deal would not have been offered in the way it had a few years earlier but Prince at this time, on the back of *Diamonds and Pearls* and the recent world tour, was sitting pretty as the biggest star in the world. He had also shown that if he wanted to he could easily produce a smash hit album at will. The tabloid press reported that it was a '100-million-dollar contract' dwarfing that previously given to Michael Jackson and Madonna. The details however are a little more complicated. It's a significant contract as it set the way forward for the breakdown in the relationship between Prince and the record label that had been threatening for many years.

This is what was allegedly offered at the time.

In basic terms, the new contract was an extension of the previous contract that Prince had, but it was reconfigured. The reconfiguration amounted to a $10million advance per record, given ahead of release; this was twice that of Michael Jackson and also twice that of Madonna, which was allegedly set at $5million per album. There was also a royalty rate of 20 percent, but there were reports this could have been up to 25 percent; if this was the case it was three times the previous percentage. This of course meant that if Prince sold more albums he would get a higher return. The rub however was Prince would only get the $10million advance if the previous album had sold at least 5 million copies, so it is an advance on sales, or basically an interest-free loan. This would have to be paid back to the record label if sales were lower, and actually deducted from royalties on older albums.

This is an important clause, especially from Prince's point of view. While Prince's previous 13 albums had sold nearly 53 million to this point, which equates to an average of 4.1 million each, a large chunk of that was due to 1984's *Purple Rain*, his bestseller to date at 14.7 million at this time, August 1992. Only three of his albums had sold more than 5 million copies and one of those was *Diamonds and Pearls*, his last one. Prince, being the complete workaholic musician, would consciously and frequently produce artistic albums that he knew would not sell in the region of the *Purple Rain* or *Diamonds and Pearls* bracket. This tactic by the label would nudge him into producing more 'hit albums' instead of the more experimental albums and projects he was famously inclined to veer into. The large advance was seen as an attempt by Warner Bros to motivate Prince to invest the same effort into future releases as he'd done for *Diamonds and Pearls*, and of course they wanted him to release albums less frequently and promote them heavily through singles, videos and extensive touring.

Another key strategy by Warners was a further $20million to be used to make Paisley Park Records a joint venture with Warner Bros; to combine the two together. This would ultimately force Prince to become more involved in the running of the label. Previously Paisley Park Records would simply supply the master recordings to Warners, who would then manufacture, distribute and promote the releases. Prince simply made and created the music and then gave it to Warners. This was where Prince sometimes took issue with the label: his view was he was recording and giving them the music, so it was their job to then promote the releases. Now this, as a joint venture, meant that the label would decide on what to invest on videos and promotional efforts. Warners and Prince would share the initial investments and also the profits. Prince would have to decide 'with the label' what to invest in, and what not to.

On publishing another $20million involved another advance, this was by Warner/Chappel Music publishers. This would be a new three-year agreement between Prince's music publishing company, Controversy Music, and Warner/Chappel Music for the handling of his copyrights worldwide. Another agreement would involve Prince and Warners actively looking for new talent. This was cited as the reason why Warner Bros Records named him a vice president of artists and repertoire and gave him an office in its L.A. headquarters. It is assumed however that Prince only wanted this position in order to acquire Time Warner stock options. Also,

> PRINCE WOULD HAVE TO SELL 5 MILLION UNITS, CLOSE TO HIS WORLDWIDE SALES ON DIAMONDS AND PEARLS, BEFORE WARNERS COULD RECOUP A $10MILLION ADVANCE.

unlike Madonna and Michael Jackson, Prince did not receive a signing fee. Promoting new talent was an area where Madonna was particularly strong. One of the key reasons for this was that she didn't assist too much in the process. Prince wrote and recorded for all his new acts, making in essence a Prince album, with everything played by him, produced by him and even sung by him as a guide for his new artist to sing over. Warners would now take an active part in this process.

The $100million figure was quickly disputed by people in the know when certain details emerged of the alleged clauses highlighted above. Prince's own team reported that they were pleased with the deal, but went on to refuse to discuss any details of the contract. It's clear that the contract is one of the biggest in music history, but it is also clear it is based on projected revenue and the income is not guaranteed. It was also a clever tactic by Warners to restrict Prince from recording too much and to make him concentrate more on albums of hit quality.

Prince would have to sell 5 million units, close to his worldwide sales on *Diamonds and Pearls*, before Warners could recoup a $10million advance. It could also mean that any unrecouped part of the advance might be cross-collateralized against Prince's publishing income. Cross-collateralization means the collateral for one loan is also used as collateral for another loan. Whichever way you look at it the figures, however accurately or inaccurately reported, are based purely and simply on sales levels.

Prince was unhappy with some of the reports after the deal was published and had his lawyer at the time, Gary Stiffelman, respond. Prince wanted the world to know he was the biggest music star in the world and that he had the largest contract in music history. Stiffelman highlighted that the deal offered covered two record labels, a publishing joint venture and the administration of Prince's own music. He also highlighted that the deal did not, as speculated by some, cover all of the albums covered by his record deal, and Prince's employment as a VP of Warner Bros records. He stated Prince remained free to negotiate for films, television, books, and other projects. He also pointed to Prince's prolific songwriting contributions to other artists' careers, arguing that his record and publishing ventures would justify more substantial funding because his own publishing interests would generate substantially greater advances than those of the artists with whom he was compared.

To compare Prince to Michael Jackson and Madonna, which many did in connection with this deal, is difficult. Musically there is no comparison and Prince stood alone; music sales however were different and he trailed behind considerably. Earlier in the year Michael Jackson had signed a new deal with Sony Music and Madonna with Warner Bros, each one for a reported figure of around $60 million. To try to compare the contracts is problematic. Jackson's contract was for 6 albums and entertainment complex and for movies. Madonna had a deal also for 6 albums but in addition had her own entertainment company, her own record label and a film company. As far as pure record sales go, up to this point in time Prince simply didn't sell enough records to compare. Madonna had released 8 albums so far with combined worldwide sales of 76 million, an average of 9.5 million each since 1983. Michael Jackson had two of his four solo albums, *Thriller* and *Bad*, selling a combined figure of 73 million.

Prince could, because of his freakish versatility, critically and musically outshine anyone. He was also able to tour and perform constantly and stood alone as a live act that packed stadiums, arenas and small clubs all over the world. Despite this though his chart 'hit' sales were simply lower. And ultimately these chart hits were what Warners were after. The issue was simply with Prince's talent - he was too much to contain: he would create jazz, funk, rock, soul and his numerous side projects covering different musical styles would dilute the chart potential which record companies needed. For Prince writing a hit commercial record was too easy and therefore often avoided in favor of a more musically satisfying direction.

> A WEEK AFTER HE HAD SIGNED THE REPORTED $100-MILLION-DOLLAR CONTRACT, PRINCE RELEASED HIS 14TH ALBUM FOR WARNER BROS TITLED ONLY WITH THE MYSTERIOUS SYMBOL ♀

In the same period Prince had buried them all with his output, releasing 13 'official' Warner albums to this point, the 14th on the way, as well as a number of albums he had created for others and of course the albums for the ghost bands he created. There were also the albums he wanted to release but couldn't or wouldn't, the albums that were left in the vault. Prince's career to date, in contrast to Madonna and Michael Jackson, had, to some at Warners, demonstrated that if you record more you inevitably sell less. The issue was that to Prince the number sold wasn't the end game; it was the music, the creation, the hundreds of thousands of fans singing his songs and turning out to his every performance. Whether there was a major misunderstanding at the time of the contract between the parties is unknown; what is known is there was a major breakdown ahead.

To cap off the *Diamonds and Pearls* project Prince released the *Diamonds and Pearls video collection* on 6th October 1992. The video featured music videos as well as unseen live footage and concert clips. This whole album, tour and promotional activity was

Prince's most accessible for many years. He was able to brilliantly take part in promotional activity, music videos and a worldwide record breaking tour and still maintain the artistic credibility he always had. He also managed to keep his mystique with the strategy of having his band members and dancers run the mundane interviews while he stayed in the studio and worked on music for his next album. This was now ready for release. Prince was not going to leave a couple of years in fear he was producing too much music: his next album featuring 16 new songs was ready, and that was that.

On the 13 October 1992, a week after he had signed the reported $100-million-dollar contract, Prince released his 14th album for Warner Bros titled only with the mysterious symbol ♀. The album was quickly dubbed '*The Love Symbol Album*'. Apart from Rosie Gaines leaving the NPG and Mayte coming into the fold, Prince kept the same line up as for *Diamonds and Pearls*. It featured Prince on vocals, guitars, keyboards, bass, drums and percussion, Mayte on vocals, Tony M on raps, Levi Seacer Jr. on guitars, Tommy Barbarella on keyboards, Sonny T on bass, Michael Bland on drums and Kirk Johnson on percussion. There were additional personnel on the album which included Carmen Electra on a guest rap on '*The Continental*'. The Steeles, Jevetta, Jearlyn, JD and Fred Steele provided backing vocals on '*The Sacrifice of Victor*' and actress Kirstie Alley plays a frustrated reporter named Vanessa Bartholomew in two segue tracks. Long-time collaborator Eric Leeds provided saxophone on '*Blue Light*'. Also returning was Clare Fischer who added string arrangements. Most of the songs on the album were recorded from September 1991 through to March 1992 with the album having an even split between band recordings and solo recordings from Prince. '*The Max*' was an older song and originated from 1988.

The album follows perfectly in the wake of *Diamonds and Pearls* in the fact that a modern commercial trend was followed as opposed to creating new sounds in music; which of course is what Warners wanted. Interestingly this was the first album in which Prince used segues to create some kind of story in between the songs. What Prince gave was precisely what Warner Bros Records requested: another album of similar material that could be marketed in the same way as *Diamonds and Pearls*. What he hadn't given them though was a gap of a couple of years or more between albums.

The album was described as a '*Rock Soap Opera*'. There was a loose narrative that follows Prince as a rock star and Mayte as a princess who was a direct inspiration for the album. There was an original version of the album that featured many more segues and made the storyline a lot clearer; these lasted for up to two minutes and made the introduction to each song clearer and the narrative easier to follow.

Prince decided however at the last minute to chop it down to make room for the song '*Eye Wanna Melt With U*' and therefore the narrative got somewhat lost throughout. The original story sees Mayte, who is a princess and the heiress to a billion dollar fortune, involved in a plot in which a small boy unearths a box in the dirt that contains the '*Three Chains of Turin*'. A reporter comes on the scene, played by Kirstie Alley, who explains that Prince and the NPG will go on tour and perform an opera of new music. The child who found the three chains takes them home and shows his

GLAM SLAM ULYSSES AND THE SHOWS AT GLAM SLAM WEST WERE AN OUTLET FOR PRINCE TO GET MATERIAL OUT THERE THAT WOULD OTHERWISE BE SHELVED.

mother, who on seeing them recalls a Prince concert years earlier before the songs begin and the plot continues with more segues explaining the three chains, the princess, and the connection to Prince. The chains provide mystery and show the future. The short explanations link it all together before it lands squarely with the final track on the album, '3 Chains O' Gold'.

The album did well and hit number 5 on the Billboard charts, sending it platinum. Prince however was bitterly disappointed in Warner Bros and the way they handled the promotional side. Prince had five singles released from *Diamonds and Pearls* within just seven months and Warners were again concerned about overproduction. They argued that radio stations were reluctant to play any new singles from Prince so soon after *Diamonds and Pearls*: indeed many were still playing the songs from it as part of their 'daily playlist'. Warners stuck to the belief that the public could not absorb any new music from Prince for the time being.

This was really the start of the downhill spiral that was now in free fall and would not recover. Prince for the best part of a decade would not reach album sales in this amount due to his distribution and accessibility. Ironically, he would go on to sell less but in fact earn more; but for the foreseeable future his sales and career would have to suffer. It would be another four years before he could free himself completely and rebuild things again fully.

In late December 1992 Prince visited Mayte in Puerto Rico. It was during this trip that he later said he had a spiritual experience which gave him the idea to change his name to the symbol from his last album: a symbol that could in his mind free himself from any contractual obligations and give him the freedom to record and release as much material as he wanted without constraint. He was considering ways in which he could get material out without the label interfering or restricting his output. The way he saw it was that Warners 'owned' Prince. But they didn't own ♀.

Prince also recorded songs during this period to feature on the 'Glam Slam Ulysses Project' which was an idea Prince had to showcase unreleased material to choreographed dance. He drafted in Jamie King to assist on choreography of songs that would not only be for *Glam Slam Ulysses* but also for a run at his *Glam Slam* nightclubs, which could feature performances to his songs that would not otherwise be heard.

Jamie King started his career in entertainment as a dancer. He went on tour with Michael Jackson on his *Dangerous* world tour in 1992 and after worked as a director and choreographer before working with Prince at his *Glam Slam West* nightclub in Los Angeles. While

at Glam Slam West, King created a new show every week using songs that Prince was unable to commercially release due to legal obligations to Warner Bros Records - another strategy by Prince to get songs out where he wouldn't normally be legally allowed to.

Prince based the *Glam Slam Ulysses* project on *Homer's Odyssey*. *Odyssey* is one of two major ancient Greek epic poems attributed to Homer. There was a first poem attributed to Homer called *Iliad*, then *Odyssey*. They are the oldest existing works of Western literature, composed near the end of the 8th century BC. Among the most noteworthy elements of the text are its non-linear plot and the influence on events of choices made by women and slaves, slavery being significant for Prince in the years ahead. The word odyssey has come to refer to an epic voyage or epic adventure. *Glam Slam* is the name of Prince's nightclubs, which he was expanding, and *Ulysses* is the Latin name for the protagonist, *Odysseus*. Again, with the public battle ahead over the controlling of his own art it's easy to understand Prince's reference points within this ancient piece of literature, albeit very deep ones. Musical geniuses however are not like the rest of us.

The *Glam Slam Ulysses* project featured a mix of live performances and videos featuring 13 unreleased songs. This was another project that allowed Prince to work on songs that Warners would not permit him to release. It was a way of channeling his frustrations on being restricted through a project of music direct to the audience. It was a clear indication of things to come.

Prince had each song representing an element from *Odyssey*. Jamie King worked with Prince on the choreography and it eventually made a musical debut at Prince's *Glam Slam* nightclub, with shows being performed in late August to early September 1993. Prince again worked with Carmen Electra who was a featured dancer in the performance.

Glam Slam Ulysses and the shows at Glam Slam West were an outlet for Prince to get material out there that would otherwise be shelved. Here he was consciously exploring ways to release his music freely and therefore this venture is significant. If you take away the deep thought process involving Greek Poems, Egyptian Princesses and Chains of Turin, behind it all is a search for artistic freedom. Streaming services and iTunes were not around yet but Prince had already had this vision of direct access to his audience way before anyone else.

Prince's reaction to his frustration regarding his recording freedom was to hit the road. He decided to tour the US, his first US tour for five years. This would be another significant step in searching for the artistic freedom he wanted.

The *Act 1* tour was a showcase for the *Love Symbol* album and a way of promoting it through the US. *Act 1* was the name of leg one for the US which would be followed by the European leg of the tour named *Act II*. As the *Act I* tour was the first tour of the US since the *Lovesexy* tour in 1988, Prince decided to play in small to medium sized venues where he could sell out easily. Most venues would be around 4-6 thousand in capacity. *Act I* focused on tracks from the *Love Symbol* album, while *Act II* would focus more on greatest hits. Importantly this would be Prince's final tour before he would change his stage name to his unpronounceable symbol. He would make the announcements during this tour, and this can be seen as premeditated, certainly in light of his early attempts at getting around the contractual restrictions which he felt were damaging his creativeness. The tour was quickly assembled, only a short time after the end of the *Diamonds and Pearls* tour. If Prince was going to announce a decision on his future where better than in front of hundreds and thousands of fans throughout the USA and Europe?

The tour started at Sunrise Musical Theatre in Fort Lauderdale on 8th March 1993. The show was as usual lauded and praised by critics for Prince's showmanship and musicianship as well as that of his band. The difference with this tour though was Prince was making statements to the crowd about how Warners were telling him that he made too much music and that the public, or those in front of him, couldn't keep up.

It was clear as the tour progressed that something was about to happen. One month after the tour started Prince would make an announcement through a press release which would shock the music world to its very core. Many thought he had gone mad, many were confused and bewildered. Prince however was deadly serious and knew exactly what he was doing.

One of the biggest shocks in music was about to announced.

CHAPTER TWELVE

WHAT'S MY NAME?

As the tour continued so did the announcements by Prince as to his dissatisfaction with his record label in the way it was restricting him. He was met with great support from the legions of fans who attended the concerts.

The *Act 1* tour concluded on 17th April 1993 at the Amphitheater in Los Angeles. It had consisted of 25 shows from 8th March and many after-shows that went into the early hours. The reviews as ever were extremely positive and Prince had repositioned himself in the US as one of the greatest live acts and as a master showman.

The final show began with Prince reading a copy of the recent Los Angeles Times review of the San Francisco tour, obviously not to Prince's liking as he pretended to urinate on it with lighter fluid, and sent it to oblivion with a match as he launched into *'My Name Is Prince.'* The first act, as with most of this leg, consisted of songs solely from the ♀ album, the symbol itself hanging high above the stage. The early show was framed around certain scenarios: a faux sheik's daughter played by Mayte, and additional dancer Kelly Konno playing a nosy reporter, Kirstie Alley's character on the album. The second act was pure adrenaline with Prince blasting off with *'Let's Go Crazy'*, *'Kiss'* and *'Irresistible Bitch'*. The New Power Generation were top-notch throughout and were well versed for any changes Prince wanted to make. Tech work included roadies who were all choreographed to perfection. Many changes in the Prince wardrobe and a futuristic light rig, as usual designed by Roy Bennet, kept the night full of eye-popping spectacle.

Shortly after the end of this section of the tour, Prince had his publicity firm announce that he was retiring from any more studio recording to concentrate on new forms of alternative media. Many at Warners would have been a little confused by the statement in light of the new contract. However, the statement went on to say that Prince would fulfill the remainder of his six-album deal by giving them old songs from the vast collection in his vault, which at this point was rumored to be over 500 unreleased songs. In addition, he announced he would not stop producing songs for other artists.

As expected Warners were shocked and bemused, especially in relation to the fact that they would not be getting any more music from one of their bestselling artists and indeed one of the biggest stars on the planet. Prince could not contain his disappointment in the ♀ album and felt that Warner's did not do enough to promote it. He felt once he had delivered the music his part of the deal was done and that it was over to the label to promote it around the media and radio stations etc. He thought Warners' promotional work was extremely weak. Yet when the sales were not high Warners would shift the blame to Prince for his reluctance to do media interviews and for releasing too much music.

The answer to this was clear to Prince: he wanted new ways of getting his music to the public. The current system was not working. It was old fashioned with too many suited executives pulling the strings who were non-musicians. Prince would later write at the start of one his songs: How can a non-musician discuss the future of music from anything but a consumer point of view? This was his mindset. He wrote to his fan magazine *Controversy* and told them that his new music would only be given to friends. He stated music should be free, like air.

To compound things even more, Prince made an announcement that would shock the music world on 7th June 1993, his 35th birthday. His publicity firm announced that Prince had changed his name to the symbol of his latest album, ♀. The plan was Prince would honor his six-album deal as stated in his last press release, as Prince. As stated he would give them albums from songs from his immense back catalog of recordings but now, because he had changed his name, he would be recording and releasing new material under his new name, ♀. From here on we shall refer to him by this name.

For fans, this was great news and was met with excitement. He had on his last tour of the US spoken out against his label at almost every show. He was actively sharing his frustrations, asking the crowd if they felt he made too much music. He told them the label thought they couldn't keep up. He would finish his speech by saying that he felt he made *'Just enough music'*. For many this felt like they wouldn't be now just getting the album a year that they were used to, but possibly even more. This was a clear indication that fans could now have vault released music under the Prince name, as he completed his contract obligations, but there would be an almost completely new direction of music from the new creation going by the name of ♀.

♀ had thrown a master stroke into a recording contract that had never happened in the history of music, even more astonishing in that it came on the back of one of the biggest music deals of all time. Prince, beyond money and beyond even his own name, valued musical freedom above all else.

> ## THE PRONUNCIATION OF THE NEW NAME CAUSED MASSIVE CONFUSION, BECOMING THE MAIN TOPIC OF CONVERSATION IN THE MEDIA. SPECULATION SOON GREW AROUND THE WORLD THAT HIS NEW NAME WAS VICTOR.

The pronunciation of the new name caused massive confusion, becoming the main topic of conversation in the media. Speculation soon grew around the world that his new name was Victor. The symbol deconstructed could spell it out, if you really tried, and on the last album the final song was *'The Sacrifice of Victor'*. O(+> quickly issued a statement to say his name was definitely not Victor and the symbol has no pronunciation. It soon became a running joke within the media, many calling him *TAFKAP*, *The Artist Formerly Known As Prince*, or just *The Artist*. O(+> however was deadly serious and was resolute in his belief. Employees at Paisley Park were now not permitted to call him *Prince*, and after much confusion many settled on simply *Boss* as behind the scenes the legalities continued.

O(+> recorded a live video called *The Undertaker* on 14th June 1993, a week after the name change. It's a brilliant insight into the live recording session featuring The *Paisley Park* Trio of Michael Bland on drums, Sonny T on bass and O(+> on vocals and guitar. Intertwined with a very loose story and small bits of acting the video showcases the trio blasting through several blues/rock numbers with swirling camera work. There was a longer, more detailed video featuring more acting parts which featured Nona Gaye, daughter of Marvin Gaye, but this was edited down to a mainly live video. The songs featured were *'The Ride'*, *'Bambi'*, *'Peach'*, *'Honky Tonk Woman'*, *'Dolphin'* and *'The Undertaker'*. O(+> tried to release it as a O(+> recording for a picture CD, but during manufacturing Warners had it destroyed. Some however managed to escape and went into fan circulation. The *Undertaker* video became very collectable.

As the chaos continued between the lawyers it was business as usual for the new musician. O(+> planned the *Act II* tour of Europe and in normal fashion started live rehearsals at Paisley Park and around his clubs. During these rehearsals Prince had another clash with his record label. O(+> completed work on an album with the *New Power Generation* called *Gold Nigga*. Prince had been working on the album with the band since the middle of 1992, when he was Prince, and now it was completed he wanted it to be released. In light of recent events Warners immediately rejected the release. O(+> at his own expense decided to print up copies and give them away

during the *Act II* tour; another example of him going direct to the fans. It instantly became very collectable and eventually became available through O(+>'s own NPG store a year or so later.

Paisley Park was now becoming a venue where O(+> was playing more frequently to fans. He played full on concerts as if he was playing to 50,000 fans, and also played many nights with the stripped-down *Paisley Park* Trio for more rock orientated gigs. Many lasted well into the early hours. In addition, O(+> also began work on a new *Madhouse* album. He was often playing live all night and through to the dawn and then recording through the day: an exhausting pace. It was as if the frustration he was feeling was now being released through exhausting concerts, recording sessions and writing continuously without a break.

O(+> continued rehearsals for the *Act II* tour, running through songs with the band and getting the show how he wanted before leaving for England in late July 1993. O(+> changed the show so it differed considerably from the *Act I* tour of the US. 27 shows were scheduled, starting at the National Indoor Arena in Birmingham on 26th July and circling Europe before concluding back in England at Wembley Arena in London on 7th September 1993.

As before, he talked throughout the tour about his issues with Warners and his views on being restricted in his releases. He also said he would not give Warners any more recordings but instead give anything new direct to the fans. This again was unheard of in 1993 - there was no direct platform for O(+> to use: streaming or iTunes were yet to be invented, and his utopian vision of how his music should be distributed was seen by executives at record companies as pretentious and unrealistic. O(+> however was challenging the contracts and restrictions imposed and going head to head with his ambitious belief; it was incredibly brave and visionary and only through raw talent, relentless hard work and enormous musical ability could it ever work.

Prince repeated the rhetoric throughout the concerts, highlighting his new name as the huge symbol lit up above his head. On stage O(+> was becoming increasingly wild with his chants and musical style; it was clear that recent events were pushing him deeper into his performances and it was consuming all he was as the tour and after-show concerts continued through Europe. His frustrations were compounded with the realization that it was unlikely Warners would allow any more releases in the near future despite his increasing recording activity of new songs, which as usual were pouring out of him. These songs simply had nowhere to go. Even more of a frustration was the fact he learned that Warners were planning a greatest hits package, something that Prince was completely against.

On 30th August 1993, the premiere for the song *'Interactive'* was broadcast. The song shows the thought process O(+> had at the time about direct access to fans, and he would go on to develop *'Interactive'* further when it became a CD-rom released later in 1994. It was starting to become clear the direction O(+> saw the music industry going: he was looking directly at multimedia and the technology it allowed from a musician and audience perspective. Many thought he was losing the plot; he was of course completely spot on.

O(+> returned to the UK to conclude the European tour on 7th September 1993. He played a surprise set at the BBC Broadcasting

House during the Radio 1 *Simon Bates show* in the morning. It was billed as a thank you to his UK fans with just 250 people in the crowd. The short radio concert started with the 1999 medley as performed on the tour before ending with a guitar frenzy of a mix of the music of *'Chaos and Disorder'* and *'Peach'*. After the radio concert ♔ performed at Wembley for 2 nights, the last show on 8th September. ♔ performed a final after-show at Bagley's Warehouse near Kings Cross London. The club was decorated with an Egyptian theme and lasted from 10pm until around 6am with about 3 thousand tickets sold to the packed club. At the end of the night ♔ was wrapped in a cloth and carried off stage. Remarkably on the same day as the after-show party finished in London, which was the morning of 8th September 1993, ♔ showed up at his nightclub *Glam Slam* in Minneapolis USA and handed the DJ a copy of a new song *'Pope'* to have it played. ♔ was getting ever more impossible to pin down from here onwards - his appetite for recording and performing were, even by his standards, becoming hard to follow. And this wasn't just in one genre, he was mixing every musical style in every direction with an ease and hunger that even his musical colleagues were finding hard to keep up with.

On 14th September, a week after the *Act I* and *Act II* tour, the first ever collection of Prince's greatest hits, *The Hits Vol I, The Hits Vol II* was released. The two discs were available separately or as part of a three CD set entitled *The Hits/The B-Sides* featuring a third disc of B-sides spanning his career. As expected ♔ was unequivocally against its release. It was also reported that Prince/♔ charged a considerable fee for the production of the cover photos for *The Hits/The B-Sides* which again Warners needed to recoup in some way. Warners needed to maximize the return on their new $100m contract. The negotiations with this album marked the beginning of the end of the relationship, and it would be a long downhill spiral from here on.

They were now negotiating with one of the most successful artists they had ever signed, who less than a year ago signed a huge long-term contract but now wanted out. There was little they could do in respect to future albums on the contract; after all he always said he would deliver the albums they wanted. What they could do though was chip into the collectables of the back catalog, and they did just that.

It was a perfect strategy with *The Hits* compilation. They also hurt the protective element of Prince's back catalog by adding the B-sides. It proved a master move in this early standoff. They had effectively broken a hole in the vault door by giving access to some of the collectable material that fans had spent years collecting and the wider public wouldn't normally seek out. It was now conveniently all in one place and re-packaged on the greatest hits collection. Originally there was a much larger release scheduled but Warners were concerned that an inflated price would put people off; there was also a lot of material to choose from and it was difficult to edit to a 2-album disc. It was eventually watered down from five discs to three with a couple of unreleased tracks, *'Pope'* and *'Peach'*. There was also a long-awaited Prince version of *'Nothing Compares 2 U'* recorded live with Rosie Gaines. The B-sides set was the main reason for seeking out the triple-disc set; it was a way of making every credible fan want to own the collection. Tracks such as *'4 The Tears in Your Eyes'* and *'Power Fantastic'*, as well as the other collectables, were now on a dedicated disc.

The Hits/The B-Sides received a great deal of commercial success all over the world with all three sets certified platinum. As with most box sets it continued to sell over the years ahead whenever there was any future commercial peak. The 56 tracks gave an incredible insight into the past 15 or so years showcasing Prince at his commercial best - commercial when he chose to be. For ♔ however commercial success wasn't cutting it and control was what he wanted. He was willing to sacrifice commercial success to pave the way for himself and future artists to have control over what they created. Determined to continue on as ever ♔ started to record his next album *The Gold Experience*.

Prince's newly formed NPG store started taking orders directly from fans for *The Undertaker* video in December 1993. They were limited to 1,000 copies and priced at $50 each. They instantly sold out and of course made a handsome profit as there would have been no share needed to anyone but the band. With this instant cash coming through it showed very early that it was possible to reach people direct and earn thousands, and possibly millions, of dollars without having to cut it to receive a low percentage. Prince was building a future model. This sale was a small taster to what was ahead.

> # WARNERS ISSUED A STATEMENT ON 1 FEBRUARY 1994 STATING THAT WARNER BROS AND PAISLEY PARK ENTERPRISES WERE TERMINATING PAISLEY PARK RECORDS.

In this vein ♔ managed to negotiate a deal for his newly penned song *'The Most Beautiful Girl in The World'*. Warners allowed him to release it independently on his own NPG Records label with ♔ having most of the US distribution handled by Bellmark Records. It was a huge risk and could easily have backfired with the work involved in such a venture but ♔ was so sure of the path he was traveling that he kept the momentum going for the deal. He held a party at Paisley Park to celebrate his first independent release, attended by many stars and celebs mixed in with the public - around 1,200 people in attendance. His performance that night showcased the stripped-down *NPG* which would form the main band for the next 2 years: Sonny T on bass, Tommy Barberella and Morris Hayes on keyboards, Michael Bland on drums with ♔ front and centre moving from guitar to bass. Mayte was also in place as a dancer alongside ♔.

Warners, in response to the events leading to this release, issued a statement on 1 February 1994 stating that Warner Bros and Paisley Park Enterprises were terminating Paisley Park Records. Very few of the latest releases had been hits and now with Warners financially responsible following the recent contract negotiations, it was seen as too much of a risk. Previously it was a joint venture and Prince was happy to support his new acts financially as he always had belief in the music. Once he had completed the music he saw it as the label's responsibility to get it out there. Without this initial financial help that Prince had previously supported his new acts with, Warners could not, and would not, support new acts, and the label in their view would have to be closed. Some of the acts signed to the label were left high and dry as it was closed, including Rosie Gaines who had an album prepared and now suddenly withdrawn. Rosie later signed to Motown Records and released her album *Closer than Close* later in June 1995.

On the morning of the release of *'The Most Beautiful Girl in the World'* ♀ flew to LA to sign 300 CDs on Arsenio Hall's *Love Jam* program. It was a significant milestone for ♀. This was his first single - his first release - as an independent artist, and it was a gamble. If ♀ had any doubts at all prior to the release they were quickly parked as it proved to be a massive success. It flew up the charts all over the world and became a massive commercial monster single. It reached number 1 in the UK and all over Europe as well as number 3 in the US. Warners stated they were happy to accommodate ♀'s desire to experiment with different independent distributions but behind the scenes they must have realized that this success would only fuel the belief that ♀ could actually do things himself, without the reliance on any major label. He felt they were obsolete; that the system was old fashioned and unnecessary.

He had proved to all involved, and most of all to himself, that he was right: you could do it yourself and be successful. It was a hands-on project to get *'The Most Beautiful Girl in the World'* out there.

The pluggers for radio, the distribution, the video - it was all hands-on and handmade. To accomplish what he wanted ♀ had to surround himself with some brilliant and committed individuals that could bring everything together. This happened perfectly with the single, but other elements in his newly formed one-man empire would naturally start to suffer as he could only stretch himself so far. What he was doing was brand new, a new approach, and his vision was practically unheard of on such a scale.

Contractually ♀ still continued to deliver albums for Warners as Prince. His next album for them was entitled *Come* and ♀ handed them an initial draft version in March 1994. Warners rejected it and sent it back. ♀ continued work on it, taking out songs and adding ones in, as well as completing an extended collection on *'The Most Beautiful Girl in the World'* which was where his main focus was.

Following on the momentum ♀ started performing at various events and one-off TV shows around the globe. In the UK he opened an NPG store in Camden, North London before a performance on the UK chart show *Top of The Pops* with the song at number 1 in the charts. Concerts in Monaco followed at the request of Prince Albert for nominees of *The World Music Awards*. Many of the events had celebrities in attendance during the sets. ♀ played mainly new numbers and covers that led to extensive jams with his stripped-down band. He concluded his European mini tour with a performance broadcast on the *Canal+* TV channel in Paris followed by a last minute advertised concert at The

Bataclan which didn't start until 3.30am. The show was advertised very quickly through a local radio station. This was the first time ♀ played 'Gold' live, setting the way for the new album he was planning on the back of the success of the single. The concert concluded at 5am.

> **MULTIMEDIA WAS BECOMING IMPORTANT TO FORWARD LOOKING ARTISTS AND ♀ WAS LEADING THE CHARGE. HIS INTERACTIVE PLATFORM WAS MOVING THAT WAY.**

To follow ♀ around this period is very difficult. Not only was he recording and giving songs to Warners as part of his contractual obligation, he was touring, performing and distributing songs as a totally free and independent new artist, who had no name. *YouTube* wasn't founded until 1995 - 2 years away - yet ♀ was looking at computers and technologies to distribute his music directly. He had the vision of direct streaming for concerts and direct iTunes style album distribution before these platforms even existed. Again, this went back to his early recording career, when technology allowed him to create without the need for other bandmates. The introduction of programmable drum machines allowed Prince to pre-set and pre-play instruments, so he could create by himself at his own incredible pace, with complete control. His idea of using technology to distribute music directly came from a similar mindset. Multimedia was becoming important to forward looking artists and ♀ was leading the charge. His interactive platform was moving that way.

Peter Gabriel was exploring it with *Xplora 1*, *Peter Gabriel's Secret World*. The multimedia around it was intended to promote his 1992 album, *Us*. The game was first released for Macintosh in 1993, followed by Windows in 1994 and CD-i in 1995. Gabriel's project was completed in collaboration with Brilliant Media under Gabriel's own label Real World Records. David Bowie also experimented with an interactive CD with *Jump* but this was criticized as being over complicated with the end reward not matching the effort put in. ♀'s own platform featured puzzles and games after the player had crash landed. Solving these would lead to the ability to download unreleased tracks. It was of course a work in progress but forward-thinking artists like ♀, Bowie and Gabriel had noticed where things were going and they were playing around with the ideas. For ♀ though this was more serious and he was resolute that this was the future for distributing music to his fans. Although the format was developing ♀ was getting more space on the internet and this of course led to a captured audience that he could ultimately keep in touch with and regularly update.

♀ started to look closer at the *Glam Slam* nightclubs, using them more and more as a venue to test and release new songs through. He visited many times, often unannounced, in the early hours and played songs either directly through the DJ sets or as a performance. Moving this further he purchased another property for around $1 million to be turned into another *Glam Slam* in Miami, and he also set about the search for a further club in Vancouver. With the NPG ♀ started work on another album entitled *Exodus*. Most of the songs were completed at Paisley Park with the band throughout May 1994, and many segues and acting monologues were added.

♀ handed Warners the revised version of *Come*, which they had originally rejected. Now fearful that ♀ was handing them substandard material they requested that they have 'The Most Beautiful Girl in the World' and 'Shhh', feeling that both songs would be radio friendly and help bolster sales. They also insisted that it would be a *Prince* record not anything to do with ♀. ♀ rejected this and refused them the tracks, citing that ♀ recorded the songs and not Prince. Warners had no choice but to accept what they were given. In a twist however, ♀ handed them the completed *The Gold Experience* around a week later. Warners refused it. Naturally ♀ was furious, as he believed *The Gold Experience* to be a body of work in need of release: it was a new album by a new artist and he did not see the harm in both records being out there at the same time. Warners however saw it as yet again too much music. Ultimately, they wanted sales and nothing that would dilute that could be accepted. The commercial benefits outweighed the artistic element yet again.

On 7th June 1994 on his 36th birthday, or the first anniversary of ♀, the Interactive CD-rom was released. It was the first venture in alternative media for ♀. The user was drawn into an interactive tour through state-of-the-art graphics at the time. It's set within Paisley Park, giving access to lots of different rooms featuring many experiences. By unlocking certain puzzles, the user is rewarded with video clips, sound bites, illustrations and biographical information.

The Interactive CD also featured unreleased music and videos. Also included with the CD-rom was an audio CD featuring the song 'Interactive' as well as clips from 31 videos. There were 6 complete songs and samples from a further 52. It was ahead of its time for a CD-rom to feature such experiences and access to music. Showcasing 52 samples and 31 videos gave a glimpse into the mindset of ♀. Why wait for 4 years to release an album of 10-12 songs when you can simply download 52 songs and have direct access? It wasn't quite there yet but the vision was. And of course, a record label would have little or no need to be involved in such activity. On the whole, the Interactive CD-rom did very well and again demonstrated to ♀ that there was a future beyond the conventional recording contracts of the past.

At meetings and at any public event he now had the word *SLAVE* written across his face. He had a new spiritual outlook and it was growing. He felt completely disconnected from anything *Prince* related and wanted now more than ever to unshackle himself from the constraints of a record label intent on holding back albums until they thought the time was right. In this instance, it was *The Gold Experience*. They had allowed ♀ to release 'The Most Beautiful Girl in the World' but that's as far as they would allow. Prince belonged to them and they would release what they were contractually obliged to do, and when they wanted to.

Throughout July 1994 ♀ played many concerts and kept himself on the road performing new songs and covers of his favorites at the

time, notably Santana medleys, Graham Central Station and Sly and the Family Stone songs. It was a challenge for many crowds as he wasn't playing anything that they had heard before, except for when a cover version blended into one of the new songs. In this month alone, he played *Glam Slam* in Los Angeles on 3 separate occasions, *The House of Blues* in Los Angeles, a benefit concert in LA for the *Sabriya of Fun* Foundation, 2 shows at *The Palladium New York* and a benefit concert again in New York for the Harlem Dance Theatre. There was also a trip to Paris to attend Versace's fashion show and two other concerts at *Glam Slam* in Minneapolis.

♀ was not alone during this period in being in dispute with his label. Another global star had for the past year or so gone public with his frustrations relating to artistic freedom. In London in June 1994 a case was at the High Court discussing a long-term contract that George Michael had signed and now wanted out of. The case was discussed around questions such as artistic freedom and the choice of a musician/artist to leave that contract whenever he or she saw fit. George Michael claimed that he could not leave his contract and he had to give the record company exactly what they asked for which compromised him as an artist. He compared it to 'artistic professional slavery': an interesting parallel.

Of course, the tabloid British press saw it more about money and ego. The British judge in the case rejected the bid from George Michael to be freed from his long-term recording contract. He lost his case against Sony Corporation. Naturally the ruling was welcomed by industry executives, who saw the case as a challenge to the traditional practice of signing artists to huge long-term album deals, which was a way to counter the large investments in discovering and promoting new acts. George Michael naturally was hugely disappointed in the ruling and complained that his record deal left him little control over his own work and career. He had signed a long-term deal for 15 years.

The lawsuit in this case had been raised by George Michael against Sony a year and a half earlier, contending that the eight-album contract he signed in 1988 was unfair under British and European Union law. He said it bound him to the company for up to 15 years and gave him little or no control over how his music would be marketed. He testified that his dissatisfaction followed Sony's reaction to his 1990 album *Listen Without Prejudice, Volume I*. With this album George Michael made a deliberate decision to play down his sex-symbol image he had grown since his *Wham!* days and then continued on to his large hit album *Faith*. He wanted to tone this back and have a more artistic direction to his songs and public image, but this did not sit well with Sony

> ♀ WAS NOT ALONE DURING THIS PERIOD IN BEING IN DISPUTE WITH HIS LABEL.

executives who were interested only in sales and not in his development as an artist. He also testified that Sony had sought to punish him by not promoting *Listen Without Prejudice* as aggressively as it should have done, especially in the United States. The album sold five million copies, which in comparison to *Faith*, which sold 14 million worldwide, was seen as a failure. In response to the accusations by George Michael, Sony executives testified that they had marketed the album to the best of their abilities. In addition, Sony's lawyers tried throughout the trial to establish that Mr. Michael was well aware of the terms of the contract he signed in 1988, and that the deal was a considerable improvement over his earlier contracts with CBS Records.

Unfortunately for George Michael, Justice Jonathan Parker largely accepted Sony's view of the matter, saying that the contract was *'reasonable and fair'* and that Mr. Michael understood the deal. He went on to say he was satisfied with the evidence, and that there was no substance in George Michael's claim of unfair conduct by Sony, or in any of the detailed complaints which he made. George Michael held a press conference after the hearing and said that he thought there were strong grounds for an appeal and that he would probably file one. George had earlier said that he would never record for Sony again. This was in fact the case and eventually, after many years of legal discussions, the contract was annulled. This in effect cancelled the requirement to deliver six more albums and compensated the label: Sony would receive $40m and a royalty payment on future recordings, to be paid by *Virgin* and *DreamWorks SKG* which were George Michael's new record labels.

The main difference between Prince and George though was George did not record or put out anything while the dispute was in place. Prince on the other hand gave the record label albums to release while simultaneously recording and releasing albums under his new persona ♀. He also toured and performed relentlessly and the music never stopped.

Dreamworks was the new multimedia company formed by Steven Spielberg, the former Disney chairman Jeffrey Katzenberg and record tycoon David Geffen. They agreed to manufacture, market and distribute George Michael's records in North America, and Virgin would handle the rest of the world. It would be a two-album deal, for which the singer would receive advances of at least $12m and royalties in the region of 21 per cent. George Michael eventually became free but it came at a financial cost to both the record label and himself.

Recording companies have always argued that because they spend so much in the search and development of new artists they can only recoup their investments through long-term relationships with those relatively few acts who go on to major success, artists like George Michael and Prince being in this category. They argue that if artists were given freedom to break their contracts and walk away after an album or two, then companies would no longer be able to afford to spend so much on new talent. If George Michael had won the case it would have had large scale implications for contracts going forward for all major artists, as it would have set a precedent. However, George lost the case and so it didn't.

At the start of August, keen to push their new *Prince* album, Warners released *'Letitgo'* as the first single. It performed moderately well, hitting the 20s in most countries around the

COME WAS AN ALBUM THAT WAS DOOMED TO FALL BELOW THE LEVELS EXPECTED IN ALMOST EVERY WAY. ♀'S HEART WAS SIMPLY NOT IN IT.

world, and reaching number 31 in the US and 10 on the R&B Chart. The B-side was *'Solo'*, again from the album. In addition, a CD single was released in the UK containing an edit of *'Letitgo'* and *'Solo'* but also containing the extended version of *'Alexa de Paris'* which was the original B-side to *'Mountains'* in 1986. It also featured *'Pope'* which was originally on *The Hits 2* from 1993. A maxi single on CD and vinyl included several remixes of the track. Warners were clearly keen to maximize on Prince and his back catalog when pushing new songs out there.

A week after *'Lettigo'* was issued the first album on ♀'s NPG Records was released *1-800 New Funk*. The name came about as it was the number for ordering NPG merchandise. Again, it was distributed by Bellmark Records. ♀ only takes credit on one of the songs, the recently recorded *'Love Sign'*, a duet with Nona Gaye. Most of the other tracks are attributed to NPG members and former musicians from Paisley Park. ♀ was fully behind the album, promoting it where he could. He shot a video for *'Love Sign'* alongside Nona Gaye as well as putting adverts in the press. He performed the track live on the *Today* Show as well as a signing at Tower Records on Broadway.

Four days after ♀ released *1-800 New Funk* Warners released their latest 'Prince' album *Come*. It was confusing for the general public, understandably so. Prince had changed his name over a year ago and he had toured continuously at a furious pace getting the message around the world on his new spiritual calling and his belief in the new direction of music. He had released, as ♀, a huge worldwide hit and had just released a ♀ album on his own NPG Records. Now a new album was out by Prince.

The message was subtle though and on closer inspection of the sleeve of the album there are the dates of Prince's birth and his recent death, 1958-1993. It has a clear theme of death on the cover and shows Prince standing at what look like gates to a cemetery. They were actually shot outside *La Sagrada Familia* Cathedral in Barcelona. Interestingly the cathedral of choice on the cover is famous for being unfinished. The Catalan architect Antoni Gaudí died at the age 73 in 1926 when less than a quarter of the project was complete. If that was intentional it was very subtle, but as with everything Prince related, there is always something unusual and unique in the offering. *Come* as an album is inconsistent; it has a basic lack of melody in comparison to past Prince albums and relies more on grooves and rhythms. It has a natural downbeat feel to it, playing to the mood around Prince at the time. There are many segues linking the songs and a lot feature the sound of water which Prince has used many times as a symbol of spirituality, baptism, cleanliness and rebirth.

Shutterstock

Come was an album that was doomed to fall below the levels expected in almost every way. ♀'s heart was simply not in it: he was fully focused on *1-800 New Funk* and wanting to release *The Gold Experience*, which he believed was far superior - and it was. *Come* basically had no backing from ♀ and little backing from Warners. Combine this with an album that in its general feel is somewhat downbeat, and it's no wonder it didn't do as well as it could have done. Of course, this is what ♀ wanted; the album is

downbeat for exactly this reason. He now publicly pushed for *The Gold Experience* to be released and went on the campaign trail. Wherever he went and whatever he did his main focus now was to get *The Gold Experience* released. It was an album he believed in completely, and it would consume him unconditionally and exhaustingly over the coming months, even years. He would not stop performing, often 3 to 4 times a day, until this album was released.

CHAPTER THIRTEEN

ALL THAT GLITTERS AIN'T GOLD

Negotiations continued on The Gold Experience as ♀ campaigned for its release. **One avenue Warners suggested was that it would allow two smaller labels to release it just before Christmas 1994 allowing ♀ to work with them and also handle the distribution himself.**

The deal however was verbal, with nothing contractually agreed. Also, the two record labels offered were both solely owned by Warners: the *Tommy Boy* label in the US and *East West* in other areas. In addition, they would not allow the release to be part of the four albums he still owed Warners. The breakdown of this negotiation moved things into a standoff. This was the period when ♀ really started to become more inward and rebel against all that record labels stood for. His behavior would to some seem erratic and unbalanced. One thing that would be constant though was the recording and performing, as the music never stopped. Blistering Hendrix style guitar solos, funky bass solos and endless jams formed his escape from the turbulent world of ownership and contracts. As always, he retreated to the music.

October 1994 saw some interesting developments. ♀ completely abandoned the *Glam Slam* nightclub in Minneapolis after a falling out over ownership of the club. It was a benchmark in many respects for trying out new songs and projects that were in the making. All ♀ and *Prince* memorabilia were removed and returned to Paisley Park. At the same time in connection with the club's ownership ♀ fired longstanding business partner Gilbert Davison. Davison had been around in some joint capacity since around 1984 but now with the club under dispute of ownership he was fired as Vice President of Paisley Park Enterprises. He was replaced with his vastly inexperienced stepbrother Duane Nelson who was tasked with downsizing the company.

♀ started a petition with a press release requesting fans to protest for the release of *The Gold Experience* and stating that the current situation was causing him considerable stress. He also stated that he wanted to fulfill the remainder of his contract to Warners as soon as possible. He told fans that the release of *The Gold Experience* at this point was 'never'. He turned to the Internet and used this new developing avenue to communicate directly with his fans.

A complicated change happened at Warners in late October. Negotiations had been continuing with Warners, who reportedly offered ♀ $4 million for the release of *The Black Album*, which would be released in October 1994, and then *The Gold Experience* for a release in early 1995. Warners also wanted as part of this deal for ♀ to write a soundtrack, but the specific soundtrack was yet to be determined. These 3 albums - *The Black Album*, *The Gold Experience* and a soundtrack - would make up 2 of the 4 that he still owed. ♀ stood his ground on the deal but his attorney believed it was a good offer and advised ♀ to accept. Unsurprisingly he rejected it and as a result his attorney quit. He was replaced with a young attorney named L. Londell McMillan who would remain with him for years to come. McMillan was the sixth attorney since the signing with Warners, and he must have felt that he too was on borrowed time as he was thrust straight into negotiations on getting the best deal and the quickest escape from the contract. As these negotiations took place there was a regime change at the top of Warners with Mo Austin and Larry Waronka leaving the company. This meant that negotiations would have to put on hold as a new team was brought in. *The Black Album* however was accepted, and a deal of $1 million was exchanged for Warners to release it. Because of this *The Gold Experience* would again have to wait, to the immense frustration of ♀.

The Black Album was released a month later on 22 November 1994. A press release was issued stating that ♀ was 'spiritually' against the album. It had been slated for release on more than one occasion since Prince cancelled it at the last minute in 1987. *The Black Album* in 1987 was hard edged and controversial in its lyrical tone and themes, but it had lost its element of shock by 1994.

Many styles had been around for a while that were far more shocking, including death metal and gangster rap, and the 1987 shocking elements of *The Black Album* now seemed rather tame in comparison. The musical aspect of the album however was still current and showcased just how ahead of his time Prince actually was.

> # THE BLACK ALBUM IS THE MOST BOOTLEGGED ALBUM OF ALL TIME, WHICH MEANT MOST FANS AND MUSIC LOVERS ALREADY HAD IT IN SOME FORM.

Remaining true to the original 1987 release it had no title and no credited artist. It became known as *The Black Album* due to its plain black sleeve. The sleeve itself has no information on it at all apart from the catalogue number printed on the spine in peach letters. To make it easier for consumers Warners had a sticker put on it for the 1994 release; they thoughtfully labelled it *'The Legendary Black Album'*. Unlike most *Prince* albums it is essentially a compilation of individual tracks, not a thematic album. Most of the tracks were songs Prince would do on days off from tour or simply as a way of relaxing in the studio. The first track to be recorded was *'Superfunkycalifragisexy'* which was in September 1986. The bulk of the remaining songs were recorded between October 1986 and March 1987. The final track recorded was *'When 2 R in Love'* which came later in October 1987; this is probably why it survived and was put on *Lovesexy*, the only song on that album to be recorded previously. The album is commonly regarded as the most heavily bootlegged album of all time, by any artist.

The Black Album reached number 47 on the Billboard 100 and 18 on the R&B chart. When you put this in context though it's impressive: this is the most bootlegged album of all time, which meant most fans and music lovers already had it in some form. There was also the fact that the album was low key in its 1994 release, with zero promotion and no singles. It is remarkable it still held firm in the 1994 charts.

On the day of The Black Album release ♀ flew to Germany for the MTV European Music Awards. ♀ performed a set with 'slave' written on his cheek. This would remain there for all public performances until the contract was completed. The slave word was widely discussed, with many not understanding how a multi-millionaire rock star could ever call himself a slave, especially in American with its history of slavery; ♀ however meant that he didn't own his masters, his master owned him. He couldn't do what he wanted, he couldn't create what he wanted and he couldn't release what he wanted. Therefore, as a musician he saw himself as a slave.

More turmoil continued when Prince arrived back at Paisley Park and found his head of NPG Records Levi Seacer Jr gone. Levi had played with Prince from 1987 onwards on various albums and side projects including *Madhouse* before his promotion to president of NPG Records. Levi allegedly left no contact or forwarding address and had just vanished with a letter of resignation. He was having a relationship with ♀'s publicist Karen Lee at the time and she too had gone. Understandably ♀ was very upset with the sudden departure of two key members to his organization.

On 3rd March 1995 his European tour launched in London. *'The Ultimate Live Experience'* would be his seventh European tour since 1986, taking in England, Ireland, Holland and Belgium. After 5 concerts at Wembley arena ♀ played an after-show at the Astoria Club in London before moving on to Manchester for 2 nights and then on to Scotland, with another 2am after-show concluding the Glasgow trip. He then returned to England for concerts in Sheffield and Birmingham. While in Belgium on the tour the second album by The NPG *Exodus* was completed, but Warners initially rejected the album so it suffered from no major label assisting with a worldwide release. Undeterred, ♀ hired independent and small record labels for licensing agreements, which meant that it was only available in England, Australia and parts of Europe. He was however proving to himself, slowly but surely, that he could release new music independently, albeit at a struggle and a cost.

Towards the end of 1994 Warners had gone through a massive restructure, this being one of the reasons why *The Gold Experience* was once more delayed. Mo Austin and Larry Waronker had both left and it's fair to say that the commercial success of Warners through the 1980s had been down to their joint leadership. It was a period of consistent success, with multi-platinum records from Madonna, John Fogerty and Prince alongside many other key signings. The label enjoyed a 51% increase in revenue; Waronker had success with REM and signed Eric Clapton, The Red-Hot Chili Peppers, Paul Simon, Talking Heads, Van Halen, Neil Young, and Dire Straits among others many others. Through large scale marketing campaigns Warners became, with the quality of these signings, the dominant force. There were however changes to come, and the major restructure landed right in the middle of the negotiations with Prince on his remaining albums and in particular negotiations for *The Gold Experience* release.

♀ met the new management team and things didn't go well. The corporate world they lived in and the music they controlled was the exact reason ♀ was fighting for ownership and freedom: businessmen - non-musicians - deciding the future direction of music. Waronker had been a great supporter of Prince and Austin was instrumental in getting ♀ his first independent release of *'The Most Beautiful Girl in the World'*. He now felt the corporate suits had little or no understanding of his music or what he was trying to achieve. Awkward negotiations took place, but an agreement was reached.

The company agreed to release *Exodus*, and more importantly *The Gold Experience*, which was scheduled for September 1995. With this in mind ♀ immediately set about plans to continue on tour with tickets going on sale in Japan from June and July. The following weeks ♀ played 16 full concerts at Paisley Park; these were charity concerts dubbed *'Love 4 One Another'* and tied in with ♀ deciding to open the doors to the public for a $5 admission fee on Tuesdays and Saturdays. Interestingly, several Prince songs were creeping into these sets which were described as 'covers'. The concerts throughout this period were unseen and unheard by the majority of fans around the world. They were unreported in the press, but they were the very essence, the very core of what he was fighting for. If streaming over the Internet was the norm like it is today this would have undoubtedly been the route to the worldwide fan base. Technology unfortunately hadn't quite caught up with him just yet.

On 26th September 1995 after a much publicized battle *The Gold Experience* was released. It was originally presented to Warners back in early 1994, the majority of the songs having been recorded at Paisley Park between September 1993 and March 1994, which meant that most of the songs on the album were over two years old on release. Even though he had changed his name over two years ago this was the first actual album attributed solely to ♔. As far as Prince albums and indeed more recently those of ♔ are concerned, it is one of the most effortless albums he ever produced. It remains one of the favorites of all time for many Prince fans. It's the most eclectic set of songs since 1987's *Sign o' the Times* and brings nearly all Prince and ♔ styles together perfectly. The sound is retro in every way and has an immense attitude within it. It has catchy riffs reminiscent of *Sign o' the Times, 1999* and *Purple Rain* and has a narrative running throughout, nodding toward *Graffiti Bridge*. The first words from the female character are spoken in Spanish and declare that Prince has died so that the *New Power Generation* may live.

> ON 14TH FEBRUARY 1996
> ♔ MARRIED MAYTE GARCIA AT
> PARK AVENUE METHODIST CHURCH
> IN MINNEAPOLIS.

Critics were very much in praise of the album, claiming it was his best by far for many years and a true return to form. It's outrageously original from start to finish and a complete renewal in sound and feel, and it put him back up in the charts on the worldwide stage. Compared to *Come* it is without doubt better in every element. As he said at the Brit Awards: *"Prince best? The Gold Experience, better"*. He was right. It was voted one of the best albums of 1995 by an annual poll of American critics published by *The Village Voice*. It was described as a mix of newly stripped-down funk and delicate balladry that reasserted his dynamic range.

The album reached number 6 on the *Billboard* top 100, if ♔ ever cared about such positioning, and was certified gold, reaching over 530,000 copies in the US. It also reached number 4 in the UK and was a major hit around the rest of the world. Ironically, after all the fighting for the release ♔ gave little promotional activity to the album, mainly due to the fact it had been over 2 years since the songs were written and he had moved on considerably. Despite its brilliance and the praise from fans and critics alike when it was eventually released ♔ saw it simply as a step towards his release from contractual obligations.

On 8th January 1996, a tour of Japan began at the *Budokan* in Tokyo. Again, the main focus of the shows was the music instead

of large stage, choreography or theatrics. The tour was renamed *'The Gold Tour'* as the album had been officially released. He could also now concentrate, quickly, on his final album to free himself from his Warners contract. The second he was back at Paisley after the tour he went straight into the studio and was adamant that he would not be submitting any really strong quality material to his last Warners offering. Anything he produced of quality was scheduled for *Emancipation* with leftovers given to *Chaos and Disorder* for Warners.

On 14th February 1996 ♔ married Mayte Garcia at Park Avenue Methodist Church in Minneapolis. It was a private ceremony, as you would expect, with just close friends and family members in attendance. After the ceremony, to avoid the hundreds of fans gathered outside, they went straight to a limo which drove them back to Paisley Park to finish the ceremony and cut the cake. Newly written song *'Friend, Lover, Sister, Mother, Wife'* was played repeatedly through the wedding and was the song the couple danced to. The track would eventually end up on *Emancipation*. Mayte reportedly pointed to a symbol shaped pendant around her neck during the vows.

Although some fans were shocked at the fact that rock's most eligible bachelor had got married, it wasn't a shock to those in his inner circle or around Paisley Park. The relationship had been ongoing for a few years since they first met back in 1992 during the *Diamonds and Pearls* tour. ♔ was notably different with Mayte than with any of his previous girlfriends. She was also there at a particularly difficult time in his career when he was fighting for musical freedom, touring with him and being by his side every step of the way. Shortly after the wedding the pair announced that Mayte was pregnant; delighted with the news, they publicly shared it and planned for parenthood. The news had made ♔ more relaxed and more patient; he became much more fun and easier to work with and be around. This coincided with some restructuring in the business affairs at Paisley Park. Firstly, he scaled back again so financially things were even more slimmed down. Paisley Park became closed as a rental facility meaning that several staff were laid off from the complex, and he also took the members of the NPG and the band's support technicians off the payroll.

Also on 14th February 1996 ♔ opened his very first website *'The Dawn'*. It would be one of many over the next few years. *TheDawn.com* linked in with the wedding and showed an eight-page wedding program titled *'Coincidence or fate?'* It was advertised as a platform to deliver unreleased music, new videos, merchandise, books, exclusive interviews, cologne, jewellery, games and tour information on ♔ and other connected artists. The technology for the site was first class at the time of launch and pushed ♔ further forward towards direct contact with his audience.

♔ could see the ending to his fight getting ever closer. He wanted to settle down, he wanted a family and he wanted to be happy again. His contract obligations were nearly over and he was entering a new chapter in his life as a truly free artist. Before this though he would deliver Warner Bros two more albums, both of which many consider to be the worst of his entire career.

It was during a meeting with Warner Bros in April 1996 that they finally saw the end of the road. An agreement was settled that ♔ be permitted, after some renegotiation, to leave the label after giving them two albums and not three. ♀ also agreed to take a reduction in the royalties he would receive. The original contract that he signed in 1992 requested six albums. *'The Symbol album'*, *Come* and *The Gold Experience* were the first three of the six he was to submit. *The Black Album* would not count towards the six so three more remained.

Movie director Spike Lee had released his movie *Girl 6* earlier in March that had the soundtrack attributed to Prince, confusing many that he had changed his name back again. The simple reason was that the songs were before the name change and were indeed *'Prince'* songs; the only one that wasn't was the actual song *'Girl 6'* which was attributed to the NPG. Therefore, in addition to *The Black Album* the *Girl 6* soundtrack would not count towards the final albums which were required to end the contract. They struck a deal however to reduce this down to two, and ♀ would then be free to move on. ♀ quickly gave them the two albums they required: *Chaos and Disorder* and *The Vault…Old Friends for Sale.*

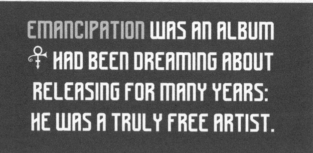

EMANCIPATION WAS AN ALBUM ♀ HAD BEEN DREAMING ABOUT RELEASING FOR MANY YEARS: HE WAS A TRULY FREE ARTIST.

This took Warners by surprise: both were complete and ready to go - even the artwork was finished with the words *'For private use only'* written on the sleeve. It was a bid to make the listener feel guilty about owning it. In essence this meant the record company were compelled to agree the deal, and they had no control over the artwork or indeed the content. They had to accept the offer which was basically 'take it or leave it'. It was a rapid attempt by ♀ to get out of the contract as soon as legally possible.

Emancipation was nearly complete and there were over 30 songs ready for the album. It was an album ♀ had been dreaming about releasing for many years: for the first time he would have no restrictions, and he didn't have to leave anything off. He was a truly free artist.

Despite all this being ready to go, and the future both professionally and personally looking perfect, he would now have to sit back and watch as the substandard leftovers he gave his record company were released as official albums.

CHAPTER FOURTEEN
BREAK THE CHAINS

Chaos and Disorder was released on 9th July 1996. The liner notes reveal that this album was intended as a demo, which give an indication to the feeling of the album. It could even have been intended as a light warning to the quality and content of the songs on the record.

The album was recorded over just ten days in January 1996. It's highly charged from start to finish: it was basically made in anger, which is no surprise, and this sets the tone of the album. There was little or next to no promotional activity apart from a couple of TV appearances, one on *The Late Show* with David Letterman and one on *The Today Show*.

The album is essentially a collection of polished demos with fragments of social commentary to cover the taunting of his record company. The lyrics cover the personal with the political. All songs recorded are attributed to the then line up of the NPG: Michael Bland on drums, Sonny T on bass, Tommy Barbarella and Morris Hayes on keyboards. While ♀ was busy alone recording and writing songs for *Emancipation*, which he clearly took his time over crafting, here he was in a room with the band and literally pressing 'record' on songs they had just created.

Despite the mainly negative reviews, which focused on the album feeling like a collection of fillers to release him from the label, which it was, there were some comments emphasizing what it actually was. It was a fun listen, a basic listen, it was what was expected and it does nothing more than rock. It has a rushed feeling; you feel it's been hurried and recorded mostly live in one or two takes. It would have been a great album if it was recorded by an up and coming rock artist, but the fact it was ♀ meant that there was a bar set higher than for most. ♀ later described the album as *'dark and unhappy'* with a similar feel to *The Black Album*.

Prince now negotiated with EMI and a deal was agreed. EMI stated they were *'thrilled and deeply honored'* to begin a working relationship with ♀. EMI's chairman Charles Koppelman was the father of Michael Koppelman who had previously worked with Prince as an engineer and mixer in 1989-1991, so there was a connection already in place. The agreement ♀ structured was for EMI to promote and distribute *Emancipation* - it would be an album by album agreement with *Emancipation* the first. This meant ♀ was a free agent to talk to other record companies and

distributors without being locked in to any forward deal. He could walk away at any time if he chose, and so could EMI. He would also have complete ownership of all master tapes, which was something he was insistent on. He had become a sort of champion on master tapes, often telling young songwriters and aspiring musicians to insist on owning masters from the start of any deal or renegotiation. *'If you don't own your masters, your masters own you'* he would frequently state.

It became known in the industry as a 'P&D' deal, where the artist, in this case ♀, pays for all production, marketing and distribution. It means the artist gets the majority of the profits and simply pays a small percentage back to the label. It basically switches the agreement around putting the artist in the driving seat. It meant that EMI made an upfront payment to ♀ who then paid the record company a percentage fee of the price retailers paid for *Emancipation*. It meant that ♀ was easily able to recoup the money he was spending as he would earn between 70-90% of each and every sale. It was extremely lucrative and although he could potentially be selling less, he was earning a huge amount more. He also had complete artistic control and had no restriction on anything he wanted to do. From here onwards his bank account on record sales simply got bigger.

On 16th October 1996 ♀ and Mayte's son was born at Northwestern Hospital in Minneapolis. Prince and Mayte were finally parents. The baby was born with severe problems which were diagnosed as Pfeiffer syndrome. Pfeiffer syndrome is a genetic disorder characterized by the premature fusion of certain skull bones. This early fusion prevents the skull from growing normally and affects the shape of the head and face. The baby had operations and interventions but was taken off life support the following week.

The baby died on 23 October 1996 and was cremated the same day. This was devastating for both parents. ♀ had scheduled *Emancipation* to coincide with the birth of his first child and had all the promotional and marketing machinery in place. The trauma of such an event is hard to imagine for any parent suffering the loss of a child, but ♀ made the decision to carry on and promote Emancipation, feeling that this was a personal affair and had nothing to do with anyone else. He would keep his private life private. Many believed that this event changed ♀ forever and his outlook going forward; this can certainly be argued to be correct.

♀ and Mayte never really recovered from this tragedy. ♀'s decision to return to music was in some ways a coping mechanism. He publicly denied that anything was wrong, even after the baby's death. He has never mentioned the event in any songs, apart from a possible interpretation on 1998's *The Truth* album if you're looking hard enough. There has been no public interview where he has once spoken about the loss or impact on him.

After this event he returned to the road, straight into the *'Love 4 One Another'* charities tour followed immediately by the *'Jam of the Year'* tour; this effectively kept him on the road for nearly all of the following year, which after such a personal tragedy cannot be seen as a coincidence. Heading straight into promotional activity for *Emancipation* ♀ held a listening party at Paisley Park, shortly followed by the infamous *Oprah Winfrey* interview special in November where he talked openly about his life, his music and the name change. He also performed on the show to the usual over the top whoops and screams of a US talk show audience.

> COMPARED TO MOST RECENT RELEASES EMANCIPATION WAS OF EXCEPTIONAL QUALITY AND FOCUS. IT'S CLEAR THAT A GREAT DEAL OF TIME AND EFFORT WENT INTO THE RECORD.

Emancipation was released on 19th November 1996, only four months after *Chaos and Disorder*. ♀ said at the time it was the album he was *'born to make'*. It's true he felt that way, especially when you look at its deeper meaning. Throughout his whole musical life, highlighted in this book, Prince had fought for the right to do things his way; this has to be to his eternal credit as he sacrificed even his own reputation to achieve this. Many thought he was a spoiled rock star throwing his toys out of the pram, but those closer could see the reasons behind the fight. He was paving the way for how contracts should be, and championing the rights of future artists.

Emancipation is something of a concept album, a massive one but a concept album nevertheless. The tracks all hold together a collective meaning and theme, much more than they do individually. There is a narrative running through the album linking to the same subjects. In this case, it was his love for his new wife and the celebration of his release from Warner Bros.

With this new creative freedom there is more experimenting within varying genres, although the production differs from previous records and masks this somewhat. There are several songs dedicated to his child, who at the time of writing and recording the album was still without noticeable problems. Another major development on the album is the use of cover versions of songs written by others. He claimed that he was tempted in the past with certain songs, which would fit in well with albums he was working on, but he had always been advised against it by Warner Bros. This may

explain why in the past few years so many covers were played live during his sets, mixed in with his own songs as he put his own personal stamp on classics in funk and rock. Four such covers appeared on the album: *'Betcha by Golly Wow!'*, previously a hit for The Stylistics, *'I Can't Make You Love Me'*, previously a hit for Bonnie Raitt, *'La-La-La Means I Love You'*, previously a hit for The Delfonics and *'One of Us'* which was previously a hit for Joan Osborne. Notably, Prince changed the chorus on *'One of Us'* from *'What if God was one of us / Just a slob like one of us'* to *'...Just a slave like one of us'*.

Compared to most recent releases *Emancipation* was of exceptional quality and focus. It's clear that a great deal of time and effort went into the record. Its sheer length of 3 discs is impressive enough but what is most outstanding is the quality of the songs. There is little risk taking on *Emancipation*; it's more of a showcase of musicianship and skill than anything else. It's a highly open and personal album with ♀'s love for his new wife dominant in many of the songs. Fatherhood, spirituality, devotion and commitment also are prominent themes throughout.

An unprecedented 36 songs cover the 3 discs, each disc at exactly 60 minutes in length. It was one of the largest albums ever released of new music. With the quality of the record and the fact it was released just four months after *Chaos and Disorder* it's quite astonishing the speed and dedication that went into it. He had proven above all else that as a songwriter and producer his ability to release frequent albums of exceptional quality was absolutely unmatched. Of course, once the forthcoming tour and subsequent promotional activity were completed, ♀ put the record behind him and, in normal fashion, quickly moved on.

The commitment to *Emancipation* kept going through the back end of 1996 with more promotional appearances. He appeared twice on *The Today Show* in the US and also on *The Rosie O'Donnell Show* where he performed *'Somebody's Somebody'*. The *'Love 4 One Another'* charity tour commenced on 7th January 1997 in Philadelphia. It was a basic warm up tour for the forthcoming *Emancipation* tour itself, with all proceeds going to various charities ♀ was personally involved with. The sold out charity tour took in 21 dates throughout the US.

In May 1997 to coincide with the charity tour ♀ opened his *'Love 4 One Another'* website. This effectively replaced *The Dawn*, which opened in February 1996. It would stay as ♀'s official website from 1997 through to 1999. Originally it started as a tool for the charity but over time it ultimately evolved into everything ♀ and Prince-related. In June 1997 songs were uploaded to the site. *'Eye Like Ur Funky Music'*, *'Funk Radio'*, *'Sadomasochistic Groove'* and *'Shoo-Bed-Ooh'* were the first to be added. It was a great new and upcoming tool to use and now was the perfect time to use it. The idea of *Love 4 One Another*, unlike *The Dawn*, was for a truly 'collaborative' fan website, these fans became known as *The Collective*. The brief from ♀ was to be inspiring and promote positivity, very much in the vein of the *Exodus* album. Incidentally, also working on the charity as this time was Manuela Testolini, who would later become Prince's second wife.

With the 35 date charity tour completed ♀ now turned his attention to his own tour of the US. He renamed the tour the *Jam of The Year* tour as he was moving away from *Emancipation*. As the tour progressed he even started to drop out *Emancipation* songs entirely and moved it towards a greatest hits style show. Before the tour kicked off properly ♀ held a press conference in New York and announced that he had a plan to build a brand-new school in Minneapolis from the money raised during the tour. He also said that tickets for the *Jam of the Year* tour would be released no more than one week in advance of the show. This was another industry first for a major mainstream pop star: he was absolutely taking control of all aspects of the music business, bringing it all in house and cutting out anyone that he felt was unnecessary. This approach for tours benefitted true fans and also gave a much larger return for ♀ himself.

Now ♀ had won the battle with Warners over ownership, and was also making a huge amount of money from sales, he was now looking straight at ticket touts and middlemen and ways around them to give genuine fans access to concerts at affordable prices. A musician's main earnings are record sales and revenue from touring. He had secured the record sales and was receiving huge percentages from this, so he now turned his attention to touring. Again, this was a system that had not changed for years and Prince was determined to change it for the better. Many tickets even now are swallowed up at face value and then resold at a much higher price.

♀ tours from here onwards were always different. He did everything possible to give fans the opportunity to see him, and at the price they were intended to be paying. It was a revolutionary approach to large scale touring. ♀'s team booked the venues at the last minute with about a week or two weeks' notice instead of the usual six months or so in advance. They handled the ticketing directly themselves through *Ticketmaster* or other sources which is usually done by outside agents. ♀ people also promoted the shows themselves from city to city using radio or other means. All the tour merchandise came direct from Paisley Park Enterprises, so no other company had a slice of the profits. This direct in-house approach in all the areas of a full-scale tour cut out many middlemen and companies who would naturally add in their own prices. This made the tour more lucrative for ♀ as he sold out 15-20,000 seater stadiums all over the US.

> ## THE ARTIST WAS PLAYING A FULL-LENGTH CONCERT AND THEN A 1-3 HOUR AFTER-SHOW PERFORMANCE IN A PACKED CLUB ON NEARLY EVERY NIGHT OF THE TOUR

His visionary business approach to records and now to touring made him one of the highest grossing mainstream artists in the world. The venues sold out quickly from city to city with many reaching capacities within hours of going on sale. This is even more remarkable considering he had been out of the mainstream spotlight for some time. The tour also raised a huge amount for charity, with many venues even opening clothes banks requesting people bring unwanted clothing to the concerts to donate. The tour played a staggering 65 full concerts in the US alone, making it his largest tour of the States since the *Purple Rain* tour.

It was during this period when 'The Artist', as he was now known, started a friendship with Larry Graham, who would go on to be a key figure in his life. Larry Graham was a practicing Jehovah's Witness and it wasn't long before 'The Artist' himself was influenced by him and his religious beliefs. Larry Graham's *Graham Central Station* opened for The Artist throughout the rest of the tour and joined the entourage. He played at many after-shows as well and quickly established himself amongst the inner circle.

Larry Graham splits Prince fans down the middle. Many believed that his influence, particularly at a vulnerable time in The Artist's life, when he was still mourning the death of his child, was unwelcome, and changed the direction of the music and his attitude. Later in Prince's career it was widely reported that he was having medical problems and was in a great deal of pain, and that these issues could have been treated quickly and more effectively if he had allowed modern treatment. The religious beliefs he was beginning to be exposed to may have prevented this intervention.

Larry Graham was born in Beaumont in Texas. His parents were both musicians. His career really took off when he started to play bass in the highly successful and influential funk band *Sly and the Family Stone*, and he remained in the band from 1966 to 1972. *Sly and the Family Stone* was a huge influence on Prince when he was younger so it's no surprise he would have been interested in meeting, jamming and playing with Graham. Prince had been playing Sly covers for many years in concert and at after-show gigs as he blended the funk in with his own tunes. Graham is famous for pioneering the art of the slap bass or slap-pop playing; this provides a percussive and rhythmic element in addition to the notes of the bass line. According to Graham, when his mother's band lacked a drummer he used the slap of the thumb to emulate a bass drum and the pop of the index or middle finger as a snare drum. This style became the quintessential cornerstone of modern funk.

The first leg of the tour concluded in mid-1997 and freed The Artist to work on tracks for his next album *New Power Soul*. It also allowed many Paisley Park concerts to take place and more benefit concerts in aid of various charities. The second leg of the *Jam of The Year* tour continued on 13th September 1997 at Buffalo with Larry Graham and his band now opening most of the concerts. His set lasted for around an hour, a long time for a support act when many, if not all, had come to see *The Artist*. Graham was also now guesting on stage on bass during the sets.

The tour continued through October, November and December 1997 with after-show concert performances through to the early hours, now with Larry Graham. In essence The Artist was playing a full-length concert and then a 1-3 hour after-show performance in a packed club on nearly every night of the tour, often finishing at dawn. The *Jam of The Year* tour had been an incredible success.

With the new business structure for touring that The Artist had in place he was taking in around 70% of all concert sales where usually this would be split between agents, managers and promoters. With the new way he was selling albums as well this meant that he was one of the most, if not the most, profitable artists in the world on record and on tour. There were over 105 full length concerts, and nearly as many after-show concerts in total, spanning the charity tour and the *Jam of The Year* tour itself. With the tour completed, he went straight back to the studio at Paisley Park and started work with Larry Graham and Chaka Khan who had both recently signed to NPG Records, as well as finalizing *New Power Soul* and the planned release of *Crystal Ball*.

Crystal Ball started to be shipped through the *1800 New Funk* website in January 1998 to fans who had pre-ordered the set. The pre-ordering went as far back as May 1997, indicating he wanted to hit a certain level of orders before distribution, or more likely a certain level of 'return' before distribution. Some fans did vent a great deal of frustration as the release date was moved several times over the period. It was the first time The Artist had truly gone direct to his fans with such a large body of work. It's easy to look at this in current day terms and think of it as just an album release but for January 1998 this was a ground-breaking, rare and a new approach in the music business. Again, it meant The Artist took nearly all the profits for the distribution.

> ## NEW POWER SOUL IS A TIGHT RECORD AND FEELS FULLY FOCUSED. IT'S FILLED WITH HIGH ENERGY FUNK WORKOUTS AND FEELS LIKE AN ADVERT FOR A LIVE SHOW.

It was also groundbreaking in its sheer size and volume: there were 5 discs in the set for those that pre-ordered it. There were 3 discs of *Crystal Ball* spanning 30 tracks, mainly unreleased material from 1985-1986 and 1993-1996. On the back of the recently released *Emancipation*, which had 36 songs over 3 discs, he now released a 5-disc album, a clear statement to a record company that wanted to slow down releases that this was how you could do it. He was proving that you could in fact release album after album, disc after disc, and still be hugely profitable.

The original *Crystal Ball* album had in the main found its way into many variations and outtakes which many collectors now owned in one form or another. It's not accidental then to find that The Artist would revive the title track and then simply call this vast collection of vault material by the same name. There was some criticism over the content of the album. As impressive as the vast amount of material is, many felt that an opportunity had been missed with the selection, and the album itself suffers from being inconsistent and jumping around from track to track without any real cohesion. It sold around 100 thousand copies and made its way onto the *Billboard* charts and, as before, The Artist's return from the album would have been vast.

Those who pre-ordered *Crystal Ball* also received *The Truth*, and *Kamasutra*, a bonus, or 'personal gift'. *Crystal Ball* can be viewed as a swipe at bootleggers and a warning that he was in control and had ownership of his own creations.

Understandably after such a marathon tour The Artist stayed

mainly at Paisley Park for the first few months of 1998, working on a variety of projects. He also opened the doors to many concerts on site and jammed with the NPG until the early hours. Around this time Larry Graham relocated to Minneapolis and moved into a property not far from the studios. He became a large influence in decisions of *The Artist* and spent a lot of time preaching the Bible. Soon after this *The Artist* announced he was joining the religion; he stopped swearing on records and also decided to stop celebrating events like birthdays and Christmas.

For many this was a major change and a big surprise; many felt that Graham's influence was unwanted and came at a particular vulnerable time in *The Artist*'s life not soon after the death of his son. He started attending interviews with Graham alongside him and also started thanking him during awards speeches, such as when he was honored at the Essence awards on 11th April 1998. Many fans felt that he was being heavily influenced and it was changing his character. Many forums had little or no time for Larry Graham and saw his constant presence as annoying.

The Artist released *New Power Soul* on 30 June 1998. The album is credited to The New Power Generation, but be under no illusions: this is an album by *The Artist*. It was marketed as an NPG album but it had *The Artist*'s photograph clear as day on the front cover. It seemed he was covering all aspects of all angles: yes it was him but HE was the NPG. More confusion for the neutral. It had only been four months since the huge quadruple-disc package of *Crystal Ball*, which followed the triple album *Emancipation* - 8 discs released over the past year or so. What would Warners have thought about that?

What is clear was that he was releasing more music than ever and making more money than he had ever done because of his restructuring of his business model for releases and touring. His vision had worked. However, his distribution and marketing could be a problem, if those who flooded to see him were unaware, or unable, to get the latest releases and keep up with the frantic pace. It was one advantage of a major global label that was hard to beat.

New Power Soul is a tight record and feels fully focused. It's filled with high energy funk workouts and feels like an advert for a live show. Indeed, this is referenced on the record when Doug E Fresh claims it's *'Coming at you live'*. It also features classy seductive ballads and plenty of the usual sound effects and pre-programmed techniques paced to entertain. It also has an order that fits in with a concert and has audience singing added to the tracks to give a live feel. What's interesting, or deliberate, is that nothing stands out and makes itself known. All the songs, as well crafted and energetic as they are, all blend and marinade together as one singular piece. This makes it feel more of a one-piece advert, or an invite, to a live show. It's the closest he ever made to a live album without being a live album.

'New Power Soul' was a phrase that had been coined many times in the past. It was heard on *Lovesexy* as far back as 1988 on *'Alphabet Street'* as well as 1989's *'Batdance'* with the repeated chant of *'Power, Soul'*. There were samples of the chant on Carmen Electra's debut album, written by Prince, and it's also on the 1992 song *'Love 2 the 9's'* from the ♀ album. A few years back in 1995 The New Power Generation's second album, *Exodus*, contained a mostly instrumental track with the same title. It was a phrase very familiar

to fans and followers, and it was clearly aimed at advertising the fact that this album was *New Power Soul* and what it actually stood for.

BMG was the chosen distributor due to the friendship at the time with the label's then owner Clive Davis. *The Artist* also made it available for purchase through his website 1800newfunk.com and clearly found this method of distribution more favorable. Through this site he made available a 3-disc slipcase set under the name *NewPowerPak*. The set included Chaka Khan's *'Come 2 My House'* and Larry Graham's *'GCS2000'*. *The Artist* clearly wanted to showcase his two new main collaborators, who he was proud to be working with at the time.

New Power Soul was recorded while on the *Jam of the Year* tour from May 1997 to the start of 1998. *New Power Soul* was made to be a fun record, a party record - the fans enjoyed it and it played perfectly to the live sound he had at the time. To celebrate the release *The Artist* spent time in New York and held a release party.

Many celebrities were in attendance including The Spice Girls, Chris Rock and Stevie Wonder. There was also an appearance on *Good Morning America* on July 1st 1998 as well as many other interviews over the next few weeks. *The Artist* again was accompanied by Larry Graham on many occasions and talked openly about the music business and his affairs. He seemed happy to talk about his new freedom and the fact he made a much higher percentage as a free agent than ever before. It was interesting to hear him talk about the money he was making and referencing this.

> HE HAD CONTINUED TO WRITE AND RECORD THROUGH THE NIGHT STACKING UP HUNDREDS OF SONGS THAT WERE STORED AWAY IN THE GROWING VAULT AT PAISLEY PARK

To some it gave the impression he was a little too focused on his own personal wealth, but others felt he was simply explaining that as a completely free artist the benefits are highly rewarding financially, spiritually and musically.

He was loving the freedom to control what he was doing and he was enjoying the fact that it was working out just as he predicted it would. Of course it wouldn't be possible for every musician: you needed an incredible work ethic and a talent to release songs continuously and perform, and you needed good business acumen to control your affairs. *The Artist* was the first high profile star to have all these things in place and he was happy to showcase that it could be done and be very lucrative.

Mayte was at this time less frequently around in *The Artist's* day to day life. Larry Graham was more involved in daily conversations and often held Bible studies and talks. His influence was clearly strong. Around this time *The Artist's* charity website *'love4oneanother'* announced that he had purchased a mansion in

Spain for Mayte. She moved over there and set up permanently, and it was reported that as a couple they were spending more time apart.

A few days later *The Artist* held a concert at Paisley Park and announced it would be his last show for a while. Larry Graham came onstage at around 1am and the show was finished around 4.30am. The final song played was a cover of Shania Twain's *'You're Still the One'*. Although *The Artist* had stated that the show at Paisley Park would be his last for a while, his activity through his websites and of course in the studio would not slow down. On 21 July 1998 *'The War'* was made available through the *'love4oneanother'* website. If evidence was needed that religious and deeply meaningful conversations had taken place, and a religious influence was in force, then this release was it.

'The War' is a dark 26-minute song with mainly spoken words and chants. There is a repeated chant of *'The revolution will be colorized'* which is a phrase referencing Gil Scott-Heron's *'The Revolution will not be Televised'* from 1970. The music is downbeat, subdued and slow with a scattering of embellishments added here and there over the chanting. The spoken words reference a threat by computers, putting microchips in your neck and a need to escape from the modern world to an underground paradise.

Although *The Artist* had been constantly on the road and had not really stopped performing for most nights over the past year, he had not toured Europe since he had left Warners and become an independent artist. In addition, he had continued to write and record through the night stacking up hundreds of songs that were stored away in the growing vault at Paisley Park of unreleased and unused material. With this in mind he decided the time was right and planned a short concert run as well as the usual after-show club concerts.

Beforehand, though, he flew to Marbella and met up with his wife Mayte. They had become increasingly estranged since the loss of their child and now with Mayte moving to Spain and *The Artist* continuing to immerse himself in touring and recording the strain in the marriage was showing. They spent time together at Mayte's new mansion in Marbella before *The Artist* began final rehearsals with the band.

When they were first married Mayte was part of the NPG, on stage with him for nearly every concert and after-show performance as well as working on her own projects. Now, after the tragedy which had struck them both, she clearly wanted to take time and assess her life. Moving to Spain allowed this to happen.

❖

For The Artist his life was music, it always was and always would be: he would not and could not stop. If Mayte, or anyone else for that matter, wasn't going to be with him on the road then they would inevitably get left behind.

It looked like the marriage would be suffering this fate as the European tour kicked off at Plaza De Toros Marbella, Spain on 8th August 1998.

CHAPTER FIFTEEN

NEW POWER SOUL

The *New Power Soul* tour of Europe was essentially a continuation of the US tour as it only had a two-month break. On paper this is slightly misleading as *The Artist* continued to play clubs and other venues like Paisley Park as and when he decided to. Nine concerts were played around Europe starting in Marbella on 8th August 1998.

The shows were spontaneous with no two the same, with a few songs added in for one-off appearances. Most of the *'Prince'* concert favorites were kept in each show with other songs changed around. A piano sit-down section was also different most nights. Considering that *The Artist* hadn't toured Europe for a while the audience reaction to the shows were incredible. He was still a huge live draw and had such a reputation that despite everything going on with his battle for ownership he was simply a must-see if he was touring.

The pace of the shows was that of a skilled veteran: he instinctively knew when to take it to full party and when to slow it down again. He also showcased the band heavily, stopping proceedings to allow the other band members to solo. On some nights he even cut songs off halfway through if he was feeling something different and would cue in another song. The band, well drilled, would fall straight into the change.

Many covers were played but the few that seemed to remain were Sly and the Family Stone's *'Thank You (Fallettinme Be Mice Elf Agin)'*, *'Everyday People'* and *'I Want to Take You Higher'*; naturally Larry Graham was prominent through these numbers, with *The Artist* on guitar. The piano sit down section usually came in after around 80 minutes. It was an impressive section and in complete contrast to the fully rounded funk party that was the show for the first hour. Mostly ballads were played here including staples such as *'Diamonds and Pearls'*, *'The Beautiful Ones'*, *'Darling Nikki'* and *'Nothing Compares To U'*. As it was him alone at the piano this section was always different and he played along to the reaction of the crowd. The concert usually ended with a medley of *'Take Me With U'* and *'Raspberry Beret.'*

As the tour continued around Europe the usual after-show concerts followed the main shows. This meant that typically *The Artist* would enter the concert stage at around 8.30pm and then proceed full on until around 5am the next morning, as he had done for the past 15-20 years. It's a completely unique and mesmerizing lifestyle when you consider that around this he was writing, recording and handling all his business affairs. *'The War'* was a favorite during these early morning shows with The Artist getting the audience to chant the main chorus of *'The revolution will be colorized'* and speaking about the war 'within yourself'.

During the London stage of the tour, on 26th August 1998, The Artist played at Wembley Arena before an after-show at Hippodrome in the centre of London. The after-show concert kicked off at around 2.30am and finished at nearly 5am.

Incredibly after this he performed the same day, within 4 hours, at a 2-hour guestlisted show at Café de Paris London with many celebrities and fan club winners. 200 of those winners were attributed to *The Truth* fan magazine. The show featured again Sly songs with Larry Graham, and Chaka Khan performed her own set accompanied by The Artist on guitar. The Artist's solo set, lasting about an hour, was sandwiched in the middle of Larry Graham and Chaka Khan.

As the tour moved away from Europe and back to the States Chaka Khan released her own album *Come 2 My House* through NPG Records. The album was released on 29th September 1998 and is the ninth studio album she released, her first on NPG Records. *Come 2 My House* was Khan's first full-length album since 1992's *The Woman I Am*, which was due to Warner Bros postponing and eventually cancelling the release of her tenth album *Dare You to Love Me* from 1995. The Artist was involved in 10 of the 13 tracks on the album, with most of them penned especially for it as opposed to being taken from the vault. Alongside The Artist other members of the NPG added music to the record including vocalist Marva King, keyboardist Kirk Johnson, bassist Rhonda Smith and drummer Michael Bland.

The Artist and Chaka began working on the album after she had signed to NPG, with the album sessions beginning back in November 1997, the songs and collaboration taking shape during the *Jam of the Year* tour. It was Chaka Khan's first full album for six years and so was met with enthusiasm when released. She worked hard promoting the album and toured continuously in support of it alongside The Artist, the NPG and solo.

As more shows and club dates continued through September and October 1998, Channel 4 in the UK broadcast an entire six hours dedicated to *The Artist*. The program started at 11.45pm and continued through to 5.50am. It showed the *Beautiful Strange* film, a mixture of music videos and live performances and the Mel B interview from Paisley Park. It also showed an acoustic video of The Artist performing *'Beautiful Strange'* while singing at the console. This was a rare treat for fans as it was well known that during his recordings he always performed vocals alone while sitting at the console desk. To have clear footage of this was indeed a rare glimpse into this extraordinary artist's everyday technique in the studio.

> MANY FANS COULD NOT UNDERSTAND WHY HE WOULD OBJECT TO SUCH A POSITIVE PUBLICATION SUPPORTING EVERYTHING HE DID.

Interestingly, at the start of November 1998 Warners issued a promo single of *'1999'* to US radio stations. The year 1999 was only a month away and what better promotional song than *'1999'* to see in the new year celebrations. It was then re-released in several countries, making it a huge hit. *The Artist* was very upset with the release but was unable to stop it as he had no control at this time over the master recordings. He vented his frustrations immediately through the *Love4oneanother* website, stating that the bulk of the profits would be going to Warner Bros. His reaction was to go head to head and record it afresh. He would be competing against his old self. Entitled *'1999 The New Master'*, he planned to re-record the song and several other versions of it for release as soon as possible. It would eventually be released in February 1999 with no less than seven updated versions that included guest appearances by Larry Graham, Chaka Khan, Rosie Gaines and Doug E. Fresh.

The Artist would hold a 1000-seater launch party for this release at MGM Grands Studios in Las Vegas with special performances and a mini concert to celebrate the launch. Although live, this was a spectacular show. It's fair to say however that on disc these updated versions are in no way comparable to the original.

The Artist flew to Europe again at the start of December 1998 for six scheduled concerts in Spain and Germany, the first kicking off in Portugal. It was announced before the tour however at a press conference that he was annulling his marriage to Mayte Garcia in a bid to rid himself completely of all contractual obligations. Although at this stage there was still a pretense that they were still a couple it was evident that they were living completely separate lives and they had both moved on. Four after-show performances were showcased in packed clubs in Lisbon, Utrecht and Cologne on 27th and 28th December with the final concert in Ghent, Belgium. After the final Ghent concert which wrapped up the *Jam of the Year* and *New Power Soul* tour a private celebration party was held just for the band members. *The Artist* flew back to the US alone the next day.

To obtain even more control over his work in February 1999 *The Artist* filed lawsuits against fan based websites and publications. This was met with a large amount of negativity and criticism from those fans who loved this source of information. They were baffled by this action, and many thought he was going after the very people who had stood by him and supported him through his much-publicized fight for freedom from his record label. He filed against the *Interactive Experience* which was a UK publication, *Uptown* magazine and a newsletter site called *The Prince Family*. He claimed they were all were either offering bootlegged recordings or unauthorized downloads of songs and photography. All were closed down. *Uptown* magazine however, which was based in Sweden, did defend itself against the lawsuit. Fans were most shocked over this particular lawsuit. This brilliant glossy publication had been a bright and positive source of information on *Prince* for many years, and many fans could not understand why he would object to such a positive publication supporting everything he did.

Around February 25 1999 Paisley Park Enterprises Inc and NPG Records ('the Plaintiffs') filed the lawsuit in a federal court in New York directly against *Uptown*. It was alleging in part unlawful use of the symbol that *The Artist* claimed to be his name. This was in addition to use of unauthorized photographs of Prince/The Artist which he claimed attempted to confuse the pubic into thinking *Uptown* was an official publication sponsored or authorized by the Plaintiffs. The contents of the Plaintiffs' complaint were publicized with the article entitled *'Call the Law'* in *Uptown* #37. In response to the lawsuit *Uptown* filed an answer and a counterclaim against the Plaintiffs. *Uptown* denied all of the allegations that it engaged in unlawful activity and that it was in any manner liable. In its defense the magazine claimed that the Plaintiffs sold copies of *Uptown* at the *Glam Slam* nightclub in Minneapolis, which as we know was owned and operated by Prince and his business agents.

The magazine defended itself with honor and eventually won the case to continue to use images and the symbol for its publications. It did however agree to no longer publish information on bootlegs. *The Artist* defended himself by claiming he was looking at launching his own magazine and therefore did not want any confusion as to what was or was not 'official'.

Despite this negativity, the concert train continued with a return after a five-month absence to concerts at Paisley Park. From April onwards in 1999, he played a total of 15 concerts at Paisley Park in and around his schedule that lasted until the dawn. All the concerts were announced through the *'Love4oneanother'* website which was now the official source of information. He clearly wanted fans to have a one point of access to what he was doing and where he was performing.

His next album *Rave Unto the Joy Fantastic* was now being assembled. It would be a collaborative album featuring many guests outside the normal NPG circle. One such guest was Sheryl Crow who *The Artist* started to work with during this time. He went to see her in concert in New York on 3rd May 1999 and guested with her playing guitar to *'Every Day is a Winding Road'* at her concert in August in Toronto.

A respected musician, Sheryl Crow has received nine *Grammy* Awards and had 32 nominations from the *National Academy of Recording Arts and Sciences*. She began her career in the mid-1980s and toured with Michael Jackson as a backing vocalist during his

Bad world tour from 1987–89. She often performed a duet with him during the tour on *'I Just Can't Stop Loving You'* with the pretense that the two were a couple, an idea designed by Jackson and embellished as they sang. She went on to record background vocals for a number of established artists such as Stevie Wonder, Belinda Carlisle and Don Henley, before launching her own solo career and enjoying global recognition as a singer/songwriter covering a wide variety of styles. She started working with *The Artist* in the summer of 1999 on a couple of songs on *Rave Unto the Joy Fantastic*, a cover of her *'Every Day is a Winding Road'* and *'Baby Knows'*. She said after her collaboration that *The Artist* was the most talented person she had ever worked with.

After a trip with Mayte to France to attend the *Versace* fashion awards *The Artist* attended the *Internet Life* awards in New York hosted by Yahoo!. He won an award for *'The War'* for the best Internet only single. He said during his acceptance speech that it was good to use a computer, but don't let the computer use you. At the awards also were *Public Enemy* who were full of praise for *The Artist*. Chuck D said that he allowed him to call him Prince, it was just the 'shysters' call him that. He praised him for writing 'slave' on his face and clearly the two had a huge mutual respect. Prince would later work on and off with Chuck D and referenced him in the title track of *Musicology* in 2004.

Just when things were going well and The Artist was getting established in his own right Warner Bros released a 'Prince' album, *The Vault… Old Friends 4 Sale*. It was initially delivered to Warners alongside *Chaos and Disorder* as a way of quickly giving them albums to free him from his obligations. Warners however decided that they would release *Chaos and Disorder* and hold back on *The Vault… Old Friends 4 Sale* until there was nothing on the market from him. This was a short window, so they acted quickly.

> # THE VAULT… IS OBVIOUSLY AN ALBUM OF OUTTAKES AND VAULT MATERIAL THAT HE HAD NO USE FOR.

Released on 24th August 1999 the album is a collection of vault leftovers and is clearly, on the first listen, an album delivered to be freed from contractual obligations. Most of the public were now aware of this as well. Critics were quick to condemn the album, especially those who did not fully understand the history and concept behind it. What they criticized it for was exactly what it was supposed to be. The album notes state that the tracks comprised of songs from between 1985 to 1994 although if you were to examine this more closely a lot of the dates are incorrect. Its artwork looks amateurish and alongside the inaccurate notes it's clear this is an album of complete leftovers for Warners to play with and attempt to market.

They did just that and marketed it as a Prince album with a statement saying it was a *'Noteworthy Musical Event'*. It has no cohesive element to it and is obviously an album of outtakes and vault material that he had no use for.

In reaction to the release of *The Vault… Old Friends 4 Sale* The Artist immediately started to ramp up the promotional campaign towards his new album - which was now nearly complete - *Rave Unto the Joy Fantastic*. As far as he was concerned, the sooner he could release this album, which was completely new music, the better. He gave more interviews in the promotion of *Rave* than at any time before. He spoke of Clive Davis and his admiration for him for allowing the album through Arista and emphasized many times that they had an 'agreement' as opposed to a contract. He also stated that he was delighted that Davis had agreed for him to own his masters.

The album however brought one main question from those interviewing him. Although the album would be attributed to ♀ or *The Artist*, it would be produced by Prince. This led many to ask how this process would work. He would usually answer this by quickly stating that Prince knew a hit and was a good editor; he then also said he wasn't schizophrenic. This did hint towards the fact that maybe he was coming around to the idea of using his birth name again at some point soon.

A listening party was held on 16th December 1999, hosted by Clive Davis in Manhattan, New York. Davis gave a speech stating how thrilled he was to be working with *The Artist* and explained how they came to meet, and their meetings in relation to the album. *Rave Unto the Joy Fantastic* was released on 9 November 1999. It was on The Artist's NPG Records in association with Arista/BMG, and it became his first major release since *Emancipation* in 1997. Now he had an agreement in place with Arista he enjoyed a non-contractual agreement, ownership of masters and worldwide distribution on a major release.

'The Greatest Romance' was scheduled as the first single, possibly due to the fact it was a huge favorite for Clive Davis. The song fared very well on the Hot R&B and Hip-Hop charts, where it peaked at 23, and lasted for a total of 20 weeks. It charted significantly around the rest of the world and in Europe, now that the label was able to push these territories. There were 8 different versions including a radio edit, the album version, an *'Adam & Eve'* mix and other remixes. In the US the CD single included the radio edit and a Jason Nevins remix of the track, plus a ten-second *'Call Out Research Hook'*. In Spain the CD single only contained the radio edit of the song.

Fully committed to promoting *Rave* The Artist took part in countless interviews and talked openly about the album and his battle with Warners. For an artist who actively avoided this kind of thing it was refreshing to see him talk so openly and answer questions on a variety of subjects. One such open interview was with *Larry King* on CNN on 10th December 1999 when he talked about a wide variety of subjects regarding his music and his life.

The album was quickly certified gold by the *Recording Industry Association of America* or R.I.A.A. The title track itself dates back to 1988 and was another abandoned project that was started but never really completed. The song surfaced as a chant on the *Batman* EP later in 1989, proving that he still was playing around with the song in some form or another. The cover caused some controversy, showing The Artist wearing a blue jacket made out of faux wool instead of actual fur. Prince described his decision with a statement on the album sleeve itself: 'If this jacket were real wool, it would have taken seven lambs whose lives would have begun like this... Within weeks of their birth, their ears would have been hole-punched, their tails chopped off and the males would have been castrated while fully conscious'. One organization was delighted that The Artist had spoken out against animal cruelty - *The People for the Ethical Treatment of Animals*, which is a non-profit organization campaigning for the humane treatment of animals, said that *'Prince deserves a lifetime achievement award based on his empathy for animals alone.'*

Towards the end of December to further promote the album The Artist held a television special from Paisley Park. *Rave Un2 the Year 2000* was a pay-per-view special which would be broadcast on New Year's Eve. The show was actually recorded over two nights, the first on December 17th when *The Time* performed at Paisley Park on the soundstage. *The Artist* joined them after 20 minutes on their greatest hits set. The next night, on the 18th December, was the full concert performance for the broadcast. Fans started lining up outside from the afternoon in temperatures that hit minus 15c. The concert kicked off at 11.45pm and blasted through until 4am. It featured guest appearances from Rosie Gaines, Morris Day, Maceo Parker, and Lenny Kravitz who played two of his recent hits, *'American Woman'* and *'Fly Away'*. In addition to the pay-per-view event, the DVD which went on sale of the concert featured a short documentary including interviews with the band members.

On the same day as the broadcast,, December 31 1999, the publishing contract with Warner/Chappell expired and *The Artist* issued a statement. He explained that the name he was given since birth, *'Prince'*, was now fully emancipated from all long-term restrictive documents. This was for him the last piece in the jigsaw to be completely free. During a pre-written speech, he explained that he would now go back to using his name instead of the symbol he adopted, or *The Artist* as he was recently called in print and in person. He explained that, as he had adopted it as a means to be free from undesirable relationships, this was no longer valid and he would now be *Prince* again. From here on in this book will call him Prince.

There isn't a musician in history that had such a journey as Prince had in this past decade. From the end of 1989 through to this point, at the end of 1999, the decade had seen a massive public battle that involved ownership, control, and artistic freedom. Many pop and radio listeners thought that he had simply vanished in the mid 1990s, and didn't re-emerge until around 2004. This of course is highly inaccurate. Ten years earlier, in 1989/1990, Prince was riding on the wave of the *Batman* soundtrack and was heading to Europe for another record breaking tour. He was arguably the biggest and most respected star in the world, and had been for many years. His albums had shown a complete one-man musical genius, and others could only watch in complete fascination as his live shows and performances were unmatched. The next year was the same until eventually he could take no more and set about dismantling himself in front of the world.

He was convinced, beyond any doubt, that this was the only way he was ever going to obtain artistic control over his recordings and releases. George Michael's struggle had many parallels, but the major difference was that Prince never stopped performing night after night, in club after club, playing songs written in the day to

perform through to the early hours. He jammed and performed endlessly, surviving on little or sleep. He was insisting that no matter what restraints he felt were held against him, he was, when performing, completely free, free to jam and free to play whatever he wanted. It made no difference to him if there were 90,000 people in the crowd or 90, it was a performance that needed to be performed and it consumed him completely, the signs of a true genius. It was almost as if he had no control over what was flowing through him. And of course, during this turmoil the song he wrote and recorded seven years earlier was the biggest anthem at the end of the decade - the song every party played, every DJ played. *'1999'* was a party for everyone, but ironically not so much for the man who wrote it. That was the past and he wasn't quite ready to reclaim it as it was, to embrace it back. That would come in a few years' time. For now, it was about the new and what could be written today, to perform tomorrow.

This decade also saw turmoil in his personal life when shortly after he had married he suffered the tragic loss of his baby. The full triple album *Emancipation* was dedicated to this new chapter in his life, *Marriage, Monogamy, Parenting, and Love*. The tragedy hit right before the celebration of the album was about to be launched. Many believe he never really addressed it and never truly got over it. Towards the end of the decade the marriage ultimately suffered. He had taken his name and killed it: he claimed *Prince* was dead and toured constantly as a 'no name' member of the *New Power Generation*, eventually settling on The Artist. His output and albums never stopped and he strived constantly to find new ways and loopholes in a rigid structure to release his albums. He had ultimately succeeded - he was financially richer and now, more importantly, he had the artistic control. He now had the opportunity to be Prince again and, as 1999 came to a close, he was completely free.

He next began work on a new website that would increase the interaction between his work and his audience. He wanted a membership scheme that would allow his true fans access to his concerts and his music. He basically formed his own early version of *iTunes*. *iTunes* itself wasn't fully formed in 2000: it would be a year later, on January 9th 2001, that *iTunes* 1.0 was released at Macworld San Francisco. Prince's early vision again was ahead of the game; of course it wasn't the platform we have today but this approach was groundbreaking as home computers began to be more accessible. And of course, his early attempts were not without issues. Many fans were often left short changed or had to wait months for material they had paid for. Prince had in 1994 launched *Interactive*, the interactive video game and song, and this was the next phase; he clearly felt this was the direction music was going in. Chart positions were getting less important and ultimately becoming ever more fragmented.

⬗◆⬖

Record companies handing out contracts to new bands and artists were still battling to keep the original model; Prince however, as the new millennium came around, was as futuristic and as groundbreaking as ever.

CHAPTER SIXTEEN

TWO THOUSAND ZERO ZERO

As the new millennium was celebrated Prince, now Prince once more, began more concerts at Paisley Park. **At many of these he took time out from the performance and expressed his opinions on matters such as dates, times and birthdays. He questioned these a lot during this period, a direct influence many felt from Larry Graham.**

The shows were mainly advertised through his website and performed in the usual fashion of starting around 1am and going through until around 4am. It again is quite astonishing the level of commitment to performing that he had. It made no difference if there was 2000 people in front of the Paisley Park soundstage or whether there were just 100, the performance was the same, a full on energetic display with blistering guitar solos as before. He played full concerts night after night, had a few hours' sleep in the morning, conducted his business affairs and returned to the studio. Essentially, he stayed here for most of 2000 before embarking on the *'Hit n Run tour'* at the end of the year, starting in November. As usual the music didn't stop and he was busy constructing his next album, *The Rainbow Children*.

Looking to evolve and stay ahead of the game Prince closed his *love4oneanother.com* website on January 1st 2000 and replaced it with a simple lyric video for *'One Song'*. This video remained on the *love4oneanother.com* website for the remainder of its existence while Prince put plans in place to launch a new website that would be more dedicated to himself and the NPG instead of the charity.

The video itself was released for download as part of the new *NPGonline* website, which would replace *love4oneanother.com*. *NPGonline* would later become the *NPG Music Club*. *'One song'* includes an introductory monologue lasting for over five minutes. It was kept specifically online and no audio version of the track was ever released. One possible explanation was that as a 'lyric video' Prince wanted his words to be noted and understood. This would make sense in the context of the deep meaningful lyrics.

While specific recording dates are not known, the initial recording is believed to have taken place in late 1999 at Paisley Park. It is not known if the song was intended for any project beyond introducing the new millennium. 'One Song' is a dark sermon type of speech

and reflects the deep discussions and study that Prince was going through at the time. *The Rainbow Children*, which was now in the making, would follow this deep thought process. Prince had always been an artist in search of the art within whatever he was doing, his talent so great that containing it was always an issue for him. With such talent it would be easy to become bored and unchallenged, so he loved the deep discussions testing his thought processes and thinking. These discussions naturally would become inspiration for his songs.

Prince wanted to give a message to the world at the dawn of 2000 about life, God, time and mankind's destiny. Prince from here onwards was an intriguing mix of opposing views. Whereas in the past there was a mix of religion and sex, which many thought were opposing but to Prince were all the same ride, now there was a larger mix of contrasting subjects. On the one hand his concerts were a mass party, a celebration of life and music and God, pure party and pure fun. On the other hand, we have anger at the music business and contracts. And there is science and religion, two subjects which have always clashed. All these subjects are shifting, clashing and rumbling away in all his work for the best part of the next decade.

He wanted the new site, *NPGonline*, to show a kind of futuristic utopia, a place where people could be actively involved and share their opinions and express their views. This was a transition phase for Prince, looking at a new way of communicating with his audience, or *'NPG Members'* as they would soon be known, and also a new way to conduct business, whether that be music, merchandise or concert tickets. It was essentially the start of what would become the highly successful *NPG Music Club*.

The first advertisement on the new site showcased the *'Newfunk Sampling Series'*. This was originally intended for sale through his retail outlet *1800newfunk.com*. Prince held a party at Paisley Park to celebrate the release on 16 September 2000 but shortly afterwards he had a change of heart and the actual release never materialized; the set was cancelled suddenly and without explanation. The *'Newfunk Sampling Series'* was intended to showcase an incredible seven discs containing a combined total of '700 audio samples' from previously recorded Prince songs; these included some of his biggest hits of the 1980s.

The tracks comprised of samples of bass, beats, voice, keyboards, loops, percussion, sound effects, and orchestral sounds that could be used. The set was a business strategy that Prince was looking into, and was a way for him to gain control, through 'payment', of his work. The set was intended for purchase by DJs and record producers for a one-off fee of $700. This meant that once it was purchased they could, without risk, use these as they wanted to.

THE GOAL WAS TO MAKE SOMETHING THAT WOULD DELIVER ALL THE CONTENT IN ONE PLACE AND HAVE IT AS A ONE-STOP FOR ALL THINGS PRINCE MUSIC-RELATED

Prince was looking at a way for people to use his music legally: he wanted to give them permission but he wanted payment for it. For the record business again this was ground-breaking. Prince was looking at a simple way, through the new technology of the Internet, to give full access to his past work within a legitimate transaction that he could approve. According to the official announcement once purchased they would be free *'of reprisal, copyright prosecution or additional royalties'*. It would give the purchaser legal use of his samples in their music. The sampling series did not comprise of any full-length songs or new material and was a clear attempt to gain control of a music industry that was increasingly using samples and other people's music, in particular in rap and hip-hop. What was also ground-breaking about *NPGOnlineLTD.com* was that it was Prince's first website to offer downloadable music and, given the infancy of the Internet at the turn of the millennium, this was a truly pioneering website. It was launched on 4th March 2000.

Starting on the 7th November 2000 and running until 9th December 2000 the first leg on his tour solely in the US was dubbed *'Hit & Run'*. It was designed to celebrate and capitalize on his return and, more importantly, the return of 'Prince' as his name. The show was as energetic as ever; gone was the extended jamming that had been prevalent over the past few years and in were the straight hits that Prince was famous for. The band as ever were well drilled for all eventualities, changing at the signals Prince gave them through the show, extremely tight but possessing the loose feeling that Prince always brought to shows. The slow set was complemented by talented jazz musician Najee on the tenor sax. Najee was also spotlighted later in the show as Prince gave him room to solo.

With another highly lucrative and successful tour coming to an end and his new revolutionary website up and running things were looking good. He had an opportunity to now focus on an album that would get a message across that combined all the elements he had been thinking about over the past year or so. The fans may have expected, in light of this greatest hits tour, to have an album that was full of mainstream pop focused on getting him back to the charts. What they got though was a new album that was his

most experimental for years, a true concept album, the brilliant *The Rainbow Children*.

There is a collection of albums within the vast expanse of the Prince catalog that stand out as a pure showcase of talent. This collection is divided amongst fans and many have personal favorites; however, musically and as a groundbreaking album, the under-the-radar *The Rainbow Children* is a perfect example of a brilliant concept album that encapsulates Prince at his very best, and his sound at this time. Released on 20th November 2001 it was initially released as a download to fan club members of the new *Npgmusicclub.com* a month earlier on 16 October 2001. It would later receive full commercial distribution though the independent label *Redline Entertainment*.

Npgmusicclub.com was launched on February 14, 2001. It evolved from *NPGonline* and would take the Internet and media platform for Prince to another level. Unlike *NPGonline*, which offered downloadable songs that Prince could put up on the site, which was pretty groundbreaking at the time, the new improved *NPGmusicclub* would also take the form of a downloadable player and also act as your download manager as well as media player. The fan would instal the player on their hard drive, and then by joining the NPG Music Club they would their get monthly downloads through the player. Downloads included an hour-long audio show which was essentially an early version of a podcast, and 3 to 4 new Prince songs, often with accompanying videos.

The *NPGmusicclub* would evolve and change and adapt as the technology improved. Once the subscription service for the NPGmusicclub was set up the goal was to make something that would deliver all the content in one place and have it as a one-stop for all things Prince music-related. Again, this was revolutionary for the time. Today we experience music mostly through closed software solutions like *Spotify, Tidal,* and *Apple*. In 2000/2001 there were many technological limitations to get over. This was many years before broadband, so most of Prince's fans were limited with what they could do online. Prince was ahead of the game. The technology wasn't keeping up with him. He was absolutely in the right place, and looking back it was the perfect set up, it just needed everyone to catch up. This was one reason why albums such as *The Rainbow Children* were available for around a month online to members of the club first, before being made available through commercial distribution.

The Rainbow Children was advertised as Prince's most controversial album to date by his press agency and label upon its release, and although this is slightly questionable it is true that it is different in every way to his past albums. The narrative, which is delivered in a slowed down voice that Prince had used in the past, follows his recent conversion to the Jehovah's Witnesses. The story is within the spoken voice and the songs follow the story through to the end of the album. Everything is consistent and it comes together brilliantly. Many albums in the past were chopped up and changed after Prince had delivered them to Warners; even the symbol album, ♀, had a narrative running through it which was chopped and changed so much that the actual dialogue segues made no sense when played from start to finish.

The Rainbow Children didn't suffer this fate. The symbol album has many similarities to *The Rainbow Children*: the segues would feed into the songs and the songs would feed the segues; it was designed to keep the music moving and become a whole piece. This was especially evident in the original version of ♀ that was changed dramatically before release. In addition, *The Dream Factory, Crystal Ball, Camille* and countless others started as ideas for unified concepts only to be slashed and changed beyond recognition. Often in the 1980s these albums simply got blended within others. This time Prince had no such interference and it played out perfectly.

The album praised his newfound faith and is a beacon of light that Prince was feeling at the time. It's clear that within all the recent questioning he had now found the answers. The narrative of the faith on the album slides effortlessly over the silkiest flowing, jazziest backing music he had made to this point.

The Rainbow Children was released through the independent distributor *Redline Entertainment*. Prince again wanted the album to be 'discovered' and therefore it was released with minimal promotion. To his eternal credit he was seeking recognition of his album above the standard industry hype that comes with ridiculous promotional activity in the media. He wanted the focus to be more on the music and less on the sales. It sold an estimated 560,000 copies worldwide, and with the distribution deal Prince had developed coupled with his high return on each sale this would have been very lucrative. He was, though, much more interested in the art and the message of the album and how it would be perceived.

The Rainbow Children was an album that was completely in sync with where Prince was in his life at this time. There was references to a Wise one, His Muse and a Sensual Everafter. Not long after Prince found his own muse and remarried again, this time to Manuela Testolini, who had previously worked on his charity website *love4oneanother.com*.

IT'S CLEAR THAT WITHIN ALL THE RECENT QUESTIONING HE HAD NOW FOUND THE ANSWERS.

The first leg of the *One Nite Alone* tour started on March 1st 2002 in Saginaw Michigan. The shows followed on from the *Rainbow Children* album and were very much jazz inspired. The tour would be followed up with the release of the *One Nite Alone* album. The album was simply piano and voice, and Prince initially released it on the *npgmusicclub.com* website. It would eventually be released and repackaged as the boxset *One Nite Alone... Live*. This would be the first ever album Prince had released that would feature new material but not have any 'official' commercial release. He clearly had enough of a following on his new website to be happy with the numbers, and of course it was going directly to his audience, the people that mattered. Because of the non-commercial nature of the release it was ineligible to chart; the charts in 2002 didn't yet recognize these types of sale. *One Nite Alone...* was recorded at Paisley Park during the same sessions as *The Rainbow Children*.

The album includes the cover of Joni Mitchell's *'A Case of You'*, a Prince favorite used as far back as 1983. Also included on the album was *'U're Gonna C Me'* which was rereleased and changed somewhat later in 2009. To coincide with the release of the *One Nite Alone* disc Prince played many concerts with an extended piano section. The album features just John Blackwell on drums and Prince playing everything else. *One Nite Alone...Live* was also in support of this tour and featured the live shows in the US; eight shows combined made up the discs, and a third disc was made up from the usual series of Prince after-show performances. It's a great audio representation of an incredible run of shows and many critics felt that this tour was one of his best, and a career highpoint.

The shows were an incredible success considering that *The Rainbow Children* was virtually under the radar as far as mainstream charts go. One perk of joining the *NPG Music Club* was that fans were permitted to attend soundchecks, and were also given the opportunity to ask him questions and meet the band. Naturally this tour was for this reason a huge favorite amongst fans. And as ever when Prince was on stage with the band you got a full-on performance, and the soundchecks were themselves small concerts so fans, being so close and intimate, felt like they had won the lottery. This tour was also perceived as a benchmark tour for Prince: it was intimate and casual and it had a creative diversity. This is one of the reasons why Prince decided to make it his first ever live album. Once the tour hit North America it began a series of concerts held at Paisley Park Studios, entitled *'Xenophobia Celebration'*. Fans paid $250 to be able to attend all the shows throughout the week of 21 to 28 June 2002.

There was a planned 7-disc set of live recordings from the *Xenophobia Celebration* in June 2002 which never got released. Just before this a live version of *The Rainbow Children* Track *1+1+1 Is 3*, was released for download on the NPG Music Club on 13 July 2002. On this release Prince added a spoken overdub at the end saying *'Xenophobia - Coming soon 2 a monitor near U'*. This gave many members to believe that there followed a possible digital release of the celebration concerts. Cryptically Prince announced on the site that the album was scheduled for release after bootleg recordings of all seven shows were becoming available.

C- NOTE WAS IN THIS WAY A FANTASTIC GIFT IF YOU WERE ONE OF THE FANS ATTENDING THESE MINI CONCERTS

The cryptic message that Prince put on the site finished with – *'YES! The new 7 CD box set of XENOPHOBIA! But wait... u already bought this set from a bootlegger. How do u feel?'* There was a mix up however, and Prince requested that his publicist clarify that details of the set were not final. A post on the NPG Music Club followed, stating that the launch story was a 'misinterpretation', but more likely it was an error that was mistakenly describing the *One Nite Alone... Live* boxset which was publicly released later in the year. It is not clear which of the songs would have been included on the album, although given that the *One Nite Alone... Live* boxset was compiled around the same time it seems likely that, other than perhaps the title track *'Xenophobia'*, there may not have been much overlap in the tracks included.

'Xenophobia' was a concert favorite for Prince as the tour progressed, a mainly jazz based instrumental where he had fun playing the part at the start, requesting fans take off their shoes, complaining that some of them look like terrorists and making the point that everyone is equal and should not be judged by appearance. The video he released for the song showed people being searched at an airport before being allowed through. It's clearly a response to 9/11 and Prince highlighting the increase in security after the event. He would often introduce the song by telling the crowd *'Don't get it twisted'.*

Although this tour is based around *The Rainbow Children* it saw Prince visiting his huge back catalogue but performing the older songs in a totally fresh and original way. In essence, he was kind of privatizing his audience by constantly selling the *NPGmusicclub* and its benefits. Those at the front of the concerts were the members of the club and primarily Prince was playing to them. The rest of the crowd further back were told to join the club to be able to reap the benefits. He had created his own world and he was in total control of it; a radio free world where the only music you needed was his. Those who witnessed these concerts agreed. The first leg of the tour concluded in Portland on April 30th 2002. The second leg toured Canada, and this also included the 7 concerts at Paisley Park for the *'Xenophobia Celebration'*, from 21st June to the 28th of June. On the 23rd of June Prince played two concerts back

to back to meet demand. Once the Canada section of the tour was completed the third leg focused on Europe with 20 concerts, kicking off in the UK with three nights at Hammersmith and two in Manchester. The final leg of the tour visited Japan for 10 concerts. A total of 71 shows were performed for the *One Nite Alone* tour (including *Xenophobia*) from March to November 2002. Many after-shows were also performed.

As usual the tour was an incredible success. He was now capturing his fan base and locking them in more than any time in his career. What fans maybe were not expecting however though was the level of experimenting he was willing to do. His next album *Xpectation* was in danger of really alienating him for the first time. Many were split on the album: for some it was too far down the road of artistry. Fans thought he was starting to produce inaccessible and unattractive music. The titles all begin with X. *'Xenophobia'* itself was removed from the album as it had been released as a live version on *One Nite Alone… Live*.

> # WHAT FANS WERE NOT USED TO WAS THAT THESE EXPERIMENTAL ALBUMS WERE NOW BECOMING THE OFFICIAL RELEASES

Xpectation was actually recorded in 2001 but held back until now for release. Prince clearly thought the time was right in 2003 now his following had amassed. *Xpectation* is a pure instrumental jazz album and shows Prince, who had jazz running through his work for many years, finally giving in and producing a pure album in the genre. Being completely free from all contracts was giving him scope to open his musical wings and experiment to his heart's content. *Xpectation* also had a guest on the album, the classical violinist Vanessa Mae. This gave the album a completely different feel. Prince was looking to bring in a classical influence and he wanted that fusion of jazz and classical.

This kind of arrangement in the past would have been passed to Clare Fischer but as the album was free flowing and with everyone in the same studio, it was all one spontaneous mix. The band that played on the album were credited as Prince, John Blackwell, Rhonda Smith, Candy Dulfer and Vanessa Mae. Also credited on the album as a player was *'Silence' 'as itself'*.

'Xenophobia' was the main hook song for the album and would have served as the showcase piece, especially as his band had it so tight on tour. Once it was removed however the album was somehow stripped of identity, especially as the song titles are meaningless. In typical Prince fashion, a week later to continue the tag line of *'New Directions in Music'* Prince released *C-Note* through the club.

C-Note was a collection of recordings from performances from the *One Nite Alone* tour. They were recordings made during the pre-concert soundchecks of shows between 25th October to 28th of November 2002, when only members of the NPG Music Club were permitted. In this way it's a fantastic gift if you were one of

the fans attending these mini concerts. It was released as five MP3s and then available individually on 3rd January 2003. It was later made available as a downloadable album a year later on 29th March 2004. This again made it ineligible for chart positioning, not that this mattered to Prince.

The first four tracks are instrumental soundchecks from the tour and simply named after the cities where the performance was recorded. Interestingly the original version of the first track, *'Copenhagen'*, contained a homage to Miles Davis but Prince had a change of heart and it was edited out on the C-Note release. The fifth track was the only officially released recording to this point in time of the fan favorite *'Empty Room'*. This full live brilliant version is worth the CD alone. This version was recorded during the soundcheck ahead of the show at Falconer Salenin in Copenhagen on 25th October 2002. *'Empty Room'* dates as far back as 1985. The remaining tracks were recorded in Japan, Nagoya on 29th November, Osaka on the 28th November and Tokyo on the 18th November. Together the first letter of each of the five tracks spell *C-Note, Copenhagen, Nagoya, Osaka, Tokyo and Empty Room*. This was also the nickname for the US $100 bill which was also the amount for a lifetime subscription to the *NPG Music Club*.

Prince released his first live CD in December 2002 based on the previous *One Nite Alone* tour. The collection was spanned across different nights of the tour: March 11th 2002 Indianapolis at the Murat Theatre, March 29th–30th 2002 Washington DC at the Warner Theatre, April 6th Lakeland at the Lakeland Centre and the Youkey Theatre, April 9th New York at Avery Fisher Hall, April 14th Houston at the Verizon Theatre, April 19th–20th Los Angeles at Kodak Theatre, April 24th Oakland at the Paramount Theatre, April 29th Seattle at the Paramount Theatre and April 30th 2002 at the Portland Arlene Schnitzer Concert Hall.

Fans were split over the direction Prince was heading in at this point. Some felt he had lost his way and some were loving the experimental music. Many critics reported that the *One Nite Alone* tour was one of his best. After this high he then released *Xpectation* and now *C-Note*, leaving some wondering what the next album would be and indeed what it would sound like. Prince had always done experimental albums, but in the past these were slotted in and around his commercial releases, *Madhouse* being one such example.

What fans were not used to was that these experimental albums were now becoming the official releases, even though they were coming through his own website. Some now wanted another commercial album, something that they could at least play in the car or through headphones when out and about, something that might be played on the radio or simply something to dance or sing along to.

❖

Unfortunately, they would have to wait. His experimental phase continued. If you loved this side of Prince then you wouldn't be disappointed in his next album; however, if you craved for something commercial, Prince was about to bring some more bad N.E.W.S.

CHAPTER SEVENTEEN

TRUE FUNK SOLDIERS

Fans wanting a return to a 'standard' Prince album would have to be patient as Prince released his next offering through the NPGmusicclub. He now released a full-on jazz-funk instrumental which was recorded in a single day on 6th February 2003. The band for this album session were Prince playing guitars, keyboards and percussion, Eric Leeds on tenor and baritone saxophone, John Blackwell on drums, Renato Neto on piano and synthesizers and Rhonda Smith playing electric and acoustic bass.

N.E.W.S, as in North, East, West and South, was written as his '27th studio album', although this is far short when you consider the amount of recording he had completed to this point. Released on the website on May 26th, and of course by *NPG Records, N.E.W.S.* contains just four tracks, each at 14 minutes. As before Prince kept the album exclusive for *NPGmusicclub* members for two months before releasing it commercially on July 29. It can be seen as a modern take on the *Madhouse* albums, with Eric Leeds taking the lead alongside a small number of NPG members for a live jam session. It's easy to look at the last three Prince albums in hindsight. A year forward from now Prince was back at the top of the charts with his worldwide hit album *Musicology*. The masses that purchased this album would have undoubtedly been reminded that Prince was still around. *Musicology* and the record breaking tour that followed was so huge that many thought he hadn't really done anything for years. It was seen as the old cliché media word: a 'comeback'.

Fans were concerned that *N.E.W.S.* was an album too far, another step inwards, another album that was isolating him. As always with the direct approach he had, and the percentages he would have made, this would not have mattered too much to him at the time. These albums were not designed for charts or for the mainstream, they were an artist doing what he wanted to do and pursuing his own direction without any outside interference. Charts were starting to become fragmented anyway - at the time of writing a 'main chart' is virtually non-existent. *N.E.W.S* became a big hit on the newly created *Billboard Internet Sales Chart*, and it even achieved a Grammy nomination for the *Best Pop Instrumental Album* at the 46th Grammy Awards, an award ceremony where Prince was due to make an appearance. Before this though Prince went on another world tour, which would be a small rehearsal and warm up run for his forthcoming large-scale plan for *Musicology*. It was performed over the winter of 2003 and was essentially a greatest hits tour and not in promotion of any album.

The tour started in Hong Kong at The Hong Kong Harbour Fest before moving to Australia for five shows. What was different on this tour was Prince's ability to showcase the hits in a different way. He looked relaxed and in control, and the balance was right between an established artist playing the crowd favorites and a new performer taking the stage by storm. Those outside his inner circle of fans were now made aware once more that he was still around, and was someone who has everything you want from a rock/pop star when they hit the stage. Gone was the inward-looking artist, gone was the perceived strange behavior on stage, preaching and sermonizing to the crowd, gone were the heavy cover versions. Prince was now playing Prince, and not in a way that felt like he was impersonating himself from before. For the first time in years, he was looking like a true iconic artist that was accessible. From this year onwards, he would fall into a legendary status: an icon, a must-see. After Hong Kong and Australia, the tour visited Hawaii. Prince was photographed on this stretch of the tour for the book *Prince in Hawaii: An Intimate Portrait of an Artist*. This also featured an accompanying CD taken from a recording of one of these shows, although the book and CD were not released until 2004.

The 46th *Annual Grammy Awards* were held on February 8th 2004 at the Staples Centre in Los Angeles. The awards opened with Prince walking downstairs centre stage dressed immaculately as ever and playing a short section of *Purple Rain* before being joined by Beyoncé. The performance then launched into a cross medley of Prince and Beyoncé hits. Prince had rehearsed with Beyoncé the week before for a short time each day, as opposed to one long rehearsal. He also went through several chords on the piano and was interested in her knowledge of musical scales as he crafted and choreographed the performance. This performance now catapulted him straight into the minds of music lovers everywhere: in short, they were suddenly reminded of him. He looked and sounded like a musician and performer at the peak of their powers. He could dance, play anything and could sing, but more importantly he looked like he was having fun. He had a massive back catalog of hits ready to go, and they wouldn't have long to wait.

HIS THREE-MINUTE GUITAR SOLO IS A PRINCE MILESTONE AND A YOUTUBE CLASSIC; IT SHOWS IN CONTEXT HIS OWN METICULOUS STUDIO CRAFT.

Not content however with the impending return to the mainstream with *Musicology*, Prince had a couple of albums to launch through the NPGmusicclub, *The Slaughterhouse* and *The Chocolate Invasion*. Both albums were released on 29th March 2004. They were originally released in 2001 and 2002 as separate downloadable MP3s available on the *NPGmusicclub*. Prince had wanted to release all the songs from the music club as part of a complete 7-CD set; however only *The Slaughterhouse* and the first volume, *The Chocolate Invasion*, materialized. There were issues with the production of the remaining five CDs and Prince encountered manufacturing difficulties.

The Slaughterhouse itself is not counted in many discography listings but it is in fact a compilation of studio songs that were released and therefore it should stand as an album in its own right. It's interesting to look at these two albums as they were written during the phase when Prince was releasing mainly instrumental albums, and so they show he was, during this period, still recording songs with some spark and Princely quality. *The Slaughterhouse* itself can be seen as a compilation rather than a collection of songs conceived for a particular album, therefore it's diverse and varied. *The Chocolate Invasion* disc had songs written and recorded between 1999 and 2001. Only the song *'The Dance'* was later re-worked and released on the album *3121*.

The month after the Grammy Awards performance, in March 2004, Prince was inducted into the *Rock and Roll Hall of Fame* in his first year of eligibility. The award was presented to him by Alicia Keys along with Big Boi and André 3000 of *OutKast*. The performance became a legendary one for Prince; as well as performing a trio of his own hits during the ceremony he also participated in a tribute to fellow inductee George Harrison. He performed Harrison's *'While My Guitar Gently Weeps'*. It was an all-star band which featured Tom Petty and two other members of the *Heartbreakers*, as well as Jeff Lynne, Steve Winwood, and George's son Dhani Harrison. Prince would play rhythm for most of the song and stood in the dark at the side of the stage, only coming in for the end solo - but when he did it became one of his most memorable solos. It's on a par with his performance at Montreux in 2009, which was a show of guitar masterclass. He completely stole the show, to the surprise of everyone in the crowd, including the band themselves who had no idea what he was going to do.

His three-minute guitar solo is a Prince milestone and a *YouTube* classic; it shows in context his own meticulous studio craft. Prince at this performance was the lead guitarist and he was given free range to roam. Famously at the end of the song he threw his guitar in the air; it reportedly never came back down and when you watch the footage it does appear to not come back to earth at all. For Prince however this was just another performance; he left immediately after the show and returned to the studio.

Musicology wasn't just an album, it was an album and tour combined as one whole package, another first for Prince as he looked at innovative ways of giving the public direct access to his music. Prince decided that the album would be given as part of the ticket price for the concert, therefore the *Musicology* tour was promoted by the album and the *Musicology* album helped promote the tour. Naturally this played havoc with the chart system as everyone who bought a ticket for 90 shows across the USA - 40-50 thousand people at each show - also in effect purchased an album. Everyone who attended the concert was handed an album on entry. There were 400,000 copies of *Musicology* handed out to every concert attendee and these counted towards the sales of the CD. The album also received a retail release and sold initially 100,000 copies, flying in to the charts at number 3, aided by its free distribution at the concerts. Prince had again messed up the system and so triggered a change in Billboard's rules, which now bar freely distributed music from their charts.

The *Musicology* album itself was released on the 20th April 2004 with the tour kicking off on 27th March at Reno in Nevada. The band continued from the warm up tour of Australia and Hawaii with John Blackwell on drums, Mike Scott on rhythm guitar, Renato Neto on keyboards, Rhonda Smith remaining on bass and the horn section of Greg Boyer, Maceo Parker, Candy Dulfer and Mike Phillips. The tour was performed with the stage in the centre and the crowd around the outside, very similar to the *Lovesexy* tour. This time however the stage was an X-shape and, as the album name suggests, it was designed to showcase musicianship over and above everything else. Prince was keen to show that real music and more to the point 'real musicians' were leading the way.

Musicology shot up the charts all over the world and, bolstered by the tour, became one of the biggest selling albums of 2004, quickly achieving double platinum status. It is not in any way as artful or as deep musically and lyrically as *The Rainbow Children*, and isn't comparable in any way. Prince now was in a different place: he had a new sound again and a new tour showcasing his talents and that of his band.

HE WAS AGAIN SITTING AT THE TOP OF THE WORLD AT THE END OF 2004.

The album and the brilliant tour were hugely profitable for Prince. The tour itself earned 87.4 million dollars and was attended by 1.47 million fans, one of the highest grossing for many years. Although the tour promoted *Musicology* only a select few tracks from the album were played during the concerts: *'Musicology'* itself, *'Call My Name'* and *'Cinnamon Girl'*. The rest of the sets were made up of Prince classics with the band and musicianship in abundance; it was one of the greatest shows he had done so far. Prince was at ease with his back catalog once again. He wasn't angry with it, he wasn't upset that the crowd instantly sprang to life on the opening bars of a past classic - he openly embraced it, he enjoyed it and he was loving it as much as the delighted crowds.

He was nominated as the greatest frontman of all time in a 2014 poll and *Rolling Stone* magazine named him as the highest-earning musician in the world, with an annual income of $56.5 million, which was largely due to the *Musicology* tour. *Pollstar* named it as the top concert draw among musicians in the US. The 96 concerts which were eventually played, as more were added because of demand, had an average ticket price for each show of $61. Remarkably he even played nearly 20 after-show concerts during the tour. The album went on to receive two Grammy wins for Best Male R&B Vocal Performance for *'Call My Name'* and Best Traditional R&B Vocal Performance for the title track.

Prince had achieved an astonishing return in 2004: he had defied all the odds as his career was considered by some, especially in the mainstream media, to be in decline. *The Musicology2004ever* tour sold more tickets than any other US tour that year. He had reinvented himself from an underground artist performing and releasing songs to his own captive audience to a global star again all over the world, and in a matter of a few months. As always with Prince though the hunger to be that global superstar was just as powerful as his hunger to perform for himself and his hardcore fans. He was again sitting at the top of the world at the end of 2004.

After the return to the charts and the success of his record breaking tour, Prince retreated and set up camp in Los Angeles. The next phase of his career was mainly spent with a new protégé named Tamar. He was first made aware of Tamar in 1994 when he heard a demo from her. She studied music business at the University of Southern California. Hungry for success, she auditioned in the fourth season of *American Idol* but she did not make the cut. While living in Los Angeles, she managed to get an invite to one of Prince's house parties and introduced herself to him. He remembered her and her past demo and asked her to audition for him on the spot, which she did.

She then went on to add vocals to a video Prince was working on at the time. Prince still maintained the operation of sticking to short term record deals that both parties could walk away from at any time. He this time signed a deal with Universal in December 2005. Tamar signed with them the same day, meaning that he could work with her and look at the possibility of a joint collaboration that he could mentor.

Social commentary has always been an important part of Prince's work. Like any talented songwriter the world around him offered much inspiration. In August 2005, Hurricane Katrina hit New Orleans, devastating the city. The images of the people of New Orleans and the resulting devastation was shown for weeks in the US and all around the world. Prince wrote the song *'SST'* directly after the hurricane and made it available as a digital download through the *NPGmusicclub* on September 3rd 2005. It reached number one on the *iTunes* R&B chart. Shortly after hitting the number 1 spot, Prince made it available as a CD single through commercial outlets. All proceeds from the recording went to hurricane relief. The title nods to Sade's 1985 song *'The Sweetest Taboo'*: Prince namechecks the song and Sade in the song itself, *Sade's Sweetest Taboo, 'SST'*. As usual with Prince there are double meanings within the songs: SST also refers to *Sea Surface Temperature*, which is used to monitor the threat of hurricanes.

Prince was now in the middle of his new album *3121* and started promoting it. At the start of 2006, Tamar toured with Prince while he made appearances promoting his new record. She appeared with him on *Saturday Night Live* on February 4, 2006, *Good Morning America*, the *Brit Awards*, and on the video for the song *'Fury'* from the album. She appeared alongside two other female dancers named *'The Twinz'* who became part of the Prince show during this period.

Twin sisters Maya and Nandy McClean, renamed *'The Twinz'*, joined Prince in November 2005 primarily as dancers and backing singers for Tamar. They would eventually outlast Tamar and continue as backing singers and dancers with Prince when he hit Las Vegas for his residency later in 2006.

> WHAT FANS FOUND BAFFLING HOWEVER WAS THAT AFTER HE HAD RECEIVED THIS AWARD FOR HIS 'VISIONARY USE OF THE INTERNET TO DISTRIBUTE MUSIC AND CONNECT WITH FANS' HE THEN CLOSED HIS WEBSITE COMPLETELY.

In March 2006 Prince supported Tamar and put together a backing band for a brief tour in support of her album. During this tour Prince played as the guitarist in the band and stood on the sidelines, only moving to the front for guitar solos. Set to be Tamar's debut album *Milk & Honey* was originally to be titled *Beautiful, Loved and Blessed*, but was later renamed after one of the other tracks. *'Beautiful, Loved and Blessed'* later appeared on Prince's own album *3121*. There were several dates rumored after this tour for a release but eventually the album was cancelled. Tamar's next album *My Name Is Tamar* was released in March 2011.

Another award was bestowed on Prince in June 2006 in recognition of pioneering Internet work for music. *The Webby Awards* honored those who shaped the Internet with their groundbreaking work, recognizing their influence and lasting impact on digital culture, communication and technology. Prince was given at the ceremony *The Webby Lifetime Achievement Award*. The speech went on to say that Prince had forever altered the landscape of online musical distribution as the first major artist to release an entire album – 1997's *Crystal Ball* – exclusively on the Web. Prince's leadership online has transformed the entertainment industry and reshaped the relationship between artist and fan. Long before *Myspace* and *iTunes*, Prince used the Web to premiere videos and new music, challenge distribution practices, and connect with his fans through his groundbreaking site *NPGmusicclub*. The 10th annual awards ceremony held in New York on June 13, 2006 gave Prince an opportunity to say something when accepting his award. Prince was among dozens of winners in categories from Blog to Retail who in turn took to the stage and gave lengthy self-absorbed speeches. When Prince hit the stage to receive his award he was greeted with a standing ovation. He said one line: *'Everything you think is true'* before he performed an acoustic performance of *'Don't Play Me'*.

What fans found baffling however was that after he had received this award for his *visionary use of the Internet to distribute music and connect with fans* he then closed his website completely. All fan members who had paid lifetime subscriptions were no longer members. It just closed overnight and was no more. Whether Prince, after receiving this accolade, was satisfied that he had accomplished all he could from the *NPGmusicclub* is unclear. The NPGmusicclub had gone through several changes and updates over the years, including the *'Musicology Download Store'* which was made available in 2003. It then had an upgrade in 2004 which gave it a glossier, high-tech feel.

The main element was a mixing console on a mixing board which showcased each Prince album on a different fader. In 2006 the Download Store was added which had a type of studio rack system again making it visually impressive. At the time of the Webby Award the *NPGmusicclub* was flying and sales were very strong. With videos and singles Prince had the only artist-owned music distribution hub at the time and he had just received one of the biggest accolades for his pioneering work and distribution to his fans. He then seemed to have gone home and pulled the plug out.

All was not entirely lost however as a new site was now emerging. Shortly after Prince closed down the *NPGmusicclub* in the summer of 2006, he started using a new site, *3121.com*. This eventually grew and became his new official website. The closing of the *NPGmusicclub* was a big blow to fans, as it had been a constant source of music and updates since its inception. He left a closing message to subscribers and with that the *NPGmusicclub* closed completely, and Prince moved on.

> ## PRINCE STROLLED ONTO THE STAGE WITH THE TWINZ COMPLETELY UNANNOUNCED, AND IT TOOK A WHILE BEFORE THE AUDIENCE ACTUALLY REALIZED IT WAS HIM.

The title of the new album was discussed amongst fans; many forums discussed what the number represented. Some thought it was a reference to the address of the house Prince was renting at the time of his residency, a mansion owned by NBA player Carlos Boozer, who reportedly filed a lawsuit against Prince for changing the property. However, this had an entirely different address, 1235 Sierra Alta Way, not 3121 Sierra Alta Way.

Prince has repeatedly referred to the property though as *'3121'* and the lawsuit which Boozer filed against him alleges he painted *'3121'* on the exterior of the property. The inner notes also indicate that the album was recorded at Paisley Park Studios and *'3121'*. Another more accurate explanation is within the Bible. A particular verse, Psalm 31:21, states: *'Blessed be Jehovah, God/Yahweh. For he has rendered wonderful loving-kindness to me in a city under stress.'* Another simpler reason could be that it was Prince's 31st release with a release date on the 21st. Or maybe, as it's Prince, it's a combination of all those three explanations.

To promote the forthcoming album Prince gave a performance of *'Fury'* on February 4th 2006 on *Saturday Night Live*. It had been over 24 years since Prince had last played on SNL and *'Fury'* had not been heard anywhere before this performance. Prince's guitar work was incredible, as he performed with his new look band with The Twinz and Tamar flanking him, dancing tightly to the grooves that Prince was shredding. Prince had a new look guitar stand that he favored for this period, angled towards him as opposed to a standard straight stand.

Continuing with TV appearances, Prince this time made a very surprising one. On May 24th 2006 he strolled on to the stage on the final of the hit TV show *American Idol*. At the time the singing show was pulling in an estimated 47 million viewers and was huge in the US. Prince, dressed immaculately as usual in a purple suit, strolled onto the stage with The Twinz completely unannounced, and it took a while before the audience actually realized it was him. He wasn't billed to perform and even the presenter Ryan Seacrest seemed surprised when he walked on.

There had been much speculation to who actually would perform at the final of the show, which was by far one of the biggest in the US at the time. The performance took everyone in the building by complete surprise, and by the time the audience had realized it was actually him and were just getting into his performance it was over, he was gone. Reports later said that he walked off the stage and kept going straight into a waiting car and was gone. No interviews, no meeting the contestants to give advice, just in, perform, go.

There were some hints of the performance when, on the eve of the show, news feeds received an email of a photo of Prince with the inscription *First Corinthians 10:14*. The exact text for the biblical passage reads: *'Therefore my brothers, have nothing to do with the worship of idols.'* Many believed that Prince was persuaded to perform in promotion of *3121* by Universal who he signed the deal with for the album. Artists in the past that have appeared on the final of *American Idol* have gained tremendous public exposure from just one performance and seen an instant spike in sales.

For a unique artist such as Prince this kind of show would be the last place you would have expected him to perform on. Any winner of the show would undoubtedly sign a contract which would give away all the artistic freedom that Prince had recently spent years battling for: the kind of contract the winner would sign would be the absolute opposite to what Prince would have advised.

3121 was released on March 2 2006 through NPG Records and Universal. Sessions for the album date back to November 2004 through to early 2006. Prince launched a competition on the release by putting a limited number of 'purple tickets' in with the album. Winners were flown in from Europe, Asia, Mexico and the US to attend a semi-private performance, along with a long list of celebrities, at Prince's home in Los Angeles. *3121* continued the success enjoyed by *Musicology*, in fact it became even bigger and was the first Prince album ever to debut at number 1. It sold over 180 thousand copies in its first week, sadly knocking the soundtrack for *High School Musical* off the top spot. This meant that it became Prince's first number 1 album since 1989's *Batman*. Eventually it was certified gold by the RIAA.

The new movement Prince brought with *3121* was that of 3121 the destination. He decided the time was right for a residency.

Prince opened a nightclub in Las Vegas which he called Club 3121. It was based within The Rio. The residency started in November 2006 and went through until April 2007. The run itself was called *'Club 3121'* for this series of shows. This wasn't really a tour as such - he wasn't traveling around from state to state or from country to country - it was more a package around the *3121* theme. He had the *3121* Album, the *3121* residency and the *3121* website. Within this he had all kinds of *3121* memorabilia. One night on the run Michael Jackson attended and watched the show; Prince spotted him and played a bass solo in front of him.

> ## THE SIX MONTHS PRINCE PLAYED AT CLUB 3121 IN LAS VEGAS FOR THE RESIDENCY MADE AN INDELIBLE IMPRESSION.
> ## IT WAS VOTED ONE OF THE GREATEST RESIDENCIES EVER IN LAS VEGAS

The after-shows would continue at a smaller nightspot next door, renamed *The 3121 Jazz Cuisine*. The six months Prince played at club *3121* in Las Vegas for the residency made an indelible impression. It was voted one of the greatest residencies ever in Las Vegas with many confirming that he was the greatest artist of his generation. The only complaint during his stay at The Rio was that he didn't stay long enough.

Once the contract expired with the Rio Suites on the 23rd June 2007 Prince then moved the club to a temporary venue at the *Hollywood Roosevelt Hotel*. Here he played an additional nine shows, which were slightly different and served more as a warm up for the forthcoming *Earth* tour. *3121* became a brand that Prince would use for at least another year and a half during his residencies in Las Vegas and his next planned residency, which would be in London. He also released a fragrance as well as other merchandise that was now being sold through his new website *3121.com*. It was while Prince was performing in Vegas that the site started to grow and develop into his next official site. He started an online newsletter which highlighted all the activity going on during the residency, featuring interviews and photos from the shows themselves.

The main feature on the site as this time however was the ticket information for the residency. This sent the traffic to the site and hooked them in on the show and the overall brand. After the shows were finished, the residency had ended, and the promotion of the *3121* album was complete, the website was then relaunched on Prince's birthday on 7 June in 2007. It then switched its promotional stance to promote his 21-night residency at London's O2. The website came offline in December 2007, and Prince then would have a gap in online presence until 2009.

Prince was again on top of the music world. The album was a massive hit around the globe and his residency for six months in Vegas was both a financial and critical success. In November 2006

Prince flew in to London to be inducted into the UK Music Hall of Fame. He was always huge in the UK and Ireland and the two-way love affair made him one of the biggest selling live draws there whenever he toured. He appeared to collect his award but did not perform. The award however got him thinking of a return to the UK. He started to draw up plans for England for later on the following year.

On the 25th December 2006 James Brown died of heart failure, resulting from complications from pneumonia. He was 73. James Brown was one of the most singular inspirations for Prince and his early sound. If Prince was indeed a blend of all styles of popular music, with an ability to create it at will, then James Brown was the most influential for him. He invented funk in its true form and created the style that many tried to replicate but simply couldn't.

What James Brown added to his songs was simply James Brown: it couldn't be copied or imitated, and without this ingredient it simply wouldn't be the same. Prince was the closest to James Brown in his funk sound and stage performance - the way he moved, danced and felt the music was Brown. But aside from that Prince had Brown's work ethic and inherited Brown's legendary drilling of his bands, rehearsing them for hours on end to perfect them, readying them for any changes the bandleader may make.

Brown's death was a huge loss to music but he lived to a good age and his legacy will always remain. Prince had always had James Brown's music somewhere in his performances, and he now started incorporating more Brown hits into his sets in tribute to *'The Godfather of Soul'*.

The residency in the US had given Prince the idea of taking it somewhere else. The Vegas stay was in a small venue by Prince comparisons, which was why the shows were so spectacular, as they felt more like an after-show than a large-scale concert performance. What if now he could stay at one venue for a residency, but instead of a small club this time have a residency at a large-scale arena? It would mean selling hundreds of thousands of tickets 'repeatedly' over a period of weeks, if not months. And all in one place.

Did he have enough of a fan base to achieve such a venture? Could it possibly happen? Or was Prince just in need of being brought back down to Earth?

CHAPTER EIGHTEEN

EARTH

If 2006 and its achievements were not enough, Prince hit 2007 with one of the most breathtaking and legendary performances he had done so far on mainstream television. On February 2nd 2007 Prince played at the *Super Bowl XLI* press conference. He then performed the *Super Bowl XLI Halftime Show* in Miami Florida two days later on February 4th. The event was watched by an estimated 140 million television viewers. It was ranked as the greatest *Super Bowl* performance ever.

At the press conference on 2nd February 2007, Prince walked on to the stage and asked the crowd of mainly sports journalists, who were not interested in anything musical at all, if they had any questions. The second someone asked a question Prince blasted his Telecaster and performed an incredible set as if he was in a full concert venue in front of 100,000 fans. Many wrote after the event calling it the greatest rock and roll moment of their lives.

If ever you could have choreographed a performance of Prince's most famous song, *'Purple Rain'*, for the biggest audience of his life, then the Super Bowl performance had the 'stageset gods' on hand. The rain poured, sheets of it lashing sideways throughout the performance. Prince was absolutely drenched playing his *Symbol* guitar, on the *Symbol* stage, with the lights, the audience and the world watching. It was the perfect accompaniment to the song. Was it divine intervention or just a storm? Either way it was the perfect dramatic backdrop for Prince's *Super Bowl Halftime* performance.

Prince next planned his residency at the *London O2 Arena*. Initially he planned 16 nights but demand was so high that he went straight for 21 at the 23,000 capacity arena. He purposely kept ticket prices down, each one at just £31.21. The tour residency itself in London was to be called the *Earth* tour. On the 8th May 2007 Prince took to the podium for a press conference and announced that he intended to play 21 nights at the former *Millennium Dome* in Greenwich, which was about to reopen as the *O2 Arena*. The announcement was preceded with a montage of Prince music videos and concert footage of his career to date. It would mean playing to an astonishing estimated total of around 400,000 people in August and September, at one single venue. He had performed in large arenas before over many nights but nothing on this scale.

Prince's next album, *Planet Earth*, was released on 15th July 2007 by NPG Records. It was distributed by Columbia Records in the UK as a free cover mount with The Mail on Sunday national newspaper. This was followed by the album's worldwide distribution. The deal Prince came up with was again something that the record industry had not experienced before. It's fair to say he ruffled a lot of feathers with this one.

Prince came to an agreement with Columbia Records to distribute the record worldwide. Prince had worked with Columbia before on the release of *Musicology* in 2004 so was familiar with the agreement in place. In a twist though, Prince and his management struck a deal with newspaper *The Mail on Sunday* to give *Planet Earth* away free with the July 15th edition. As expected this earned Prince a huge amount of criticism from UK record stores who were already battling against online and other media that was turning people away from physical records. One of the world's biggest stars giving away an album for free was the last thing they needed, especially if this set a precedent for others.

Prince's decision resulted in Columbia refusing to distribute the album in the UK, though its release in the rest of the world remained unaffected. The practice of giving albums away for free was of course not new for Prince. In 2004, again with Columbia as distributor, he gave free copies of *Musicology* to all concert goers during the *Musicology* tour. In addition to the free giveaway with the paper Prince also gave *Planet Earth* away with tickets to his record breaking concerts in London. Everyone that entered the concert was handed a free copy. This resulted in Sony BMG not distributing the album in the UK at all and also made it ineligible to chart.

HMV decided that it would stock the 15th July 2007 edition of *The Mail on Sunday* in lieu of the CD, saying that this was the only way that they could make the album available to their customers. Unfortunately for Prince, on July 10th, with just days to go before the official release through the newspaper, a poor-quality version of the album was leaked. It was reportedly recorded from a stream and was then leaked onto the Internet. This allegedly cost Prince $4.6 million in licensing fees. Prince though would not have to wait too long to get this hit back as the forthcoming 21-show concert run at London's *O2 Arena* reportedly earned him a gross of $23.4 million, and thus an $18.8 million profit. Not bad for 21 days.

Planet Earth has collaborations with quite a few new and old musicians, the new being singer Bria Valente who became the latest Prince protege at this time. It also features the former *NPG* members Marva King, Sonny T, and Michael Bland. Sheila E also makes an appearance as well as Wendy & Lisa. As *Planet Earth* was practically given away, coupled with the fact that it promoted an entire tour, it gained an incredible amount of attention in the media, especially in the UK. On release *The Mail* received its highest sales since the death of Princess Diana. Over 600,000 extra people rushed out to buy the paper proving that whatever criticism he received from the standard record company platforms, the strategy was a success.

Although *Planet Earth* debuted at No. 3 on the *Billboard* Top 200 in the US the sales overall were hampered because of the free giveaway. Prince viewed the album as a pure promotion for his 21-night stand in London rather than the tour supporting the album. He had reversed the standard marketing and promotion approach. He was successful though as the 21 night tour was a complete sell out, and when you add in the additional crowds who flocked to the after-shows at the nightclub inside the O2, *Indigo 2*, he actually played to a staggering 'half a million people' in under seven weeks. All this in one city without having to travel. He had, a few months earlier, played to the biggest TV audience of his career and now he was playing to his biggest live audience.

> # PRINCE HAD NEVER PLAYED HIS HITS LIKE THEY ARE ON RECORD: HE WAS A LIVE PERFORMER WITH A REAL BAND.

The band for the record-breaking residency was Cora Coleman on drums, Morris Hayes and Renato Neto on keyboards, Joshua Dunham on bass guitar, Shelby Johnson and Marva King on backing vocals, Greg Boyer on trombone, Maceo Parker on alto sax, Mike Phillips on saxophone, Lee Hogans on trumpet and the dancers Maya and Nandy McLean, The Twinz.

Prince played for two to three hours on each night, with after-show parties at the *Indigo* Club next door, and true to his word every night was different. The intro remained the same each night, this being the video that inducted him into the *UK Hall of Fame* voiced and narrated by Beyoncé. There was no real set list, just Prince conducting the band through the changes with what looked like pure spontaneity, but which was of course drilled and meticulously rehearsed.

On the opening few nights many newspapers and publications sent journalists and pop stars to see the show and submit a review. All praised his musicianship and showmanship with a few lesser known talents not fully understanding what was going on. One woman who had had a couple of hits wrote that she was frustrated that he didn't play his hits in their entirety, clearly not understanding the length and sheer scale of a 21-night run at a major arena. Prince had never played his hits like they are on record: he was a live performer with a real band. It was clear that this reviewer was so used to a backing track she didn't understand the talent that was in front of her. On the whole though, as usual with Prince, the reviews were incredible with some even saying that it was the greatest concert they had ever seen.

The record breaking run of concerts began on Wednesday 1st August. The stage was the trademark *Symbol* positioned in the centre, with the audience filling up the gaps all around. The large screens were suspended above it in all directions with the main band positioned all around and moving constantly. Prince entered the arena when the lights were dimmed inside a tall black music box. After a few nights, fans came to realize he was inside and tracked the box as it was pushed in. He then entered the base of the *Symbol* to join the band. Entrance to the stage was typical Prince, with dry ice all around and then a platform falling before it slowly came back up and he rose from the base of the Symbol launching into the first song. On this opening night it was *'Purple Rain'*. According to some reports the first night's scheduled running order of songs had been leaked, so Prince purposely changed the entire show at the last minute.

The band were in constant motion filling the Symbol like a musical playground. The main staples of the band, Renato Neto, Morris Hayes and Josh and Cora Dunham, all remained in the centre of the Symbol. Vocalists Marva King, Shelby J with The Twinz kept the crowd partying as they moved around at will with the horn section. It gave a full-on show of musicianship and crowd participation. If Prince was on one side of the Symbol they would venture instantly to the other giving the audience something to watch at all times. This was very important and clearly well drilled with every section of the Symbol covered at all times. As usual with Prince, many thought that the show was over and had left the arena after the standard encore, or had run straight to the internal nightclub with the anticipation that he would be performing another couple of hours; instead, though, a third encore was given with *'Little Red Corvette'*, *'A Love Bizarre'* and *'Le Freak'*. This set the tone for other nights with fans never knowing if it was truly over or not - they had to wonder whether to risk joining the queue for the after-show or wait to see if another encore was in the offing.

The first night's after-show was, as with every night on the tour, rammed to capacity. Entrance to the club was £25 and Prince's website *3121* encouraged fans to come along, but didn't however guarantee that he would be performing every night. It was a full two hours after the main show when the curtains opened revealing the full band, in fact the full band apart from Prince. The band played brilliantly for well over an hour and then, just as the crowd in the club were almost dropping with exhaustion, the man himself walked on stage dressed in a strawberry suit and launched into a guitar solo that almost blew the roof. Many had been in the club for over seven hours by the time Prince casually walked on stage. He ripped through songs by the JB's, The B-52's and Billy Cobham's *'Stratus'*. By the time it ended it was completely light outside. The musically frazzled crowd wandered out into the morning London air having witnessed the first night's experience by this extraordinary performer.

And so the shows continued; night after night through August and September Prince packed the O2 Arena to capacity with fans jetting from all over Europe to be part of the party. Elton John guested on the 13th September during the main show and joined Prince for a version of *'Long & Winding Road'*. He joined the after-show to watch Prince blast on for another two and half hours covering Hendrix, Led Zeppelin and many of his own early hits such as *'Dirty Mind'* and *'Partyup'*.

Naturally fans saw repeated shows during the residency, and one recurring comment was that they seemed to get better as the show went on, Prince omitting songs that he felt were not fully working and replacing them with others. By the time he had performed a few shows he was fine-tuning the pace and had gauged the reactions of the crowd to perfection. The acoustic sections were also varied, as sometimes he would play on the guitar and sometimes at his now infamous pre-programmed piano. The rehearsals were non-stop during the day with the band ready and fine-tuned to keep with the constant changes. With the after-show finishing in the early hours Prince would have a few hours' sleep at his hotel, The Dorchester, and then would return for soundchecks and arrangement of the next night's show.

While at The Dorchester Prince had photography taken which was later released in a glossy book about the residency in London. The book, entitled *21 Nights*, came with a disc containing after-show songs from various nights at the Indigo club entitled *Indigo Nights*. The 256-page book contained poetry and lyrics to new songs and photographs of rehearsal footage as well as staged pictures of Prince in his hotel suite.

The final show of the run at the O2 was on Friday 21 September 2007. The show was this time filmed live on *Sky News* for the first 30 minutes. Everyone in the packed arena had purple glowsticks for the performance and it was a truly magical night, a celebration of the achievement of the past 21 nights. He played again his after-show at the Indigo later in the early hours, and again it was packed to capacity with fans still not knowing if he would perform or not. After an hour or so the music started from behind the curtain and Prince's voice gave the cue - at last the audience knew he was there. The band went into the intro of *'Love is a Losing Game'*, a Prince favorite at the time. As the curtain rose it revealed the composer herself as Amy Winehouse stood front and centre with Prince alongside for a moving version of the song. Prince had been calling for Amy to join him during the stay and she eventually did. Prince, visibly moved by the performance, put his shades on mid song.

Prince was now increasingly getting frustrated with the Internet. He saw the sharing websites and the associated technology as a direct threat to musicians and bands when albums, songs and videos could be shared for free. He instructed his lawyers to start legal action against these sites. On November 5th 2007 several Prince fan sites formed *'Prince Fans United'* to fight back against the legal requests they claimed Prince had made. The claim was to stop all use of photographs, images, lyrics and even album covers. It basically requested that anything linked to Prince's likeness should be taken down and stopped.

He was also looking to sue *YouTube* and *eBay* because he claimed they *'appear to choose not to filter out the unauthorized music and film content, which is core to their business success'*. The claim was that the infringements could be reduced down to zero and then the next day 100 or 500 would be back up again. Prince's lawyers had claimed that the use of such representations constituted copyright infringement, but the newly formed *'Prince Fans United'* fought back and claimed that the legal actions were in fact blatant attempts to stifle all critical commentary about Prince. Prince again turned to music in response and, on November 8th 2007, the site received a song named *'PFUnk'* which gave a 'Prince like response' to the new movement that he felt had been created against him. Later, on November 20th, the song was released on *iTunes*, retitled *'F.U.N.K.'* It's a brilliant song and once again demonstrates the ability of Prince to walk into a studio and create a piece of music, playing all the

instruments and hitting a subject head on. It was sent to the site within two days of it opening, Prince describing it as a *'gift'* in response to the site's criticism of his approach towards his fan websites. The initial recording dates for the song go back to the *Musicology* album around 2003 or early 2004 but Prince re-recorded the track and completely changed the lyrics on 7th November 2007 and sent it to *Prince Fans United*.

The *Coachella Valley Music and Arts Festival*, commonly referred to as *Coachella*, is held annually at the Empire Polo Club in Indio California, located in the Inland Empire's Coachella Valley in the Colorado Desert. It was co-founded by Paul Tollett and Rick Van Santen back in 1999 and is organized by *Goldenvoice* which is a subsidiary of *AEG Live*. As with most festivals it features a wide variety of music from many genres including rock, indie, hip hop and dance music, as well as art and sculptures.

The grounds of the festival are vast and the event has many stages which over the period of the festival keep the music in continuous motion. The main stages are the Coachella Stage, The Outdoor Theatre, The Gobi Tent, The Mojave Tent, and The Sahara Tent where the main acts would be performing. The history of the festival goes back to a 1993 concert that *Pearl Jam* performed at the Empire Polo Club; at the time the band were protesting against *Ticketmaster* and were actively boycotting venues that they controlled. The show then validated the site for large scale events which resulted in the *Coachella* Festival's being held over the course of two days in October 1999. There was no event the following year in 2000 but *Coachella* returned on an annual basis, beginning in April 2001 as a single-day event. In 2002 it returned to a two-day festival. Since then it has been expanded to a third day, which was in 2007, and eventually a second weekend in 2012. At the time of writing it is held on consecutive three-day weekends in April. Ticket holders were eventually permitted to camp on the grounds from 2003. It fast became one of the largest, most famous, and most profitable music festivals in the United States and indeed all over the world.

Every festival season, Prince would inevitably come up on the list of rumored headliners for one of these major festivals. Usually he was never part of the circuit and many wondered if he ever would grace the stage to headline one of these huge events but now, in 2008, he decided it was time. Many reviewed his appearance in 2008 as the greatest headline so far for *Coachella*. On April 26th he headlined the festival and performed for over two hours. He effortlessly mixed covers of other songs into his setlist, playing snippets of *Santana*, *The Beatles* and *The Time*. All were interwoven through his own songs and were so tightly slotted in it was difficult to even spot the changes the band were making on his cues. One cover Prince did play however made the headlines shortly after: a cover of Radiohead's *'Creep'*. This got many headlines for Prince's guitar work during the song, but it soon became clear that another headline was emerging as Prince immediately had this performance taken down from streaming sites, something his lawyers often did around this time as Prince was becoming increasingly protective of where his performances were going, and the quality of what was being shown. This caused a backlash from *Radiohead* themselves who, as it was their song, requested it be left alone.

Eventually Prince gave in and let it stay on sites for all to see. Alongside Prince headlining this year were Roger Waters (whose inflatable onstage pig sadly flew away during his set), Jack Johnson,

Portishead, The Verve, M.I.A., Kraftwerk and Aphex Twin.

The 2008 festival had an attendance of over 151,0000 people and it grossed $13.8 million.

DESPITE THE PRESS SPECULATION, THE COLD TRUTH WAS THAT THERE WOULD BE NO HUGE CONCERT IN DUBLIN FOR THE SUMMER OF 2008.

Prince had planned another major concert event in Ireland for 16th June 2008: over 55,000 tickets had been sold for a concert at *Croke Park* in Dublin. Unfortunately, another situation regarding promoters and money had come to be an issue, very similar to the events of the cancelled Blenheim Palace concert. For the Irish fans, and of course the many thousands that were traveling from all over the world and had paid for hotels and flights, the news of the cancellation just ten days before the concert was met with much anger. The statement read very simply that the concert was cancelled *'due to reasons beyond the control of Prince and promoters MCD Productions'*. Of course, with such a late cancellation the press were hungry for the reasons why. Prince had headlined *Coachella* only a month before without issue, he had played the *Super Bowl*, and 21 nights the year before in London, without any cancellations or problems at all. Despite the press speculation, the cold truth was that there would be no huge concert in Dublin for the summer of 2008.

Naturally an incident like this ends up with lawyers fighting it out behind the scenes. MCD took legal action to recover their alleged losses in 2009, a reported $1.66 million. During the case it emerged Prince was set to be paid an alleged $3 million for the show and the promoters had paid half of that upfront as a deposit. In fact it was alleged that Prince was offered a staggering $22 million for seven concerts through 2008. As expected, Prince did not appear in court but there were some eyebrows raised regarding Prince's relaxed attitude when the negotiations were heading in the wrong direction in the run up to the concert. Despite the legal argument there was no real explanation given for the cancellation. The matter looked like it was going to be eventually settled out of court, but everyone again was back in court a month later for a €2.2 million judgment against Prince.

Allegedly Prince, or more to the point his team, were reluctant to pay, which resulted in MCD taking out a European Enforcement Order. They began legal proceedings in the Los Angeles Superior Court in 2011 to get Prince and his team to comply with the terms of the judgment. It wasn't until May 2011 that Prince finally settled the bill. Shortly after the trial Prince eventually played what would be his final Irish show, at Dublin's *Malahide Castle*. This time though the concert was promoted by John Reynolds and POD Concerts.

Shortly after cancelling the show in Ireland, Prince played another two concerts at his Beverley Hills Residence, this time on June 22nd and June 25th. It's clear that despite the headlines that were surfacing regarding the reason behind the cancellation, he was simply just playing on as usual. He had a team of lawyers who handled such matters, so for Prince it was back to the studio and to the stage: the music, the parties and the performances carried on regardless. His schedule was always free flowing, he never stopped and would travel consistently all over the world performing. Within days of the cancellation he was performing the next scheduled concert and busily planning the next album and website. The two shows he performed in Beverley Hills were now starting to incorporate new songs from his next planned release, in particular a version of the 1968 song *'Crimson & Clover'* written by Tommy James and the Shondells, later made famous again by Joan Jett in 1982. Prince leaned heavily on his guitar work during the track and he incorporated lyrics from The Troggs' *'Wild Thing'* into the song. Another performance at the Beverley Hills residence on September 20th saw him again perform the song.

On September 30th the *21 Night*s book was officially released with the accompanying *Indigo Nights* live CD, containing 14 live songs in total, of which there are eight live versions of previously released Prince songs, four cover songs, two new songs, and a monologue. Prince next flew to New York for two shows at The Rooftop Lounge which were performed on October 10th and 11th. These two shows also featured *'Colonized Mind'*, another new song scheduled for the new album, the name of which was now leaked, to be called *Lotus Flower*. Fans soon got very excited about this next venture as it was rumored through various sites that it would be another large-scale ambitious project similar to *3121* with a website and album all combined together.

At the start on January 2009 Prince started to put together this next project, *Lotus Flower*. It was on January 3rd 2009 that his new website *LotusFlow3r.com* was launched. It was the site now dedicated to all Prince activity from streaming, selling and concert tickets. Towards the end of the month Prince released several songs that would eventually make it on to the album itself, *'Disco Jellyfish'*, *'Another Boy'*, *'Chocolate Box'*, *'Colonized Mind'* and *'All This Love'*. The website was a major launch for Prince and he had high hopes and many aspirations for the site; unfortunately during its brief opening he fell out of love with the Internet and became upset with the digitization of music, which he felt devalued it. Once he was the pioneer of this platform, but during *Lotusflow3r.com* he lost faith in it and turned his back. As a result, the site would only be open for around a year.

The site was made open to subscribers from 24th March 2009, when Prince launched three albums: *LotusFlow3r*, *MPLSound* and an album by his new protégé Bria Valente named *Elixer*. He had been formulating and recording the songs over the past six months. All three were made available for download both in MP3 and WAV formats. Prince was again looking at ways to distribute his albums away from the standard traditional format. This time he made all the physical copies of the 3-album set available in the US exclusively through *Target* stores. At this time the *Target* Corporation was the second-largest discount store retailer in the United States, the first being Walmart. It also incidentally has its headquarters situated in Minneapolis. The set sold for $11.98, which was around the price of a single disc at the time, so to have this price for a three-album set was good value. With the accompanying website now launched the whole package was now up and running and if any fans had not paid the $77 entrance fee to the site they still had the chance to purchase a physical copy from *Target*.

Things didn't start smoothly though and it became clear the site had some issues. The first issue with the website was that once you had paid for the subscription with your $77 you were then required to solve a puzzle. The mystery built up inside but didn't really go much further. Also, a t-shirt was offered but many complained that they never received this. There were, in addition, many promises of other material from the site to the members which never really came. Fans naturally started to vent their frustrations but the website developers argued that Prince was very sporadic in his schedule and wasn't giving them material to put up on the site. Many for this reason headed to *Target* and gave the site a miss, once rumors spread on forums about the lack of content.

This wasn't a good time for Prince with his online community. He had hit the headlines over the past few months in his pursuit of taking on anyone that displayed his image online or used his songs where he didn't want them. He was right in some cases as some were actually illegally sharing his recordings, but Prince's team of lawyers also dragged in many fans and harmless sites and gave the false impression he was going after his own fanbase. A dancing baby on *YouTube* at 29 seconds was one such instance that hit the headlines along with many more.

Prince released the physical CD set of *LotusFlow3r* with its two other albums on the 29th March 2009. He made it only available inside the USA. The album is Prince at his guitar best; it starts with a slow instrumental but soon kicks in with a breathtakingly effortless collection of songs that seem to flow smoothly and confidently through the album with masterful ease. If you're looking for an album of Prince in Hendrix mode then this is the one for you. It's accomplished and heavy in rock and jazz, and runs with many radio friendly tunes; it is both musically and lyrically an album of supreme quality.

Songs such as *'Colonized Mind'* and *'Dreamer'* are Prince at his lyrical and guitar best. The album has a live edge to it, indicating that the songs would be easily added to the huge live arsenal that Prince now had. The album is extremely coherent and uses Prince's array of creative talents, in fact it's one of the most coherent albums he has ever produced. It could be seen as a concept album: it certainly has elements of concept within it both with the strength of the production and the running themes. Musically it comes together perfectly. It feels like an album created in one sitting while all the elements are fresh and musically connected. If you're looking for a theme it's one of pure power, a search for higher knowledge, lust for the world to be a better place. It's about longing, a passionate pursuit for wanting more. It takes you through a concise collection of polished songs before leaving you back where you started with the final instrumental *'...Back to the Lotus'*.

Minneapolis Sound or *MPLSound* was the second CD in the set. It's far more mainstream than *Lotus Flower* and of course it's meant to be. While *Lotus Flower* starts with a jazzy dreamy instrumental that sets you up for the quality that lies ahead, *MPLSound* starts with *'There'll Never Be Another Like Me'*, and instantly it's clear that this disc is going to be different to the last. Prince said of the third disc in the *Lotus Flower* set, *Elixer*, 'We got sick of waiting for *Sade* to make a new album'. Ironically Sade must have heard him because a year later she released *Soldier of Love*, her sixth studio album; it was however released 10 years after her last album *Lovers Rock* so maybe he had a point. As a surprise bonus disc, it sits well and gives some more value to the set. If you want an album that's nice just to chill

to, if indeed that was the intention, then it's quite happy here. If however Bria was trying to release an album of the quality of Sade then it unfortunately falls way short. Sade has this area well and truly covered, every ten years.

Prince did a couple more TV shows in April and May 2009. First, he guested on *The Ellen DeGeneres Show* where he performed a rousing version of *'Crimson and Clover'* and then the following month he appeared on *The Tonight Show* with *'Somewhere Here on Earth'*. It was then back to Paisley Park for recordings and rehearsals for another major show.

On June 25th 2009 Michael Jackson, the self-proclaimed king of pop, died. He was 50 years old. Over the years the press had linked Michael and Prince as bitter rivals bidding for the crown of the best singular performer in the world. Michael was reported heavily in the press as having financial and legal issues prior to his death and, at the end of 2008, he was advised to close his *Neverland* Ranch which he had as collateral for loans, which allegedly ran into tens of millions of dollars. There were also numerous repackaged albums released in the past few years, a clear strategy to gain income. In March 2009, the month when Prince released *Lotus Flower*, Michael held a press conference at London's O2 Arena to announce a series of comeback concerts entitled *'This Is It'*. What Prince had done two years earlier Michael would now do the same.

The concert series would have been Michael's first since 1997 - a full 12 years of not touring since the *HIStory* tour had ended. Michael also said that he would be retiring after the concerts, a common announcement to gain ticket sales. The series of concerts was soon increased from the initial reported 10 nights much in the same way as when Prince had announced 21 Nights; it would have commenced on July 13th 2009 and finished on March 6th 2010. Prince and Michael, despite the press reports, were in fact good friends and watched each other closely, but apart from their level of fame they cannot be compared. Michael was probably the most famous performer that ever lived, his fame outshining his talent. He had long gaps between releases and tours and relied on songwriters and producers for his work, Quincy Jones and Ron Temperton (who actually wrote *Rock with You*, *Off the Wall* and *Thriller*) being examples. This was a world away from Prince and how he musically worked and performed. As with the death of James Brown, Prince immediately added some Jackson songs into his shows, notably *'Don't Stop Till You Get Enough'* as a tribute to Michael.

The album set did very well for Prince and landed at number 2 on the Billboard top 100. It's fair to say that if it hadn't had the exclusivity agreement through *Target* it would have done much better. It also topped many more charts in the increasingly fragmented chart system. It was also an interesting time for Prince as he was now becoming more disappointed with the internet and starting to turn against it. The webmasters were left frustrated with the lack of Prince interaction with them and maybe Prince was feeling frustrated with what was produced.

The once pioneer of this medium, who used it to such effect and successfully steered the music industry towards it, was now starting to turn his back on it completely.

CHAPTER NINETEEN

THE INTERNET IS OVER

It now looked like the latest website, Lotusflow3r.com, the one with a major launch and the promise of so many great things, was in fact on course for closure. Prince was not adding anything substantial to it, and coupled with his recent claims that 'the Internet is over' it looked like a foregone conclusion that he was moving on.

This statement of course was not meant to apply generally, as some reports suggested; he was speaking from his own perspective and from a musical one.

Prince now traveled to Europe for a string of concerts and festival headline performances. The first was two nights headlining the *Montreux Jazz Festival*. Prince headlined on July 18th 2009 and went through probably one of the best guitar led concert performances he had ever done. He closed the *43rd Montreux Jazz Festival* with two stunning free flowing tailored performances that fitted the occasion perfectly. Overall it was an amazing set showcasing a versatility unmatched in the music world; the band were incredible and Prince showed just what an incredible guitar player he was throughout. The Montreux 2009 performance is, as of the time of writing, on most streaming sites, although a lot show certain songs and not the full performance; nevertheless it's well worth watching.

In May 2010 Prince performed another surprise concert at *Bunkers* in Minneapolis before heading to New York. He performed there on May 5th at *Village Underground* and after this performance he headed back to Europe where he was booked to play more festivals. First was the *Roskilde* festival held in Denmark, the first of many that would form part of Prince's next tour. There was a brief tour of the European festival circuit timed in conjunction with the release via newspaper channels of the album *20Ten*. The tour went through two phases over the summer and autumn of 2010.

Prince appeared next at the *BET Awards show* and received 'The Lifetime Achievement Award'. He was dressed in a white suit with his own image on the front; this image would be the cover of his next album *2010* or *20Ten*. *20Ten* was again distributed in unique fashion, away from the standard format. It was released on July 10th on NPG Records but this time Prince negotiated a deal with the UK newspaper *The Daily Mirror*. It was given as a free cover mount with the *Daily Mirror* and *Daily Record* in the UK and Ireland. The album itself did well and the reviews were also positive in the main; many of course had to be, as he was distributing through publications which needed the increase in sales to return on the upfront cost of having the album in the first place. A publication was never going to give a bad review to an album they would be giving away.

Prince now closed the *Lotusflower* website completely. He simply wanted this album to get out there easily and without any fuss; he said simply 'No charts, no internet piracy and no stress'. He even refused to give the album to any digital download platforms.

Although the *Lotusflower* website had held such promise it was clear that something had changed in Prince's mind and he claimed the Internet completely over as far as he was concerned. It's fair to say he had received a fair amount of bad press over the past few months and his battle with his fanbase also added frustrations from his followers. Many were also unhappy with the high price they had paid for the *Lotusflower* website which simply did not deliver on the promises that were made. There was also the battle with *YouTube* which, with the blanket battle to take things down that were not permitted, caught a dancing baby in Prince's purple net. The continuous battle with piracy and lawsuits against those who used his image and songs without permission also demonstrated his growing contempt towards the Internet and the threat he saw for artists and their work. Many were getting tired of this as they felt they were not in any way doing anything wrong, they just wanted his music.

As before, he was of course correct in this early battle; his stance may have looked confrontational but looking at the years ahead he saw the threat coming. It would of course for many artists in the future get worse - they could expect to earn little for their albums, compared to past artists, as more and more albums could easily be shared, and therefore not paid for. Prince was also criticized around this time for not letting others cover his songs. Warners allowed the awful Tom Jones cover of 'Kiss' to be released, but since then Prince had been steadfast on any request that he had power over.

He said of song covers that it was the only art form that frequently allowed this type of thing to happen; he said that he wouldn't be allowed to write his own version of *Harry Potter*, so why should it be any different? Prince used covers frequently in his live sets, but on record there were hardly any, apart from a few exceptions. *20Ten* was in response to all this, and it worked.

On July 4th 2010 Prince began his *20Ten* tour of Europe starting at the Roskilde festival in Denmark. It then moved to Germany, France, Belgium and Austria and, as with most Prince shows, the set was changed almost every time. The tour visited *Super Bock Super Rock* in Portugal before returning to France again. Norway, Denmark and Italy followed with the usual after-show performances throughout. Prince without any break planned the next leg of the tour through America; first, though, he had another award to receive. Prince was inducted into the *Grammy Hall of Fame* on December 7th 2010. Rehearsals and recording then continued at Paisley Park before the next tour commenced

Welcome 2 America, as this section of touring was named, started on December 15th 2010. Prince was in a charitable mood and gave $1 million dollars to the *Harlem Children Zone*, $250,000 to *The Uptown Dance Academy* and another $250,000 to *The American Ballet Theatre* during this leg. Amazingly, smack in the middle of the *Welcome 2 America* tour Prince planned to perform like he did in London; this time he would go for LA and announced another 21-night run, this time at *The Forum*.

> ## AT 52 YEARS OLD, PRINCE WAS OUTPLAYING AND OUTPERFORMING ANYONE ON THE MUSIC CIRCUIT.

Prince started his residency on April 14th 2011 with an amazing 3-hour show. He shouted *'Inglewood is mine'* before starting the first night of the 21 that were scheduled. The show, as before on this tour, was as energetic as ever with each song blending into the next, extended jams giving the band room to showcase their individual talents as Prince cued them in at will. The opening two hours were thrilling and full of showmanship, guitar playing and musical mastery. At 52 years old, Prince was outplaying and outperforming anyone on the music circuit. The concerts were completely sold out and demand was incredible. And of course, there were the after-show performances to attend as well, if you had the energy to keep up with him.

As with the residency in London, the LA residency was an incredible achievement from a musician who could simply perform endlessly night after night. The run finished on May 29th.

A month later Prince headlined the *Festival International de Jazz de Montréal*, or the *Montreal Jazz Festival*, for two nights on June 24th and 25th 2011. The festival holds the Guinness World Record as the world's largest jazz festival and every year it features around 3,000 artists from over 30 countries. It holds more than 650 concerts, with 450 free outdoor performances, and welcomes over 2 million visitors every year. Prince kicked off the three performances with an electric performance of Jimi Hendrix's *'Foxy Lady'*. Luxembourg, Italy, Finland and Holland followed before Prince finally put the previously cancelled concert in Ireland to bed

with a concert in the grounds of Malahide Castle in Dublin. He openly apologized for not performing before, and made amends with a three-hour set.

The tour continued through Europe with concerts in Norway, Germany and three nights in Denmark including an after-show performance that continued until the early hours. Prince's band was changing around this point with more female band members joining him. One who would remain and become a key member was bass player Ida Neilson who would go on to stay with him and be part of the trio *3rd Eye Girl* that Prince would be part of in the years ahead. Prince during this tour was starting to feature Ida more on bass solos and was actively jamming with her during his sets. Prince next travelled to Sweden and Switzerland before moving the tour across to Canada for the *Welcome 2 Canada* run.

The *Welcome 2...* tour was by all accounts a world tour, with Prince now simply changing the name to the country he was visiting. He also changed the show accordingly and worked and rehearsed the band for hours at a time pre-shows to fine tune the changes to suit the venue. It gave Prince the option to stop the tour if he felt the need at any time, but they were so incredibly successful he just kept rolling it on from country to country. The tour had now been going since he announced it back in October 2010 and now having toured America and Europe, including many Festival headlines, he launched it again for Canada. The US tour alone was reported to have made him over $20 million.

Continuing the theme and the process the tour became *Welcome 2 Canada* and marked Prince's first shows in the country for 11 years. Prince next travelled home and spent a few months recording and of course performing regularly at Paisley Park before embarking on the Australia leg of the tour, *Welcome 2 Australia*, commencing in Sydney on May 12th 2012 before heading for Melbourne and then Brisbane. The run of concerts ended at *The Rod Laver Arena* on May 30th before Prince headed back to Chicago for another run of concerts in the city.

On October 23rd 2012 Prince performed live on *The Jimmy Kimmel Show* for a concert. He performed a new song *'Rock n Roll Love Affair'* which would later be released with an updated version on *Hit n Run Vol 2*, before launching into a mini concert with full backing band and horn section. He also performed *'Don't Stop Till You Get Enough'* as he closed the set. Kimmel said afterwards that the new song Prince performed, *'Rock n Roll Love Affair'*, would be available soon through his website. It would be a while though before it actually surfaced. The music video for the song also featured Andy Allo whose own album with Prince was about to be released. *Superconducter* is her second album after 2009's *UnFresh*.

She had been in Prince's touring band previously and they wrote the album together while touring. Prince wrote three of the songs on the album: *'Long Gone'*, *'The Calm'* and the album's title track, *'Superconducter'* which became the lead single and had its own music video. Prince makes reference to the song *'When Stars Collide'* in the lyrics of *'Rock n Roll Love Affair'*. The album debuted at number one on *Amazon.com*'s soul and R&B charts in France, the United Kingdom and the US. As well as Prince the album also features Maceo Parker and Trombone Shorty.

Around this time Prince once again started to venture back online after a long break. It was no secret that he had fallen out of love

PRINCE - THE LIFE, THE GENIUS, THE LEGEND

with the Internet but there was a growing trend for live streaming and this was something Prince was particularly enjoying. It was instant and meant fans could access concerts and short studio sessions at will; it also meant they could not record or reproduce it. Prince had the control. Digital music and streaming were now dominant in the market and the physical CD or record was very much falling behind. It would of course make a comeback later on, particularly in vinyl, but for now this was the new thing and the foremost way to watch and purchase new music.

Prince was looking at streaming but as ever added his own stamp on the technology. His new band were in place and he had the vision that streaming and bypassing the current standard would be the way forward. He developed a new website entitled *20PR1NC3.com*. Like some of his sites before this one would be short-lived.

Again, this was Prince looking for alternatives to the standard set up bypassing the major distribution online platforms that were dominating at the time, namely *iTunes*. The site evolved initially from the lyric video for *'Screwdriver'*, which was the catalyst for the site development. Prince was impressed with this and wanted more of the same to develop. The whole website was created in just four days and was, like his new band, a stripped-down website allowing for instant purchase and streaming of videos and music.

The new band were named *3rd Eye Girl* and were basically an all-girl rock band with Prince at the helm. Drummer Hannah Ford grew up in Louisville Kentucky. She was previously a member in a trio band named *Pandorum*. She was in a relationship with percussionist Joshua Welton at the time of the band forming and would later marry him, changing her name to Hannah Ford-Welton. Guitarist Donna Gratis grew up just outside Toronto and was playing guitar from an early age. She was invited to Paisley Park earlier in November 2012 for auditions and was successful, although 'auditions' are a loose term as this would be extended intensive jamming as Prince felt his way around his new potential set up. Donna proved her place and alongside Hannah Ford and former NPG bass player Ida Neilson, they formed a new backing band with Prince. Prince took them on the road, initially in North America along the West Coast.

> ## HE PUT ON A FULL 3-HOUR COMPLETE CONCERT OF DIFFERENT MATERIAL, AND A DIFFERENT BAND, EVERY NIGHT.

The tour was called *Live Out Loud* and was basically a stripped-down concert. Shortly after the end of this tour Prince announced he had made a deal with *Kobalt Music* to market and distribute his music. *Kobalt Music Group* was founded in 2000 and is an independent rights management and publishing company. It would have been of interest to Prince as it is mainly an administrative publishing company meaning that it doesn't own any copyrights. It developed a successful online structure that could provide royalty income and activity to artists; the artists themselves would manage their own rights and royalties directly.

Prince now created a new website around his new band, which saw the end of the short lived *20PR1NC3.com*. This was an evolution from the previous site and continued Prince's desire to bypass traditional channels and go his own way with the idea of tracks and videos going directly to the public, avoiding *iTunes* to do so. Prince added the new *'Screwdriver'* and the *'3rd Eye Girl'* logo which was drawn up; other tracks and videos were then added. This became the main site as Prince toured with his new all girl band.

With the US tour completed they now headed to Europe and again hit the festival circuit. First though Prince would showcase his incredible genius and unique versatility by performing yet again at *The Montreux Jazz Festival*, followed by festivals in Sweden and Denmark. For now though this section of his European tour was simply entitled the self-explanatory *'3 Shows, 3 Nights'*.

Starting on July 13th 2013, Prince headlined all 3 nights at Montreux with a completely different show every night. He had rehearsed three separate bands at Paisley Park before the Festival and put on a full 3-hour complete concert of different material, and a different band, every night. He had *3rd Eye Girl* with him rocking the Festival, the NPG line up and he had his full horn section crossing over everything.

It was, for those who witnessed all three shows, a truly unique and individual display of pure musical talent that could not be matched. He repeated the process again at *The Stockholm Music and Arts Festival* on August 4th and then performed at *Smukfest* in Denmark, again with 3 completely different shows. A week later he started again with *3rd Eye Girl* for shows in Amsterdam on August 11th and 12th. The final leg in Europe was in Portugal at *Coliseu dos Recreios* in Lisbon on August 17th before Prince and the band headed back to the US.

Also in August 2013 Prince released a new solo single for download through his new *3rdeyegirl.com* website. The single *'Breakfast Can Wait'* had cover art featuring comedian Dave Chappelle's impersonation of Prince from a sketch that was on the show in 2000. It featured on the *Comedy Central* series *Chappelle's Show*. Later Prince made it available on *3rdEyeTunes.com* on November 5th 2013.

The reviews of *Prince and 3rd Eye Girl* live were brilliant; his new band were the perfect accompaniment to him as he showcased his guitar work more than ever before. His new look with the growing Afro gave him that 'Hendrix appearance' and when he blistered through his guitar solos it was the obvious comparison from critics watching. Prince was completely reenergized with the band and it showed in all the performances. He also 'named them', giving them an identity of their own: they were not just a backing band, which was significant. Just three girls, and Prince, rocking the stage around the world.

⬥⬥⬥

His new touring band were becoming more polished live and their reputation was growing. Prince now started writing with them for the band's first, and as it turned out, only album.

CHAPTER TWENTY

BACK TO THE PIANO

Back in the US Prince continued with appearances before launching his next tour, which would be entitled *'Hit n Run'*. These concerts however didn't start officially until February 2014, leaving Prince time to perform at various places in the US. He played for two nights in New York at The Winery on August 23rd and 24th 2013 before spending some time writing and recording back at Paisley.

Shortly afterwards Prince headlined three nights in California at Mohegan with a huge backing band and full horn section. *3rd Eye Girl* also joined him on set and it became a full-blown rock show. Many speculated after the brilliant Mohegan Sun show that Prince would launch a full-scale tour showcasing the expanded band of the *NPG*, his band leader skills, and the pure rock element he enjoyed with *3rd Eye Girl*. For now though it would just be the girls.

In February 2014 after more recordings and rehearsals Prince traveled to the UK with *3rd Eye Girl* for the start of some *Hit n Run* style concerts. *Prince and 3rd Eye Girl* kicked off at The Electric Ballroom in London on February 4th 2014, then played again the following day with two shows on February 5th. Shepherd's Bush Empire followed before Prince and the band played another two shows at Kings Place. They moved again to Koko in London for another two shows before heading to Ronnie Scotts for a final two shows on 18th February.

As announced at *The Brit Awards* and following in the same *Hit n Run* style Prince and his new band played Manchester with two shows at The Manchester Academy on the 21st and 22nd February. The reviews were incredible as Prince and his new rock outfit brought the short run of concerts in the UK to a close. He would be back in the UK in a couple of months as a larger arena tour was planned, but for now Prince and the band headed back to the US where Prince made an appearance on *The Arsenio Hall Show* on March 4th. Sadly this was to be his last talk show appearance. He spoke openly to Arsenio and the audience and of course performed on the show with his extended band. He performed *'Funk n Roll'*, *'She's Always in my Hair'* and *'Mutiny'*.

After *The Arsenio Hall Show* Prince stayed in California for concerts throughout March before planning a return to the UK, to commence in May. He first though returned to Paisley Park with some important business to take care of. In April 2014 Prince went back to to Warner Bros Records after an 18-year absence. This would be a deal that would give him back ownership of his vast back catalog of music. The so called 'classic albums' he released through Warners would still be licensed through Warner Bros but now would be part of a new global agreement. One part of the deal was that *Purple Rain* would be re-released in a remastered deluxe version, to coincide with the 30th anniversary of the album and movie. There would be other planned re-issue projects and Prince would also produce a new album as part of the deal.

The deal was made because of the ability to terminate master recording copyright after 35 years: this was in the Copyright Revision Act of 1976, which became effective in 1978, which was the year of Prince's debut album, *For You*. When 2013 came around on the music calendar many record labels, artists and managers were unsure as to how copyright terminations and ownership reversions would play out. They were waiting basically for a court case to set a precedent. There was a grey area as works created under work-for-hire contracts were not eligible for copyright reversion.

Privately though some label executives thought that it might be better to negotiate the reversions; this way they retain control of issuing artists' catalogs that would be eligible for such copyright terminations. Again, Prince negotiated a landmark deal. He decided to remain with the label, the one that he was in constant battle with all those years before, because it would ultimately avoid any risky and costly legal battle that could lie ahead. It also allowed him to regain ownership of his catalog.

The actual financial terms and length of the licensing deal were not disclosed; also, Warners' announcement did not make clear whether Prince would be gaining ownership of his back catalog all at once or in stages. It was likely though that it would be in stages, as each album became eligible for copyright termination after the 35 years. The Warner Music Group declined to provide further comment on the details of the deal but they did issue a statement: *'Everyone at Warner Bros Records is delighted to be working with Prince once again: he is one of the world's biggest stars and a truly unique talent. We are also very excited about the release of new and re-mastered music from one of his greatest masterpieces.'*

New deal in place, *Prince and 3rd Eye Girl* started the arena tour of

Europe beginning in the UK at the LG Arena in Birmingham on May 15th 2014. 12 shows were scheduled all over the UK and Europe. Entitled *Hit n Run II*, the tour was an expansion of the smaller tour he did in February but this time it had a schedule and performed at large arenas. Prince and 3rd Eye Girl played Birmingham, London, Manchester, Leeds and Glasgow before heading to Holland and Belgium. They then played in Paris before a return to London starting at *The Roundhouse* on June 4th. He played for two shows that night before heading the following night to the Hippodrome. A final concert in Vienna closed the European tour.

> ## ART OFFICIAL AGE WAS CREDITED TO HAVE A CO-PRODUCER, JOSHUA WELTON. THIS IS A RARE OCCURRENCE FOR A PRINCE ALBUM.

Prince returned to Paisley Park after the European leg of the tour and continued recording. He was contemplating releasing an album of his own alongside the album he had ready to go with *3rd Eye Girl*. Both albums, *Plectrumelectrum* with 3rd Eye Girl and a new Prince album *Art Official Age*, were planned for a September release and throughout August he finalized the two albums.

Prince released *Art Official Age* on September 26th 2014. It was an NPG Records release but formed part of the renewed license deal with Warner Bros Records. This made it only their second collaboration since 1995's *The Gold Experience*. *Plectrumelectrum* with 3rd Eye Girl was released on the same day.

Art Official Age was credited to have a co-producer, Joshua Welton. This is a rare occurrence for a Prince album. It does raise a question as to what degree the new album was truly *'co-produced'* knowing what Prince was like in the studio. *Art Official Age* is another concept album and provides a totally different listening experience to the album released on the same day with 3rd Eye Girl, *Plectrumelectrum*. One song that stood out for many was the remix of *'Funknroll'* which stood proudly in place on *Plectrumelectrum*. This song was remixed and placed at the end of *Art Official Age* and seemed to be a weaker variation of a solid track. There were of course others who disagreed and thought this version stood on its own and worked well with the album as a whole.

Art Official Age has the usual qualities that Prince fans loved: it was strong on the minimalist funk sound that he had made so unique and on point over the years, it had the modern element of the Prince electro funk capable of club tunes and of course the usual smooth seductive Prince ballads and R&B arrangements. As a concept album the songs all flowed and belonged together; this wasn't an album for the 'shuffle' generation - it flowed from track to track and held together as a single piece. Many critics were in favor of the album, if that ever mattered, and saw it as a true return to form.

For Prince though, flying high above these reviews, it was just another example of a new direction he was heading in. The concept itself is sometimes hard to follow but Prince is inviting us into a new state of mind. The opening track leads this and the song *'Clouds'* shows the future 45 years from now. All other songs follow the narrative, which starts with Prince saying *'Welcome Home Class'* at the beginning of the album. It moves into seduction and sedation before taking us on the journey with the tracks then following this musical ideology. There are moments with Prince at his funky and creative best and when you lay this alongside the conceptual theme it's a great album to add to the Prince collection. It was also a chart success, landing at number 5 in the US and number 1 on the R&B Chart, reaching number 8 in the UK and again number 1 on the UK R&B chart. It also charted all over the world, not that this mattered to many as the charts were now irrelevant in the cross-media frenzy of album releases.

Plectrumelectrum had been delayed many times so this was the album that fans were really waiting for. Prince had toured with the band all over the US and Europe so fans were now familiar with the line up and saw the girls as his new backing band. The band provided Prince with a new energy; the girls were young and hungry and had the stamina to keep up, a trait needed when working with Prince. It is sad to note in hindsight that this debut would also be the last with 3rd Eye Girl. *The Revolution* managed three albums and with the NPG it was only two (as a named album backing band).

There was a difference with 3rd Eye Girl in comparison to the others: this was a rock outfit and they could trade well with Prince both on record and live. They seemed to be true musical collaborators. They are equal to him on stage and on record; Prince was openly sharing the music with them and not, as he had done in the past, taking control over every element of the sound. *The Revolution* were great at embellishing Prince's songs and adding new elements to them; the NPG were great in the studio at recreating Prince's vision of the songs and putting them on record; but this band seemed to be true musical creators in the raw sense of songwriting. Prince clearly enjoyed being around them and it showed when they toured. The album therefore was much anticipated.

Prince shares the vocals but can't be heard on some of the tracks; as with The Revolution on *Parade* his vocals are not there but the musicality is, and you can hear his style behind the vocals of the girls. It's a strong quartet from a tight, serious rock band. The songs such as *'Plectrumelectrum'*, *'Aintturninaround'*, *'Marz'*, *Anotherlove'* and *'Pretzelbodylogic'* all have the feel of a truly no-nonsense established rock band firing on all cylinders. The other tracks on the album are more experimental but not at any time does it veer off course. It flows perfectly as a rock album should and is a standalone statement of what this band is.

Ida Nielsen has said over 100 songs were recorded by 3rd Eye Girl - that's a lot of songs and for any other band it would be taken with a pinch of salt; but this is Prince, so the statement is completely believable. It's very sad this band did not get the chance to continue. They brought Prince back to songwriting basics and a raw quality that he loved, especially when performing. There was nowhere to hide, no backing track, no lip-syncing, miming or singing over your own voice. It was pure, and showcased musical skill and raw talent. Originally Prince just wanted an all-female backing group; perhaps he underestimated what was to come because over the course of the recording sessions this changed and became a new collaborative approach, and then a new band with Prince at the front.

With the two albums released at the same time, there was a valid argument that they hurt each other as far as record sales were concerned. They competed with each other. Most music album reviews took on both at the same time and compared them. And of course, critics disagreed as to how they compared. This is probably exactly what Prince wanted and expected. It would have been easy to put the two together as a double album or indeed to pare it down to one pure masterpiece and have the remaining songs as a collection of B-sides. That though would have been too simple; Prince was about the creation as he had always been. The two albums were separate projects. They reached the people that mattered and he had delivered two albums that were completely different, even if one may indeed have damaged the other by competing from the commercial perspective.

To promote the two albums Prince and 3rd Eye Girl performed on *Saturday Night Live* in the US on November 1st 2014. Prince next headed to Kentucky and played four shows in March at the Louisville Palace Theatre before returning briefly to Paisley Park. Shortly afterwards however, an event would occur that would grab Prince's attention and get his activist juices flowing.

On April 12th 2015 a 25-year-old black man by the name of Freddie Gray was arrested by the Baltimore Police Department for possessing what the police alleged was a switchblade. Such blades are banned under Baltimore law. While they were transporting Mr Grey in the police van he fell into a coma, and was then taken to a local trauma centre. He died later on April 19th 2015. His death was later attributed to injuries to his spinal cord. On April 21st 2015, pending an investigation of the incident, six Baltimore police officers were suspended with pay. Many reports then followed regarding Freddie Grey's arrest and alleged treatment, resulting in a series of street protests in the city; it also made headlines around the USA.

> PRINCE PLAYED A SECRET GIG AT THE WHITE HOUSE ALONGSIDE STEVIE WONDER. THE GIG WOULD HAVE GONE UNREPORTED IF IT WASN'T FOR A SINGLE TWEET THAT WAS SENT AFTERWARDS

On April 25th 2015 a major protest in the city centre of Baltimore turned violent. It resulted in 34 arrests and many injuries; 15 police officers were also injured. Freddie Gray's funeral was held on April 27th 2015 and again civil disorder intensified. There was looting and burning of local businesses throughout the city and this resulted in a state of emergency declaration by Governor Larry Hogan. There was also Maryland National Guard deployment to Baltimore and the establishment of a curfew. The events were reported around the world and many linked them to past similar incidents in the US. The *Black Lives Matter* movement grew during

the following months. Prince responded to the events by putting on a benefit show on May 10th 2015 at *The Royal Farms Arena* in Baltimore. Prince called the show *'The Rally 4 Peace'*. Joining Prince backstage were Alicia Keys, Beyoncé and Jay Z who all wore grey for the occasion and posted pictures through their social media channels for the event. Prince played for over two and half hours and included a new song, *'Baltimore'*, written in tribute.

The day before the concert Prince made the song available to stream on a newly-created *Prince3EG* Soundcloud account on 9th May 2015. He added additional orchestral and horn overdubs later in the month and made it a digital single. On the following day the same new platform hinted towards another new release which would more than likely have been *'Free Urself'* which has the same theme as *'Baltimore'*. *'Baltimore'* was recorded on 30th April 2015 at Paisley Park Studios after Prince had watched the story unfold on TV. Prince was moved by the events and alongside 3rd Eye Girl and Joshua Welton they recorded a live cut of it at the Paisley Park Studios soundstage on 29th April 2015. Directly afterwards they recorded it alone in Studio A. It was then quickly mixed and later Eryn Allen Kane added vocals.

Prince continued touring in the following months in the US and Canada. While touring he played a secret gig at The White House alongside Stevie Wonder. The gig would have gone unreported if it wasn't for a single tweet that was sent afterwards, which was picked up by *ABC news* and reported the next day.

Prince now had another album ready to be released: *Hit n Run Phase One*. After the Baltimore Rally for Peace, Prince talked to Jay Z about his *Tidal* streaming platform and agreed to use it as a release mechanism. *Hit n Run Phase One* was released exclusively on the *Tidal* streaming service on September 7th 2015. It was then released on CD on September 15th by NPG Records. The title was originally reported to be just *Hit n Run* but Prince had so much material already recorded it was confirmed by Prince's publicists as *Hit n Run Phase One*, leading fans to correctly assume that *Phase Two* would shortly follow.

The *Tidal* streaming service claims to pay the highest percentage of royalties to musicians and songwriters within the streaming marketplace. It had agreements in place with all of the major music labels as well as many independent labels. Jay-Z acquired it in March 2015 and a large-scale marketing campaign followed as it made a major relaunch. At a large press conference in March 2015 artists were introduced as 'co-owners and stakeholders' in *Tidal*. *Tidal* was heavily promoted as the first service to be artist owned. Prince was on board with this vision and had no hesitation in offering *Hit n Run Phase One* to the service.

Hit n Run Phase One was essentially a collection of songs that had already been released in some form and most true fans had most of the tracks already; in fact only two songs from the eleven on the album were brand new: *'Like A Mack'* and *'June'*. Judith Hill also featured on the album and her vocals are prominent throughout the opening track *'Million $ Show'*. She had performed with Michael Jackson previously and was his main duet partner for his *This Is It* tour that was scheduled for 2009: she had rehearsed with him up until his death in June that year. She then came to the attention of Prince, who wrote and co-produced her album *Back in Time*, recorded at Paisley Park and released in March 2015.

Before the release of the album, Prince invited a selection of representatives from *Fox 9*, *City Pages*, *89.3 the Current* and the *Star Tribune* to preview the new album at Paisley Park. Prince told the journalists that it was the fastest album he had ever made, taking around two weeks from start to finish. *Back in Time* was officially released on *Tidal*, *iTunes*, and *Spotify* on October 23rd 2015.

Hit n Run Phase Two was released on December 12th 2015. It would be Prince's last album. As before with *Phase One* it was initially released exclusively on *Tidal*. The physical CD was released shortly after. The album later became a complete continuation of *Phase One* and was made into a two-volume bundle through the *Tidal* website.

> ## PHASE TWO IS FOREVER TINGED WITH SADNESS ON EVERY LISTEN, KNOWING IT WAS HIS LAST.

As with *Phase One* most hardcore fans already had the songs in some format. To keep it fresh, Prince added some new songs to the mix and therefore ensured everyone was happy. It was better received than *Phase One* and is a much stronger album in every way. *Phase One* and *Two* are simply a collection of songs written over the past few years and packaged together for a release; they are the other end of the spectrum to a *Lovesexy* or a *Rainbow Children*. It is an album of genuine quality, especially if you have not heard any of the tracks previously. The two new tracks on the album '*2Y. 2D (2 Young 2 Dare)*' and '*Look at Me, Look at U*' were particularly well received by fans. All other tracks were known to fans and therefore some felt they sounded out of place when Prince chose them for a collection and one song ran into another.

The reviews for *Phase Two* were largely very positive; it left fans contented that he had delivered a collection of songs yet again full of strong tunes, imagination and creativeness beyond anyone of a similar age or standing. It stands well in the huge Prince catalog, although it is also forever tinged with sadness on every listen, knowing it was his last.

With the album released Prince headed into the new year. He agreed to host a celebrity party on New Year's Eve with a concert as the guest of Roman Abramovich. He played at the *Estate* at Gouverneur Beach on December 31st and January 1st. Prince was photographed leaving a helicopter propped up with a cane when arriving on the island.

Prince now planned his next tour, which sadly would be his last. It was a solo tour with Prince returning to just himself and the audience. It's a perfect visual image for a musician whose life was completely and utterly dedicated to his music and performance; Prince never stopped and here he was performing again in a totally unique way. Entitled simply '*Piano and a Microphone Tour*' it would be just Prince, a piano and a microphone. It would be the most intimate series of concerts that he ever played. Prince premiered

the tour at Paisley Park on 21st January 2016, a month before he launched it as a world tour. A website link was set up at *Paisleyparkafterdark.com* and showed the stage at Paisley Park being set up for the event with a piano. At the premiere show he told those in the crowd that he was looking for a new challenge; he said that he rarely gets bad reviews because he has perfected his craft for over 30 years, and he now wanted something new. The piano performance would be more naked and more pure as an experience. He had, in all the years of touring, never performed a full concert alone.

His hair was in the same Afro style as the young boy who first started learning the instrument all those years before. In fact, many pictures were circulating comparing just how similar he looked to the young teenager who first came to the music world's attention. Now, he was back sitting at the piano, and performing alone. It was, in hindsight, for many millions of Prince fans an extremely sad tour. The concerts in fact raised the question of his health: he looked incredibly thin, almost fragile in appearance, and the fact that he was mostly sitting added to rumors of some kind of pain, possibly in his hips and ankles. It would also be a hugely personal tour for Prince: he would talk openly to the audience about his life, and talked a lot about his father and his influence.

It was by far the most personal tour of his life and again in hindsight looked like he was saying goodbye to the life he had. He was completely immersed in the songs and was visibly emotional through many of the performances. His entire life had been in the spotlight, a life at the top; Prince had nobody equal to him musically and he had achieved everything he ever wanted to. The *Piano and Microphone* tour was a return to basics, the purest musical form that you can get, and he was showcasing it for the last time.

That said of course, all his concerts were pure celebrations, a complete party from start to finish with the crowd fully engaged. If before with 3rd Eye Girl and his other countless tours he had demonstrated he was one of the greatest guitarists of all time, this was another showcase of his genius, just alone at a piano. He again changed the songs to fit in with the show, re-arranging the compositions for the piano, and he blended in his hits and other songs seamlessly in a unique and unrivaled display of talent. It was fascinating for many to witness the songs played in this way. This showcased the lyrical side of Prince, as the songs were condensed and simplified, which highlighted this side of his outstanding ingenuity.

The tour was originally intended to begin in Europe in December 2015 but because of the terrorist attacks in Paris it was postponed. The attacks actually happened on the same day the tickets went on sale. Instead the tour was scheduled to start in Australia and New Zealand, then moving on to the USA and returning to Europe later. Sadly of course the tour never reached the rescheduled European stage.

Just before the first concert Denise Matthews, aka Vanity, died of renal failure, on February 15th 2016. She was 57 years old. The first show was on February 16th in Melbourne Australia, and Prince dedicated performances of '*Little Red Corvette*', '*Dirty Mind*', '*The Ladder*', '*The Beautiful Ones*' and '*Adore*' in special tribute to his ex-girlfriend. He also shared many memories about her to the audience and was visibly upset during the performances.

The first two concerts were played in Melbourne on February 16th with two more concerts the following night, all at The Arts Centre. All four shows were exceptional, and the reviews were outstanding. Each of the concerts was different and Prince showed his unique virtuosity and versatility as a pianist within the performances. Reports also commented on the variety of styles Prince bought to the performances, ranging from boogie woogie, blues, jazz, pop, classical and of course funk. His skill and musicianship for melody allowed him to segue from one song to another beautifully. As an example, during the opening night he played the first verse and chorus of 'Little Red Corvette' and then went into the first verse and chorus of 'Dirty Mind'. He would go from the pop of 'Strange Relationship' to the rhythm and blues of Ray Charles' 'Unchain My Heart' and then end the medley with a classical instrumental version of 'Question of U'. This kept the crowd fully engaged as the melody would change so effortlessly that they were constantly surprised by the blending. It all melted into one show of pure skill and ingenuity.

He also played the hits but these felt new and refreshed. Prince spoke about his parents and told the audience he loved his mother and his father. He said that he learnt to play the piano by watching his father play. He also told a story of how when he was a boy he loved the movie The Wizard of Oz and learnt how to play all the songs from the movie. While he was telling this story, he was playing 'Somewhere Over the Rainbow'. He used the audience as an instrument, clapping when cued, finger snapping when cued and singing along and dancing when cued. The audience would get up to dance on the up-tempo songs and then sit down during the ballads. Prince's musicianship and interaction with the audience showed that he is the ultimate live performer. A performer of such calibre rarely comes around in any lifetime. Prince was giving so much back during these intimate affairs that in hindsight it's hard not to wonder whether he knew things were coming to an end.

After Melbourne, Prince continued to Sydney and played two concerts at The Sydney Opera House. The Opera House was lit purple during the concerts on February 20th. Again reviews were outstanding and Prince performed different sets for each show. Two more concerts followed, this time at The State Theatre in Sydney on February 21st, before Prince flew to New Zealand for his first ever concerts on February 24th. He performed once more in Perth, Australia before heading back to the USA. Another poignant tribute during the concerts was Prince singing 'Dolphin' and blending it into David Bowie's 'Heroes' and back again. It was a beautiful tribute to a songwriter who is often compared to Prince. The footage of this is also on streaming sites as it was performed a couple of weeks after Bowie's passing on 10th January 2016.

Prince arrived back in the USA and was seen at a basketball game on 3rd March 2016. He arrived and strutted to his seat with model Damaris Lewis before the scheduled shows the following day. He looked well and smiled during the game, wearing shades and a Princely cool suit, walking with his trademark cane. The USA leg officially started in Oakland on March 4th before another concert in San Francisco on March 5th. He made a brief appearance in New York on March 18th before continuing on to Canada. He played three nights in Montreal and then two shows in Toronto on March 25th.

Prince's next scheduled concerts were in Atlanta on April 7th; however, he cancelled the shows. This was extremely rare and social media lit up with speculations. When it was announced he had influenza, this again raised a lot of questioning from fans around the world. Prince simply did not get ill; it was as if he didn't even age. His musical life was always moving, he didn't have children, hadn't been married for years, had a new backing band and had just released another brilliant album. He was now performing a world tour in a superb intimate setting and fans were calling it the best Prince tour they had ever seen. So, a sudden cancellation and an announcement of influenza meant something wasn't right.

> ## WHEN THIS INFORMATION CIRCULATED THERE WAS WIDESPREAD CONCERN FOR HIS HEALTH.

The shows were rescheduled for April 14th 2016, and he performed the two shows again back to back. Prince apologized for the cancellations and performed as he had always done. After the concerts he flew back on his private jet to Minneapolis. On board was singer Judith Hill and Prince's assistant Kirk Johnson. Prince became ill during the flight and became unresponsive and unconscious, so the flight made an emergency landing at Quad City International Airport in Moline Illinois. He received medical treatment at a local hospital.

It was alleged that Prince was treated with a shot of Narcan and when conscious discharged himself to return home to Paisley Park. Narcan is a medication used to block the effects of opioids, especially in overdose, so again when this information circulated there was widespread concern for his health.

The main thought at the time was that Prince was suffering from hip pain caused by years of performing, and that he was taking drugs to ease the pain but something somewhere had slipped through and he was now getting into trouble. Of course, as his religious beliefs were very strong he would refuse any type of surgical intervention like a hip transplant as this would involve blood transfusions, something Prince was against. This belief stems back to Larry Graham and the religious study Prince was exposed to by Graham after the death of his child.

The following day, back in Minneapolis, Prince was seen on a bicycle riding around Paisley Park. Social media channels talked about the relief of seeing him out and about and looking good. The following evening, he was snapped again at a Minneapolis record store called The Electric Fetus. Prince tweeted a link to the store that evening. The store had a 'Record Store Day' and Prince had stopped by in support. The CDs Prince bought were of course of interest and the record store manager Bob Fuchs revealed what he purchased: Stevie Wonder Talking Book, Chambers Brothers The Time Has Come, Joni Mitchell Hejira, Swan Silvertones Inspirational Gospel Classics, Missing Persons The Best Of Missing Persons and Santana Santana IV. The same evening on April 16th 2016 Prince held a dance party at Paisley Park as a way of showing fans he was

okay and in good health. He made a brief stage appearance and told everyone he was feeling fine. He reportedly told the crowd to save their prayers for a few days.

On April 20th Prince's representatives called for help and contacted a California based specialist in addiction medicine and pain management, Mr Howard Kornfeld. Kornfield cleared his schedule and planned to meet Prince on April 22nd. In the meantime, he sent his son to Paisley Park, who had flown in with buprenorphine that morning to devise a treatment plan for opioid addiction. At Paisley Park Prince was discovered unconscious in an elevator. Emergency responders were called and performed CPR but a paramedic said he had been dead for about six hours. They were unable to revive him and pronounced him dead at 10:07 am on April 21st 2016. It was reported afterwards that there were no signs of suicide or foul play and a press release from the *Midwest Medical Examiner's Office* in Anoka County on June 2nd stated that Prince had died of an accidental overdose of fentanyl at the age of 57. It is not yet known whether Prince obtained the fentanyl by a prescription or through an illicit channel.

Prince was reported afterwards to not have made a Will. Therefore his estate would be divided between his siblings. This to many was a complete shock: how could a musician who absolutely controlled every aspect of his musical life not have put provisions in place for it after his death? Prince was fully aware of the legal fighting that followed such events: James Brown's estate for example had

virtually nothing left after the legalities had begun. Many were completely surprised by the absence of any Will but, at the time of writing, nothing has been found.

After the announcement of Prince's death, the music world came to a standstill. Prince was an artist who for decades had been a pioneer, a musical genius in the true sense of the word, at the top of the game; he had shaped his image and shaped popular culture. Many tried to replicate small elements of him but he was completely unmatched. His music will be studied for generations to come and many will ponder just how exactly he did it. How can one person be so talented in all areas of music, how can one person be so driven in the belief of musical freedom to take on the establishment and win?

And he won by still playing music and creating music, he didn't wait around for court decisions, he played, built his army of fans and played with complete freedom. He of course had ups and downs but at the end of the day his talent was so strong he could never really fail. He produced album after album, song after song, and performed relentlessly around the world to record-breaking audiences wherever he went. A truly global star adored by millions for one thing: his raw talent. Prince Rogers Nelson was only with us for 57 years but within that is so much music, and music yet to surface - his impact will be felt for decades, if not hundreds of years to come.

Put simply, a talent like Prince will never be seen again.